GRIFFITH TAYLOR

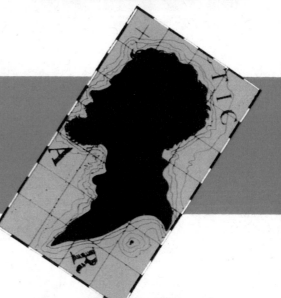

Antarctic Scientist and Pioneer Geographer

Marie Sanderson

GRIFFITH TAYLOR

Antarctic Scientist and
Pioneer Geographer

©Carleton University Press Inc. 1988
  Ottawa, Canada

ISBN 0-88629-068-6 (casebound)
ISBN 0-88629-066-X (paperback)

Printed and bound in Canada.

Canadian Cataloguing in Publication Data

  Sanderson, Marie
    Griffith Taylor

  (The Carleton library ; 145)
  ISBN 0-88629-068-6 (bound) —
  ISBN 0-88629-066-X (pbk.)

        1. Taylor, Thomas Griffith, 1880-1963.
  2. Geographers—Canada—Biography.   3. University
  of Toronto—Biography.   I. Title.   II. Series.

G69.T39S26 1987   910′ .92′4   C87-090286-5

Distributed by:
  Oxford University Press Canada
  70 Wynford Drive
  DON MILLS, Ontario, CANADA, M3C 1J9.
  (416) 441-2941

GRIFFITH TAYLOR

Antarctic Scientist and Pioneer Geographer

Marie Sanderson

CARLETON LIBRARY SERIES Nº 145

CARLETON UNIVERSITY PRESS
OTTAWA CANADA
1988

Acknowledgements
Carleton University Press gratefully acknowledges the support extended to its publishing programme by the Canada Council and the Ontario Arts Council.

Table of Contents

List of Figures

Acknowledgements

Grateful thanks are given to Griffith Priestley "Bill" Taylor, the older son of Griffith Taylor, who graciously gave me all of Grif's personal diaries when I was in Australia in 1980. Grif began to keep a daily diary when he was 21 years old and kept up the practice for more than 60 years until his death in 1963. Bill Taylor also gave me some family pictures, several of which appear in this volume. In addition, I was allowed to copy an historical account of Grif's parents, handwritten by Grif's sister Dorothy, a document that provided invaluable information on Grif's early family life. These sources gave an insight into Grif's private life which does not appear in any of his writings.

The main sources of Taylor material are in collections at the National Library of Australia in Canberra, and in the Scott Polar Research Institute in Cambridge, England. There are minor holdings at Sydney University, Australia and at the University of Toronto in Canada. Details of these collections are listed in Appendix I.

My personal thanks are due to the librarians who helped me with this material: John Thompson, Manuscript Librarian, National Library of Australia; Director G. de Q. Robin, and Harry King, Librarian, of the Scott Polar Institute; Pamela Green, Thomas Fisher Rare Book Library, Sydney University and the staff of the Fisher Rare Book Room, Robarts Library, University of Toronto.

A great many individuals have helped me with their personal recollections of Grif. I will begin with Australia, since that is where Grif also began his life's work: the late Dr. Marcel Aurousseau, himself a distinguished geographer who worked with Isaiah Bowman at the American Geographical Society offices in New York and who wrote several of the obituary notices for Grif, and was a great friend and companion in his retirement years in Australia. He and his charming wife Cecily gave generously of their time when I visited them in 1980 and recalled many happy times with Grif and his wife Doris. Mr. Brock Rowe of Sydney was a former student of Grif's who efficiently organized itineraries for me in Australia and whose kindness will long be remembered. Sister Nell Stanley of Holy Cross College in Sydney was one of Grif's first female students and loved talking about the early days of Geography at Sydney. Professor Trevor Langford-Smith and Dr. Philip Tilley and librarian Muriel McInnes of the Department of Geography at the University of Sydney knew Grif when he retired to Australia and continued to visit him until he died. They also knew Grif's sister Dorothy. All were most helpful in supplying details about the Taylors. In Canberra, Professor O.H.K. Spate was a source of much interesting "Griffiana" and his comments on Grif's work appear in this book. Other Australian geographers who helped the author with references and articles were Dr. Wayne Hanley, formerly of the University of New England (Armidale, NSW), and Dr. Joseph Powell of Monash University.

In England, Dr. C.L. Forbes of the Sedgwick Museum, Cambridge University, provided information on some of Grif's Cambridge professors. Since one of the highlights of Taylor's life was his Antarctic experience with the Scott expedition of 1910-12, it was especially moving to discuss the expedition and its members with Scott's son Sir Peter Scott at his home at the Waterfowl Trust in Slimbridge.

In North America, special thanks are due to (the now late) Dr. George Tomkins of the Centre for the Study of Curriculum and Instruction, University of British Columbia, for his kindness in loaning a microfiche of Taylor's unpublished MS *Journeyman at Cambridge*. The original is in the archives of the Scott Polar Research Institute in Cambridge. I especially enjoyed talks with (the now late) Dr. George Tatham of Atkinson College, York University, who was one of my professors at the University of Toronto and a colleague of Taylor's. I thank Dr. Tatham for granting permission to hear a recent tape in the Robarts Library of the University of Toronto of an interview with him concerning the early days of the department at Toronto. For their help in locating sources and for their encouragement, I gratefully acknowledge Gary Dunbar of the University of California, Los Angeles, Geoffrey Martin of Fairfield, Connecticut, Keith Fraser of the Royal Canadian Geographical Society and John Jacobs of the University of Windsor.

Many of Grif's former students at Toronto kindly provided anecdotes of their relationship with him: Brian Bird of McGill University, Richard Ruggles of Queen's University, Lloyd Reeds, now retired from McMaster, Bill Wonders of the University of Alberta, and Don Innis of SUNY at Geneseo, New York. Special thanks also are due to Dr. Chun-fen Lee of the East China Normal University in Shanghai, China, who remembers his days in Toronto with great pleasure and who sent a photo of himself and Grif. The list could have been much longer but I contacted only the students from Grif's early days in Toronto and those who kept up a correspondence with him when he retired.

As far as published works are concerned, I owe much to Grif's own autobiography *Journeyman Taylor* although the final publication was an emasculated version of his original MS because of the changes made by his editor, Alisdair MacGregor. Much use was also made of George Tomkins' Ph.D. thesis "Griffith Taylor and Canadian Geography."

Of course, the extensive writings of Taylor himself were an essential source of information. A (hopefully) complete list of his publications is given in Appendix II. These tell us about the professional Taylor, but his diaries and his thousands of letters, written and received, provide some knowledge of the private Taylor.

Finally, I acknowledge a great debt to my sister, Joan Lustig Stanford, also a geography graduate of the University of Toronto, who helped to locate all of Grif's published material, and whose support and encouragement will always be remembered.

Preface

Griffith Taylor was a man who had that quality of greatness that is undefined but unmistakable. His contribution to the Scott Antarctic Expedition and to the development of geography in three countries during the 83 years of his life are reasons enough for the present volume.

Grif wrote an autobiography *Journeyman Taylor*, but when it was published in 1958 it was an emasculated version of his original manuscript and contained little of his private life. In 1965 George Tomkins wrote a Ph.D. thesis for the University of Washington entitled "Griffith Taylor and Canadian Geography" but it was never published, and again, contained little of the private Taylor.

I was a student of Grif's at the University of Toronto and he was the reason I became a geographer. He had that rare ability of being able to transmit to his students his excitement and curiosity about the world around him. In this book, I try to show the complete Taylor since I had access to his private papers in the National Library at Canberra, and was given his personal diaries (from 1901 to 1963) by his son, G.P. Taylor. I have used many quotes from Taylor's diaries, his journals and from the large collection of his letters in the National Library. I hope in this way to let Grif himself speak to the reader.

Griffith Taylor's first claim to fame was his considerable contribution as chief geologist in the scientific team on Captain Robert Falcon Scott's 1910-12 Antarctic Expedition. To all students of Antarctic exploration and science, Taylor's name will be remembered and a glacier and a dry valley in the Antarctic bear his name. His account of the Expedition *With Scott: The Silver Lining*, published in 1916, tells the story from Grif's point of view and is interesting reading. Unfortunately, few copies of this book are now available.

Grif founded the first departments of geography in two countries — in Australia at the University of Sydney in 1920 and in Canada at the University of Toronto in 1935, a very considerable accomplishment. He was an inspiring teacher, probably because of his immense enthusiasm for and dedication to his chosen field. Geography was his life and his curiosity about the world was insatiable. He was also kind and generous to his students and colleagues who gave him an enduring loyalty, and the departments in Sydney and in Toronto were hardworking and happy places.

His production of scientific writings was remarkable, some 20 books and 200 articles. Much of what he wrote seems out-of-date in today's geographic circles, but created a flurry of excitement at the time of publication. He wrote the first climatology and regional geography of Australia and made many enemies by identifying the arid heart of Australia. He is probably most remembered for his writings on environment and race, and environment and nation and was often maligned for his deterministic views. However at the time of his writings on cultural geography, as he was the first to name it, his ideas were most stimulating and gained a wide audience among geographers and non-geographers alike. His works were read and appreciated by Arnold Toynbee, H.G Wells and H.L. Mencken. However, from the point of view of the 1980s, he is not seen as the archtype environmental determinist since his approach was always pragmatic, and eminently sensible — to view the affairs of man against the background of the natural environment.

He was fortunate to have as life-long friends scientists who became famous in their own fields, among them several who were also "Antarctickers". He grew up in Australia with Frank Debenham and Douglas Mawson, both Antarctic explorers. At Cambridge he roomed with James Simpson and was a friend of Charles Wright, both of whom were with him on the Scott expedition as was Raymond Priestley who, with Charles Wright were later to become his brothers-in-law. He was fortunate also in having as his first geology professor and great supporter the famous Australian geologist Sir Edgeworth David, and to make the acquaintance early in his career of such famous geographers as William Morris Davis, Isaiah Bowman and Ellsworth Huntington in the United States and A.J. Herbertson in England. He did not receive the honours that were his due, as his obituaries record. Most of the other scientists who were survivors of the Scott expedition and who made subsequent contributions to science were honoured with knighthoods — Wright, Priestley and Mawson; Taylor was being considered for such an honour by Australia when he died in 1963.

Grif was born when Charles Darwin was still alive and he died in the year that President Kennedy was assassinated. His life span saw incredible changes in our little planet, and he kept up with the changes. All his life Grif kept his motor running, travelling, writing, lecturing, walking. In 1911 Captain Scott called him a "remarkable character" and in 1972 Oskar Spate wrote "we shall not soon see another like Grif".

Marie Sanderson

CHAPTER 1

Early Years

Griffith Taylor's father, James, was the youngest of eight children, born in 1849 to Henry and Martha Taylor in a place called Back Dirken St. in the poor quarter of Oldham in Lancashire, England. Henry repaired looms in the cotton mills and was known to drink to excess at times and to beat his wife. According to her son James, Martha was an amazing woman, working from 6 a.m. until 6 p.m. in a cotton mill while also managing to feed and tend her eight children.

James was a young man of very strong conviction. Because of his wayward father, he developed an almost fanatical hatred of fermented liquor and tobacco, both hatreds inherited by his son Griffith. Grif's sister Dorothy wrote a short biography of her father after his death. In it, she stated that his main stimulant, developed in early boyhood, was ambition. After working all day in a machine shop in Oldham, he attended classes at a technical school in the evenings, and achieved an almost unheard-of reward, the Whitworth Scholarship to Owens College, now Manchester University. He couldn't believe his good fortune, to obtain £50 a year for three years to attend college. At Owens he managed to lose his broad Lancashire dialect and to gain a "correct" pronunciation and an extensive vocabulary. James was a brilliant student at Owens, achieving a notable array of prizes and medals. Chemistry was always his first love and his most esteemed professor was Sir Henry Roscoe for whom he was a laboratory demonstrator in his senior year. James was a friendly, outgoing youth who made many friends at Owens, among them Alfred Griffiths, whose father Thomas was an accountant in Henry's — a Manchester cotton firm. Alfred's home life was considerably more affluent than James Taylor's, and he often invited James to his home where he was welcomed and entertained by Alfred's large affectionate family, including his youngest sister, Lily. Lily was to become James' wife and Grif's mother, and Taylor was very proud of his ancestors on his maternal side. Lily's father was a pillar of the nonconformist church and often conducted the service. The family said that Thomas Griffiths could trace his line to the Llewellyn of Wales. Lily's mother, Elizabeth Hawkins, was a striking looking woman with a powerful brain and a good deal of character. She was a descendant of the infamous John Hawkins, who introduced slavery into parts of America. Taylor stated in his autobiography that this probably accounted for his own buccaneering character.

After graduation from Owens in 1873, James spent six months in Germany, visiting Leipzig, Karlsruhe and Heidelberg, where he worked with Bunsen of Bunsen burner fame. During this time, he managed to acquire enough German to translate Landauer's book on blowpipe analysis into English. He then returned to England and became a student at the London School of Mines, but did not complete his course. He was attracted by an advertisement for a chemist to manage a nitrate plant in Antofagasta in Chile and with the help of Sir Henry Roscoe's recommendation, was the successful candidate. James did not seem to have difficulty in learning his second foreign language, Spanish, in order to carry out his duties at the mine. During the year he spent in Chile, he invented a process to greatly speed up the production of the mine; but evidently the owners did not approve, for they presented James with a £1000 bonus and terminated his contract. James then returned to England.

Lily meanwhile also had been travelling. In 1873, when only 17 years old, she went with her brother Alfred to Australia and remained in Toowoomba, in the Darling Downs district of Queensland for four years with some of the Griffiths relatives. When she returned to England she again met James, and although she said she was more in love with continuing her career as an adventurous young woman, a rare thing among her contemporaries in those days, she consented to marry him in February 1880. James then returned to the School of Mines in London to finish his course, and the newlyweds set up housekeeping in a tiny house at number 9 Green Leaf Lane in Walthamstow in Essex, northeast of London. This was to be Grif's birthplace and he tried to find it when he was in England in 1912. He had heard from his father that it was at the southern end of the great Epping forest, with Waltham Abbey, founded by Harold in 1066, as its most famous landmark. But Grif confided to his diary that he was never able to find the house since the street names were changed.

Lily found life a little lonely and difficult in Walthamstow, especially since she almost immediately discovered that she was pregnant. She had to be a careful housekeeper, making do with a few shillings a week in order that James' South American savings would last until he graduated and found a job. Lily trouped from suburb to suburb to find the cheapest groceries, and the couple's first serious disagreement arose when James accused her of plunging into excess and luxury when she had spent an extra twopence on watercress!

The baby born to Lily Taylor on 1 December 1880 was a boy who was named Thomas Griffith after Lily's father. His digestive system was defective, and since Lily was unable to nurse him, cow's milk had to be obtained from a location on the other side of London. However, he and his parents survived, and James finally achieved his degree, "Associate of the Royal School of Mines" (A.R.S.M.).

After graduation James accepted a job as mine manager of a small copper mining company in Serbia, in the tiny village of Majdenpek, south of the Danube River. The village was a dozen miles from Milanovatz, and about 80 miles from Belgrade. Here the little family had a happy time with three servants, a substantial house, and cows, horses and a vegetable garden. Here, too, Dorothy, or Doubla, as her father always called her, was born in 1881. Probably the move from the impoverished conditions of Walthamstow to the beautiful Danube countryside saved the infant Grif's life! The village accepted the English family with cordiality and they joined in all the festivities. This idyllic arrangement lasted about three years, when the family trekked back to England, Grif just under four years of age and Dorothy not quite three. James had obtained a position as analytical chemist at Firth's Steel Works in Sheffield, and the family set up housekeeping in a large comfortable stone house which they called Shirecliffe Cottage.

The Taylors always kept one general servant in Sheffield, although the rent and upkeep of so large a house must have been out of all proportion to James' income in any eyes but his own and his wife's, since his income at Firth's never exceeded £250 per year. James was happy in his laboratory job at Firth's. He had two or three assistants, one of whom was Henry Brearly who became famous as the inventor of stainless steel. Many years later when Grif was a student at Cambridge, he visited Brearly in Sheffield at the Taylor Institute, an establishment named in James' honour.

James Taylor was a small man with long black hair and a beard. As his children soon learned, he was an apostle of the simple life. He bathed every day in cold water and ate sparingly. Often his lunch at Firth's consisted of brown bread and a few dates. Throughout his lifetime, he preferred porridge with milk and molasses to any other food. Grif inherited his father's lack of interest in food and was quite content with a meal of bread and milk!

James and Lily were faithful Unitarians by conviction, and with Grif and Dorothy in tow would walk several miles from Shirecliffe to the chapel. Later in life, Grif disavowed any religious convictions, but Dorothy maintained a church affiliation all her life, and later in Australia, was a member of the Congregational church. James and Lily were also keen travellers, and took the children on trips every year to different parts of England and Wales, visiting castles and cathedrals. They were also enthusiastic cyclists, James perhaps more than Lily, and they frequently took to their wheels for a few days and the children were parked with their maternal grandparents. It was on these occasions, when the parents were separated from their children, that the practice of exchanging letters began, a practice continued throughout Grif's long life. The first letter that has survived was one from his mother to Grif, written when he was five years old, obviously in answer to one of his.

> My dear Griffith — I liked your letter very much. You must write me another. You must try to read this yourself (1).

When it was time for young Griffith to go to school, he was sent to Miss South's school in Pitsmoor. He kept his first geography textbook from that school and it is now with other Taylor books in the Rare Book Room, Thomas Fisher Library, at the University of Sydney. It was *Gill's Geography* (Oxford and Cambridge: George Gill and Sons, 1886). Grif was a precocious child and was encouraged by his mother and father to write. His first words in print were in a letter to the editor of the Manchester Weekly Times when he was seven years old, a letter which was carefully preserved by his father and is now in the National Library in Canberra. Two further contributions by Grif appeared that same year in the Manchester paper.

A third child was born to the Taylors in 1886, a boy who was called Rhys, and in 1889 another son. On this occasion, Thomas Griffiths wrote to his daughter, Lily, that the child should be called John Hawkins after his ancestor Admiral John Hawkins, a contemporary of Raleigh, Drake and Frobisher. There is no record of Lily's reply, but the child was not named John Hawkins, but Evan. About this time Sheffield youngsters were subjected to epidemics of chickenpox and measles and James and Lily had their own treatment for their children's diseases, as Dorothy related. It was to "sweat it out." They were "hydropathists" and dispensed with all doctors and medicines, but relied on water and the action of the skin. The treatment was as follows.

> The naked patient was rolled in a sheet wrung out of water at boiling temperature. Then layers of blankets were wrapped around the child and tucked in tight all around. Then a cold sponge bath followed (2).

This treatment was given for indigestion, sore throat, fever, for any and all childish ailments. In spite of this unorthodox treatment and the fact that James and Lily never allowed the children to be vaccinated, they were a healthy lot and never suffered any serious illnesses.

Lily early taught the children not to waste time. The boys were given bowls of porridge for breakfast which they were expected to eat on the way down the drive toward school, and leave the bowls on the gatepost for their mother to collect later in the day.

When Grif was ten years old, he was sent to Pitsmoor College for two years and here he started German and Latin. In his autobiography, Grif stated that he didn't know what first influenced him in geography, unless it was his father's maps. James kept two drawers in his desk filled with maps of every description and Grif's early delight even at age ten was in poring over these maps.

In 1892, when Grif was almost twelve, James answered an advertisement for a government metallurgist in New South Wales, Australia, and he was the successful candidate. It would appear that James, like his son Grif after him, was possessed by a spirit of wanderlust. Perhaps the advertised salary of £1000 per year offered further enticement. The family packed their belongings including a piano in seventy large cases and sent them off by freighter, booking passage for themselves on the palatial Orient liner Ophir out of Naples. It must have been quite an expedition for James and Lily, with four children, crossing the channel and travelling by train through France and Switzerland to Italy. They seemed to have been inveterate easy going travellers all their lives, another trait certainly inherited by Grif. Although Lily was seasick during the long trip to Sydney, the others loved the ocean voyage. Dorothy tells an interesting story about brother Grif on the ship.

> He realized, sometime during the voyage, that he would be sent to school in Sydney and that he did not know the counties and county towns of New South Wales, and the rivers on which they stood. Appalling, since geography was his best subject. Since the age of five

or six he had been drilled day by day on the counties and county towns of England and their rivers — Northumberland, Newcastle on the Tyne: Cumberland, Carlisle on the Eden etc., and here was Grif, an embryo geographer, quite innocent of the rudiments of NSW geography. Yet he still had some weeks to go. On the Ophir he got some Australian Statistical Registers, and found a list and a map of NSW showing counties. They were feebly supplied with county towns, and rivers seemed for the most part nonexistent. But he did his best. I bet he could draw a map and fit in every county from memory before he finished (3).

In February, 1893, the Taylor family arrived in Sydney and rented a house in Double Bay, a two-storey, slate-roofed, stone-walled house they named after their Sheffield home "Shirecliffe, Edgecliff." Grif and Rhys were at once installed in a boarding school with Miss Macauley of Darling Point and here Grif remained until 1896.

Grif at thirteen was four inches shorter than his younger sister and he kept a stern eye on Dorothy so that she should not get "uppish." His expression was "Now don't you come the elder sister over me." He always made it clear, wrote Dorothy in her 69th year, that

anybody with my face should walk humbly and not claim prominence in any way. I suppose that is the function of elder brothers (4).

However, a great affection existed between Grif and "Pal" (as Dorothy was usually called), which is very much in evidence in the Taylor papers. Grif kept copies of all his letters to his family and there were thousands during his lifetime, to Pal, Mater, Father, Rhys and Evan, but the majority were to Pal. Dorothy wrote as often to Grif. When he was in the Antarctic, she wrote faithfully every week, keeping the letters for him to read on his return. She was his first "demonstrator" when the department of geography was formed in Sydney under his leadership, and one of Grif's students from those days, Sister Nell Stanley, wrote that Dorothy adored her brother (5).

Grif was sent in 1896 to the Sydney Grammar School, which he liked, but did not stay long, since the family moved that year to Parramatta. James and Lily had always dreamed of a country house with horses and gardens, and now purchased a part of the Adderton estate three and a half miles from Parramatta, two hours by horse and cart from Sydney, which they christened Blaen Crai after the home of a Welsh ancestor. James was rarely at home. He had to travel all over New South Wales, inspecting mines, so Lily early learned to cope with the problems of a house and four children. She also had the problems of a domestic staff, a general handyman and two women in the house, but no refrigerator, no town water, no electricity, and no gas. The Taylors had two horses. One was hitched to a victoria, and with a coachman in livery, often an ill-fitting hand-me-down, Lily would drive into Parramatta to collect James at the station, Dorothy from Abbotsleigh School and Grif from the King's School where he was a student from 1896 to 1898.

Kings was undoubtedly the best school in Sydney to which the children of the wealthy were sent, but Taylor stated later in life that his days at Kings were the unhappiest of his life. He said that the chief interest of the masters seemed to be in sport rather than work, and because he didn't care for sports, he was bullied. Yet it was at Kings that Grif met Frank Debenham who was to be his sledging mate in the Antarctic and his life-long friend. A report from Kings School in 1896 stated that Griffith Taylor was

> excellent in divinity, excellent in geography, but in Latin and Greek
> he was attentive, but must be careful not to overwork himself (6).

Although Grif did not win the prize in geography, he won a special prize for Greek testament. It was at Kings that Grif obtained the hatred for classics which he carried the rest of his life, stating later

> how can educationalists justify the waste of some 4 hours a week for 4
> years (not to mention the time devoted to preparation) which was the
> experience of so many of us in the field? (7)

In 1897 When Grif was seventeen and Dorothy sixteen there occurred in the Taylor household an event which Dorothy said "shook us up to our foundations." It was the arrival of a fifth child, christened Jeffrey. Dorothy stated,

> I was astounded. I was speechless. So was Grif and I dare say he also
> shared my sense of impropriety. We thought three children in a
> family admirable, four a little numerous and verging on common;
> five became almost vulgar. And we had thought our family finished
> and static. We would slink about after we got home from school and
> we would say, "did you tell anybody" and the other answer "no, did
> you?" Evidently our baby was unmentionable (8).

But, of course, little Jeffrey became the darling of the Taylor household, spoiled by parents and brothers and sister alike. In the Taylor family album, there is a cherished photo taken of the last time the complete family was together at a Christmas gathering in 1912. It shows James at 63 with his hair and beard white, Lily 56, Grif 31, back from the Antarctic, Dorothy 30, shortly to travel to England with her father, Rhys 26, soon to marry Linda and live in Ashfield, Evan 23, soon to marry Dorothea and live in England and Jeff 14, a beautiful youngster, who unfortunately was to die in 1916.

James gave up his position of Government Metallurgist in 1900 and became a mine manager at Peak Hill. From this time on, he was rarely at home but his letters to his family were unfailing and frequent. As Dorothy stated in 1950,

> He had more years in one-horse mining communities than he ever
> enjoyed in comfort and affluence such as his family enjoyed. Yet he
> never grumbled but cherished a philosophy of cheerful content (9).

6

It was about 1910 that James was engaged by a Mr. Gillies as a chemist for the Complex Ores Company in a scheme for the electrolytic extraction of zinc. In this position, he lived in Melbourne for several years. He also was in Tasmania for a time in connection with the development of electrical power for use by the company in its projects. Dorothy recalled:

> It was during this visit that James made an excursion over Mt. Wellington from the north to Hobart. Having arrived at the top at dusk, (there was no road then and only an ill defined track), he decided it would be risky to attempt the descent in the dark, so he camped on the top with only a newspaper for bed clothes. It would be safe to say that son Grif would have approved! (10)

Lily suffered greatly from the summer heat at Adderton, and in 1912 while James was away, made the decision to sell the house for which she received £1500, and bought a plot of land at Drummoyne on which a small house was built which she called Cartref. It was here that James retired and looked after his garden and rode his bicycle. When he was 70 years old, he rode from Sydney to Melbourne, some 600 miles, in three days, a feat which was reported in the local newspaper and of which son Grif was very proud. In her journal, Dorothy records that James died in December 1927 "always young at heart and a jolly companion."

After Grif graduated from Kings in 1898, he was persuaded to try the Public Service examination and was appointed to the Correspondence branch of the Treasury of New South Wales. He kept the job for a year and during that time became quite proficient at typewriting, an accomplishment which stood him in good stead later in life when often without the benefit of a secretary, he was to type all his own letters and manuscripts for publication.

In 1899 he enrolled in the University of Sydney, in the Arts course. He found that mathematics was not for him, and failed the Christmas examination, changing then to the Science faculty. Here, as chance dictated, he was to meet the man who played the most important role in his career — Professor Edgeworth (later Sir Edgeworth) David. In his freshman year, during Michaelmas term, he attended David's lectures on physiography. He kept his notes from those lectures all his life and they are now preserved in the Thomas Fisher Library at the University of Sydney. On the flyleaf, he wrote many years later:

> My first introduction to geography and geology. Professor David's lectures on physiography in 1899, which led to my earning the University Prize — and in fact, to my lifework (11).

Professor David was an extraordinary man. Born in 1858 in England and educated at Oxford, he went to Australia as Assistant Geological Surveyor for New South Wales. He was instrumental in finding several coal fields, and while on these prospecting trips became interested in the causes and effects of glaciation. In 1891 David was asked to fill the chair of geology at the University of Sydney, where he remained for 33 years.

When Shackleton was organizing his expedition to the Antarctic in 1909, Professor David was an obvious choice as one of the geologists. Discussing his appointment, Mrs. Shackleton wrote,

> Professor David is perfectly charming, always helpful, a great acquisition to the expedition. He has a powerful intellect and is a most clever geologist . . . and will have such a good influence over all the men (12).

David was a great addition to Shackleton's team. Although he was 54 years of age while in the Antarctic, David travelled 1,200 miles on foot and led a party to the summit of Mt. Erebus (13,200 ft.) and to the south magnetic pole.

David was a successful lecturer at the University of Sydney, delivering his well-prepared and illustrated (he was an amateur artist) lectures in a well-modulated voice. He was liked and respected by his students and colleagues alike. His high ideals and Christian principles are evident in a story quoted in his obituary in the *Proceedings*, Royal Society, Vol. 99. In August, 1914, at a geological meeting he was conversing with Dr. Albrecht Penck of Germany when the press asked about the war which had just broken out. He put his arm around Penck and said "All men of science are brothers." David was knighted in 1920, and when he died in 1934 was given a state funeral, a most unusual honour for someone not in government.

Taylor enrolled in Science (Geology and Physics) and his second year at Sydney was spent as a Deas-Thomas Scholar, doing research in physics on the element selenium. Taylor recounts in his diary:

> For a year I had the largest lump of pure selenium in the world, lent, I believe, by the Royal Society of London. I spent monotonous hours testing this black slab, six inches across, to find its electrical properties. I made no important discoveries (13).

Grif had begun the practice of keeping a daily diary in 1901, a custom he continued faithfully until his death. The diaries are filled with a mixture of his personal activities, his accounts, and also notes on his travels, sketches of the landscape and even sketches of people — W.M. Davis and Captain Scott among them. Little of this material made its way into Taylor's books which he kept strictly free of personal data. In the diaries we see a very human person — who had trouble with insomnia, who didn't like to get up in the morning, who loved dancing and bridge and movies and who was loyal to old family friends.

During his years as a student in honors geology and physics, Grif began the field trips which greatly increased his knowledge of New South Wales. One of the first trips, led by Professor David was to the Yass district near present-day Canberra, and the second in 1902 to the Mittagong area, with fellow geology student Douglas Mawson, who was to be another of Taylor's distinguished and life-long friends. This resulted in his first scientific paper, "Geology of Mittagong" with Mawson as co-author, published in 1903 in the *Journal of the Royal Society of New South Wales*. The notebook he and Mawson used on this first field trip is preserved in the National Library, and it is typical of all Taylor's notebooks, with very detailed notes, cross-sections, and very fine block diagrams, the technique for which he had learned from Professor David.

Grif joined the Sydney University Science Society, and in 1904 along with Douglas Mawson, was one of the secretaries, while Professor David was vice-president. He obtained his degree in Science in Geology and Physics from Sydney University in 1904. He then enrolled in the mining school at the university, perhaps because of his father's advice or perhaps because he hoped that it would advance his career in geology. As Grif stated later,

> We had merry times in the mining school, especially in the assay laboratory. Here we sampled ores and crushed them, and I was also busy trying to purify some gold bullion with unsatisfactory results. But chiefly I remember our meals. We would let the fires die down, and then broil mutton chops or steak on them to the pitch of perfection. A curious drink was water with a slight addition of acid from the reagent shelf (14).

After graduation, Grif was employed as a school teacher for a few months at Newington College, in charge of a class of senior boys, an experience he did not greatly enjoy. When Professor David asked him to join his staff as a demonstrator he joyfully accepted. About this choice he states

> If any young scientist were to ask my advice as to the best way to advance in his chosen field, I would tell him what was the best move I made. Obtain a position, however junior, on the staff of a well known leader in your field. Take notes of whatever you see. In earth sciences, sketch everything (15).

He learned from David the methods of successful lecturing which he was to put into practice successfully later in life.

> He spoke loudly and I have tried to follow this rule even if my voice and diction were nothing like so melodic or polished as David's. How many famous scientists have I known who failed in two major respects. They could not remember the low intelligence level of the student body, and they *would* mumble! (16)

As the junior staff member, Taylor helped Professor David arrange specimens and visual exhibits for lectures. Not all of the demonstrations succeeded. Taylor describes one which David meant to use to illustrate Hawaiian volcanoes and the phenomenon called Pélés Hair, formed when wind blows the ejected lava into long strings.

> David procured a deep assaying pot, filled it with a mixture of ground-up lava and the inflammable powder called Thermite. He

Taylor's slides at Mac-

ignited this and when it was glowing, took a steel capsule of CO_2 and dropped it into the glowing mass. He then stirred the mixture with a long slate pencil. It blew up and scattered liquid fire all over the room, igniting a heap of cotton waste, but mercifully missing the two operators. For years afterwards one could still see fragments projecting from the metal ceiling but David had no Pélés Hair to exhibit that evening (17).

Taylor also discovered during the preparation of some of David's specimens that he was red-green color blind, so he found teaching classes in palaeontology more attractive than preparing specimens.

Taylor had two other geological papers published while at Sydney University, one with Professor David, "The Occurrence of Pseudomorph Glendonite in NSW" in the *Geological Survey of New South Wales* in 1905 and "The First Recorded Occurrence of Clastoidea in NSW" in the *Proceedings of the Linnean Society, New South Wales* in 1906. Later in life, Taylor decided that his first geographical paper was one published in 1906, with W.G. Woolnough, "A striking example of river capture in the coastal districts of NSW." He stated later:

> Professor David had the kindness to criticize it for me which links it up with the man who is responsible for a geography department in the (Sydney) university (18).

In the year 1904, a professor of geology at Melbourne University, J.W. Gregory, without knowing it, influenced the young Taylor in his choice of careers. Gregory had published a book on the geomorphology of Victoria, which Taylor stated:

> opened my eyes to interesting research on which a knowledge of the origin of landscapes is based. This realm of science has been one of my chief studies all my life (19).

The publishers of Gregory's book wished to have a companion volume on New South Wales. They naturally approached Professor David and he agreed to edit such a work, asking Grif to do the section on environment and mines. To aid in this work, Grif built a large relief model and on it plotted rainfall and structure. This led to the writing of his first climatic paper "A Correlation of Contour, Climate and Coal, a contribution to the physiography of New South Wales."

This paper very directly affected Grif's career as a geographer. The famous American geographer-geologist William Morris Davis wrote a criticism of it in the U.S. *Journal of Science*. Consequently Grif corresponded with Davis and his association with Davis was of great help to him later in his career when he was a student at Cambridge. It certainly was a factor in his being chosen as geologist on the famous Scott Antarctic expedition.

The story of how Taylor came to be a student at Cambridge is an interesting one, told by him in an unpublished book called *Journeyman at Cambridge*. It was the last book Taylor wrote and he sent it packed in a cornflake box to the Scott Polar Research Institute in 1961, just two years before he died. He wrote in the flyleaf that he would be agreeable to its publication and the following material on Grif's life at Cambridge is based on that manuscript.

In the first chapter of this *Journeyman*, Taylor stated that his friend Dudley Stamp claimed that his (Taylor's) career was based purely on chance.

> The great exponent of determinism (i.e., environmental control) is himself the product or victim of possibilism in that his life is shaped by a series of accidental happenings. There is truly some basis for this remark; for my four years at Cambridge were largely due to a stout old lady who had the distinction of sending graduates to Cambridge with the "Exhibition of 1851 Scholarship" for three years in succession (20)

The profits of the Great Exhibition of 1851 in England were spent, at the suggestion of the Prince Consort, in bringing young students from all parts of the Empire to do postgraduate work in England. The scholarship, worth £200 per annum, was confined to scientists, and the subject of the research was to be of some practical value to the country from which the candidate applied. Rutherford of New Zealand was the first '51 scholar.

During his years at Sydney, Taylor was a paying guest in the home of one of his fellow students — Thomas Laby. Mrs. Laby, the stout old lady in the above quotation, encouraged her son, who was a brilliant student in chemistry, to apply for the scholarship in 1906 and he won it, leaving Australia to work at the Cavendish Laboratory in Cambridge. Mrs. Laby then insisted that Grif had a good chance, and he sent in his application for the scholarship on 26 February 1907, although he was worried about the condition of the "practical value" of his research. His field was geology and he decided on a study of a little known fossil organism *Archeocyathinae* or "ancient cups" as Taylor described the fossils.

In South Australia, a geologist (W.H. Howchin) had traced a series of Canberra limestones for a distance of over 400 miles north of Adelaide. These steeply dipping rocks contained innumerable fossil organisms, *Archeocyathinae*, which appeared as white rings about one inch or less across in the darker limestone. Their biology was very uncertain for some scientist claimed them as corals, other as sponges, while a palaeontologist in Russia was of the opinion that they were "relics of a calcareous seaweed." Grif gave a paper on these fossils to the Eleventh Meeting of the Australian Association for the Advancement of Science in Adelaide, and it was published in their proceedings in 1907. Professor David was very interested in this fossil reef and suggested that Grif go to South Australia and collect as many specimens as possible. With friend Doug Mawson and Professor Howchin, Grif collected six packing cases of the fossils at a place called Sellick's Hill, a few miles south of Adelaide.

11

Professor David wrote a letter in support of Grif's application for the 1851 Scholarship, although he advised Grif to go to Oxford rather than Cambridge. On March 27 Taylor received the good news that he had been awarded the scholarship. He was elated that the scholarship and the princely sum of £200 per year would be his for two years' study at Emmanuel College at Cambridge. In June, he packed his fossils for Cambridge and his last day at the University was June 27. The department had a dinner for Grif on July 8.

At the time Grif left Australia for Cambridge, he was a very studious and very innocent young man. His friend Mawson at Sydney teased him about his lack of interest in female undergraduates, and Grif states in his book, "I blush to state that I only remember speaking to one co-ed in my undergraduate days." The co-ed to whom he referred was probably Maud Scrutton who was also a student of geology — a rather unusual choice of profession for a female in those days. Although Grif does not make mention of her by name, he kept in his papers a postcard she sent to "T. Griffith Taylor, Esq. B.E., BSc. Passenger per SS Zealandia, Sydney." On the postcard was the very clever poem reproduced below. It describes the ambitious young scientist setting off for Cambridge.

When Paddy goes a-wandering from Ireland
He takes a bit of peat with him, 'tis said.
So now you're straying forth you're taking with you
A ton of other little things instead.
There's Archaeocyanthus on your shoulder,
And Reciptacellites in your swag,
While Microphyllum nestles in the corners
And Phillipsastrea bulges out your bag.

You've left the mountains' influence behind you,
The unfair pull they've got upon the plains,
The arid parts of your adopted country,
Where it never, that is, hardly ever, rains.
But there's one thing to console you; — I would wager
You could shout it loud enough to beat the band, —
In your journey off to Cambridge from Australia,
You cannot be compelled to go by land.

While gathering 'ruptive rocks at Rotorua,
Or slithering down Mt. Eden's crater round;
While figuring Fiji's continental features,
Those tell-tale granite outcrops Woolnough found,
While studying stratigraphy at Stanford,
Or demonstrating Barrier Reefs on terms,
Just take a little respite in between whiles,
Lest ere you reach the Cam you feed the worms.

When writing your address upon their letters
Your friends put only two degrees as yet;
But when you're through your Exhibition lectures
There'll be more calls upon the alphabet.
A special size in envelopes they'll need, then,
To carry all your scientific rank,
To hold the many letters that will prove you
A well authenticated coral crank.

Your friends have spelt success for you in plenty,
And prophesied a brilliant career.
Emmanuel and Cavendish will surely
Endow you with a name the world will hear
Ambitious is your watchword. — Here's a better,
Whose claims all worthy scientists confess
Be TRUTH your guiding-angel, goal and lode-star!
She'll bring you all you need of happiness (21).

Maud Scrutton knew Grif well enough to know that he was very ambitious and wished "for a name the world will hear." She correctly labelled him as hard-working, ambitious, and above all, curious about the world. Taylor was 27 years old when he left Australia for Cambridge in 1907 (Fig. 1) and had already made considerable contributions to science. He had earned two university degrees, had published several papers and had worked with one of Australia's most distinguished scientists. Although a graduate in geology, his special field of interest was physiography, or the origin of landscapes. He was interested in climate and the way in which climatic factors affect the landscape. He never used the term geography or thought of himself as a geographer, but already he was beginning to think in a geographical way and was on his way to being a pioneer in physical geography. His paper that related the actual landforms with climate and with coal formations show that he was already beginning to associate man's activities with climate and landforms.

Established professorships in university departments of geography occurred during the nineteenth century, first in Germany, later in France. Previously in these countries as well as in Britain and the United States, university geography lectures had been given by various scholars, including some from other disciplines. In England the first full-time university teacher in geography, Halford Mackinder, had been appointed Reader in Geography at Oxford University in 1887; the School of Geography at Oxford was established in 1899. In the United States, William Morris Davis was appointed Assistant Professor of Physical Geography at Harvard University in 1885. The first separate graduate department of geography in the United States was established at the University of Chicago in 1903.

Davis was an international figure in geography and Taylor greatly admired him, and looked forward to meeting the great man whose background in geology was similar to his own. He had written to Davis and was planning to visit him at Harvard on his way to England. Life for Grif was taking a new direction and he was eager and excited to get on with it.

References

1. National Library, Canberra, MS 1003/1/31.
2. National Library, Canberra, MS 1003/1/34.
3. Taylor, Dorothy: Unpublished biography of James Taylor, 1969.
4. Taylor, Dorothy: Unpublished biography of James Taylor, 1969.
5. Letter to the author from Sister Nell Stanley, Sydney, Australia, January 1984.
6. National Library, Canberra, MS 1003/1/14.
7. Taylor, Griffith: *Journeyman Taylor*. Robert Hale, London, 1958, p. 25.
8. Taylor, Dorothy: Unpublished biography of James Taylor, 1969.
9. Taylor, Dorothy: Unpublished biography of James Taylor, 1969.
10. Taylor, Dorothy: Unpublished biography of James Taylor, 1969.
11. Thomas Fisher Rare Book Room, University of Sydney. Griffith Taylor Collection. Box 1.
12. Taylor, Griffith: "Journeyman at Cambridge," Unpublished MS, Scott Polar Research Institute, p. 124.
13. Griffith Taylor. Private Diary, 1902.
14. Taylor, Griffith: "Journeyman at Cambridge," p. 6.
15. Taylor, Griffith: "Journeyman at Cambridge," p. 7.
16. Taylor, Griffith: "Journeyman at Cambridge," p. 8.
17. Taylor, Griffith: "Journeyman at Cambridge," p. 10.
18. Thomas Fisher Rare Book Room, University of Sydney. Griffith Taylor Collection. Box 1.
19. Taylor, Griffith: "Journeyman at Cambridge," p. 10.
20. Taylor, Griffith: "Journeyman at Cambridge," p. 1.
21. National Library, Canberra, MS 1003/9/7/07.

CHAPTER 2

Cambridge

Taylor left Australia for Cambridge in August 1907, and, as he was to do throughout his lifetime, lost no opportunity to see as much of the world as possible while travelling to his destination. In this case, going from Sydney to Cambridge, he first spent a week in New Zealand. He went from Auckland to the volcanic area at Rotorua by bicycle and stated that the pumice roads were hard on bicycles! From New Zealand, Grif journeyed to Tonga, keeping a daily journal as well as a personal diary, and writing long newsy letters to his family. August 1st saw him in Samoa where he set out alone, since he could not find anyone to accompany him, on a 25 mile walk to the western end of the island of Upola. Fiji, and Viti Levu was his next port of call, and again a walking tour — this time with a colleague from Sydney, Dr. Woolnough. Throughout his lifetime of travelling, Grif practised what he preached: that there was no better way to see a country than on foot!

After a few days in Hawaii he left Honolulu on the steamship *Aorangi* and arrived in Vancouver on August 30. Taylor immediately proceeded to California, since Dr. Jordan of Stanford University had invited him to give a lecture there on the Barrier reefs of Australia. Grif always seemed to have controversies with the press and he loved an argument. In Seattle on September 1st he and a travelling companion from Hawaii were interviewed by the *Morning Times*. The next day Grif wrote to the editor:

> One of your reporters interviewed me last night as to my impressions of U.S.A. and my opinion of the Hindoo factor in Fiji. His report in your paper apart from the essential fact, that the Fijian despises the Hindoo, too much to be demoralised by him — is fairly correct. But I must say I was shocked at the series of misrepresentations which he has worked out of my friend's remarks re Hawaii. The whole account is directly opposed to Mr. Heye's statements and as I was in the room and much interested in the description of Japanese life which my friend gave to the reporter, I may be permitted to contradict the whole article (1).

After a visit to Berkeley he set off by train to make a leisurely trip across the United States. As usual, Taylor travelled cheaply, usually sleeping on the train and subsisting largely on biscuits, peanuts and chocolates. He stopped for a few days in Salt Lake City, Denver and Chicago, where he had his first glimpse of the city he would live in for seven years later in his life. He was not impressed with Chicago, stating that it was like a rather gloomy cellar with the buildings and streets under the elevated railway. However, he did make a point of visiting the

15

geology department at the University of Chicago where he met geographers Paul Goode and Harlan Barrows, as well as the famous geologist Professor T.C. Chamberlin and his son, Rollin, who was to be a good friend to Taylor in his Chicago years. He visited Niagara Falls and made a sketch map of that historic site. His ultimate destination in the U.S. was Harvard. He had written to W.M. Davis that he would be in Massachusetts in September and Davis replied

> I hope to welcome you here at Harvard . . . I regret to say there are no funds for engaging lecturers . . . but I will see what can be done in the way of offering you some compensation for a public lecture (2).

Unfortunately Taylor did not receive the letter until he arrived at Cambridge and consequently was not able to take advantage of the opportunity to lecture at Harvard. He thus did not visit Harvard but boarded the *Caronia* in New York on September 24 for England.

On 1 October 1907, after 15 years away from England, Grif again saw the land of his birth. He landed in Liverpool and went directly to Oldham to visit the Griffiths relatives — the Coates clan headed by his Uncle Thomas Coates of the well known cotton firm. He toured the factory and wrote at length to his family of the process of turning raw cotton into thread. He finally arrived in Cambridge 13 weeks after leaving Sydney. Coming from colonial Australia, with its lack of history and beautiful architecture, he was immediately impressed with the beauty of this college town. All his life Taylor thought of himself as a Cambridge man, and it is revealing that his last unpublished book concerned his years at Cambridge.

He wrote long letters to his family describing Cambridge and his first impressions of Emmanuel College. He had chosen Emmanuel because it offered entrance scholarships for overseas students. He explained to his mother that Emmanuel was a relatively new college, founded only in 1584 and was not one of the illustrious colleges which bordered on "The Backs" along the river Cam, but rather was situated less dramatically in the downtown area on Clarendon St., next to Christ's College. Taylor found that the "digs" in college were not for newcomers and on the advice of the porter, found rooms that he could afford at 39 Clarendon, just east of the enclosed courts of Emmanuel. A fellow colonial, who was to be Grif's lifelong friend and who also lived at 39 Clarendon was James Crawford Simpson from Canada. Simpson had graduated from Medical school at McGill University and had also obtained a '51 Scholarship. He and Grif often joked that Taylor's study of the 500 million year old "Ancient Cups" was probably as "useful" to Australia as Simpson's study of some little biological creatures called *Holothuria* was to Canada.

Taylor and Simpson were rebels against the rules at Cambridge: that a freshman must not wear a stiff collar or a bowler hat or dark trousers, or shake hands with a man twice in a term, or walk on a college green, or omit to wear a gown, or be out after 10 p.m. (3). Already in November they were in trouble with the proctors for not wearing gowns, and Taylor's penchant for directly confronting an issue is obvious. He wrote to his mother on November 10:

> We (Simpson and Taylor) were fined for being out without gowns
> and after 11 p.m. We had a straight out talk and I told him (the
> proctor) my chief object was to be the very thin edge of a very long
> wedge (4).

The argument apparently bore fruit for in February of the next year the senior tutor informed Grif that advanced students were freed from gate fines and could stay out of rooms until midnight.

Finally, Grif's six cases of fossils arrived and he started to work. He was given space in the Sedgwick Museum which he describes as "the finest building at that time in the University, having been built only a few years before." He first had to slice the limestone and for this time-consuming work he was given a young assistant. Then he had to etch the stones with acid, and photograph and sketch them. Finally he classified the organisms and described them. He did not find this part of his life at Cambridge very exciting, but he persevered and produced finally a very thorough memoir on the "ancient cups."

Grif's tutor was a Professor Hopkins, who was a world authority in physiology, and was later to become President of the Royal Society. Grif and he got on well together. It was Hopkins' custom to invite his students — usually ten or so — to breakfast on Sunday mornings, and Grif loved these occasions since he met other advanced students, and he loved to talk. Already in November he was invited to join the highly elite Emmanuel Science Club. Grif attended Wood's lectures on fossils, and Harker's on petrology. His best lectures, he stated, were those of Marr of the Sedgwick, who lectured in general Geology and espoused Gilbert's ideas on erosion. John Edmund Marr was 50 years old when Grif first met him, and was a fellow of St. John's. He was a popular lecturer with all the students and Grif was again lucky to have such an excellent professor. Marr's almost boyish enthusiasm for his work, which included at that time an interest in glaciation, was transmitted to Grif. Marr knew and respected William Morris Davis, and introduced Grif to the great man. He admitted to his students that his views underwent modification as a result of field trips with Davis. Even before the end of his first term, Taylor asked Marr to think of some physiographic work for him to do, as he said he did not want to be tied down to palaeontology. "A nice exploring trip as a geologist would suit me," he said.

One of his Sydney classmates had given Taylor a letter of introduction to his famous uncle, Professor T.G. Bonney of the Sedgwick Museum. Although Bonney was 74 years old and retired, he still took an active interest in geology and was a good friend to Grif. He was at the time the first ranking geologist in Cambridge. Bonney was a fellow of St. John's, and an authority on microscopic petrology, and in 1904 when the Sedgwick was built, Bonney was given room in the new museum and asked to give some help to the junior students. (His desk in the Sedgwick is still used by Professor C.L. Forbes). Bonney was very severe with his students and desired to instill in them a necessity for absolute accuracy. His favourite field method was that of a traverse, sketching and making notes as he went. Grif learned this technique from the great man and it was a field method he put to good use throughout his career.

Figure 1. Griffith Taylor (about 1906) before leaving for Cambridge. National Library of Australia.

Taylor often stated that the social contacts, and especially the chance to travel, were two great advantages of a student at Cambridge. Consequently, his first Christmas holidays Grif spent with this new friend Simpson in exploring London and Paris. Simpson had been an art student in Canada and introduced Grif to the famous galleries in Paris.

Taylor kept up his correspondence with W.M. Davis, admitting that he, like many young geologists and geographers at the time, was a great admirer of Davis. He sent Davis a letter commenting on Davis' criticism of his Australian article:

> It is a poor workman who blames his tools, but we are only *beginning* to work out the physiography of Australia. Probably you know we have *not one* contour map on *any* scale, so that I am naturally grateful for the criticism of so eminent a leader as yourself (Italics are Taylor's) (5).

In his diary at this time Taylor wrote that concerning Davis' criticism of his work he felt like the English peasant who always boasted that he had been kicked by King George. Davis wrote to Taylor 8 March 1908:

> Is there any chance of your being on the continent this summer? I shall sail for Italy April 25 and spend May, June and July moving slowly northward studying various problems on the way. I hope to have a few advanced students associated in a rather free way with me. (6).

Marr advised Taylor to accept the offer and in June 1908 he was in Europe again. Taylor recalled that Cook's of London wrote his ticket for two months travel in Europe for £9! As usual, he was thrifty in his travels and described one technique he used to find inexpensive hotels in large cities.

> When reaching the usual plaza with its large international hotel 'Ritz' or 'Splendide', I would pass them by, go two blocks down the main street, turn to the left, and take the first hotel I came to (7).

Taylor's trip to Bellagio on Lake Como where he was to meet Davis, was by way of Antwerp, the Rhine gorge, Heidelberg and Switzerland, where he first saw the Jungfrau and became fascinated with Alpine scenery. He was never enamoured of mountain climbing, however, following the example of W.M. Davis, whom he asked, "Do you go in much for mountain climbing?" and Davis answered, "No, Taylor, I've always been a valley-climber." (8) Taylor was the only Britisher in Davis' party of fourteen, which included Mrs. Davis, the American geographers Fenneman and Leverett, and several Swiss, Polish, German and Italian students. With such a motley group, the problems of translation were enormous. Davis would point out some feature and discuss its character in English, then in French, then in German and finally in Italian, a regular Tower of Babel, Taylor wrote. Taylor ventured to argue with Davis, but admitted later that his theories were easily disproved by Davis. As Taylor wrote in a letter that year to W.M. Dunn in Sydney:

> Davis is a man with a keen eye — extremely keen, and a logical tongue, Oh most logical, I assure you. He is a champion teacher and a holy terror on language, too (9).

Davis told Taylor he should study the geological literature in the language in which it was written, so Taylor began studying German in earnest when he returned to Cambridge. He and Simpson often studied together from German phrase books. *U & T requirement*

> Simpson would read in German from his phrase book, "Is that the picture of your small brother?" and Taylor reading from his book might reply with the German equivalent of "no, it is a little monkey from the zoo." Sometimes the answers happened to make sense; oftener they did not, yet the method did help us with our German pronunciation (10).

Taylor found life a little dull in Cambridge in August, with only his "ancient cups" to occupy his time, so he began working on what proved to be his first textbook, an introduction to Australian economic geography. He also bought a motor bike and rode to Wales to meet Davis again and had some lively talks with him. Davis suggested that Taylor attend a meeting of the British Association for the Advancement of Science in Dublin that September. He did so and enjoyed meeting the chief geologists of the day — especially William Johnson Sollas. Sollas had occupied the Chair of Geology at Oxford since 1897 and had been a student of T.G. Bonney at Cambridge. He was the professor of Geology and Palaeontology and was very well respected. Grif was very anxious to meet Professor Sollas and asked to be introduced. Sollas was pointed out to Grif as the gentleman in the green hat, and Grif immediately photographed the man in the green hat, or so he thought. He found out later that it was the wrong man. Taylor, being color blind, had a photograph of a man in a brown hat

By the time his second year at Cambridge began in October 1908, Grif was beginning to feel at home. He made a trip to Oxford to visit Professor Sollas and Sollas also visited him in Cambridge. It was Sollas who introduced Taylor to the famous geographer, A.J. Herbertson in Oxford, with whom he had been corresponding in connection with his economic geography text on Australia. He had sent Herbertson his notes and the noted geographer had replied in a letter to Taylor, Nov. 18, 1908. *AJH - Leonard Russell 1912*

> Much of the work is both interesting and suggestive, but also here and there it is too discussive. You have hardly been critical enough either of your authorities or of your own style (11).

However, he did compliment Taylor on his "sense of map-making." Grif visited Herbertson and the School of Geography in Oxford in December and

20

was invited for tea by Mrs. Herbertson, who was a geographer in her own right. It was during these visits to Oxford that Herbertson invited Grif to write a general geography text on Australasia for English schools and this finally appeared in 1914 — *A Geography of Australasia*, published by Clarendon Press, Oxford and edited by Herbertson. Taylor's first textbook, *Australia in its Physiographic and Economic Aspects*, was also published by Clarendon Press, Oxford in 1911 with Herbertson as editor. Taylor received this book while in the Antarctic and regarded it as his "first-born." Herbertson was one of the leading British geographers of the time and was very interested in producing a series of school texts that would be more than physiographic introductions and gazetteer accounts of each state.

In the preface to the book, Taylor outlined the three stages in the growth of geographic knowledge-exploration and primary mapping, accumulation of statistics to make possible secondary mapping and finally examination of data as a whole from a "geographical point of view." He stated that he tried to follow the plan of Mackinder and Davis by laying "the most stress on the physical controls which govern the industrial conditions in our island continent" (12). Part I of the book concerned the "Physiographic Aspects" including Herbertson's system of natural regions. Part II covered the "Economic Aspects" and was based on a series of lectures on commercial geography Taylor had given at Sydney University in 1907. The concluding chapter was entitled "Future Close Settlement in Australia" and predicted a population of nineteen million by the end of the century — a view which would spark a heated controversy a decade later. This textbook set the pattern for many subsequent ones and was a very competent piece of work for its time. Taylor's extensive travels had given him a unique knowledge of Australia and this early book is still considered useful for its information on the physical environment.

Taylor was now finishing his work on the *Archeocyathinae*. He had not reached any definite conclusions about them, since he found the creatures somewhat contradictory. But he wrote up his findings and the final memoir was published by the Royal Society of South Australia in Adelaide in 1910, with Howchin the editor. The memoir earned Grif an extension of his scholarship from the 1851 Commissioners and a third year at Cambridge.

This was the year of the Shackleton Antarctic expedition of which Grif's Australian friends Edgeworth David and Douglas Mawson were members. Mawson wrote Grif when he returned to Australia that he and his companions had reached the magnetic Pole and that he had

> soon lost that acquired taste for seal oil in which they had all revelled, how decent life had been in the Antarctic, but how unmitigated the agony of sledging in anything but mid-summer. It is all a dream now, a nightmare (13).

Although Grif later tried to persuade Mawson to go on Scott's 1910 expedition, he would have no part of it.

About half the year at Cambridge was available for journeys and Grif, always the eager traveller, made full use of the holidays. During the Easter vacation, with brother Rhys (who was now attending school in England), in tow, Grif made a tour of five countries — Belgium, France, Germany, Holland and Luxembourg — in two weeks, at the amazing cost of £5 per person. He also did a great deal of weekend tramping and cycling with Simpson, and from one of these expeditions came Grif's only attempt at a short story which was entitled "Wydotter and I go Mammoth Hunting." This was written in 1909 but Grif found a publisher only in 1922 when it appeared in his old school magazine in Australia, the *King's School Magazine*. Grif's type of humour is evident in the title. The Wydotter in the story is really Simpson, the opposite of "simple" being "wise" and the opposite of "son" being "dotter."

After term ended in 1909, he was again on his way to Europe — this time with R.J. Russell, a student of philosophy and mathematics who wanted to go to Venice and let Grif decide the route they would follow. They toured for three months, mostly on foot, while Grif wrote 300 pages in his journal and reported in his diary that the 99 days cost him £39. They ate simply, usually bread and milk, eggs, sardines, chocolate and fruit, since Grif's motto, as he often stated, was to fare simply and fare farther. While on this trip, Grif received several pieces of good news — his 1851 scholarship had been renewed for an extra year, his little book on Australia had been accepted by Oxford University Press, and he had received a valuable prize from Emmanuel College. On the return trip to Cambridge they ran out of money in Munich and lived on chocolate and buns for two days. They then spent a month in Heilbronn in a special German school for foreigners at a cost of £2 per week. Ever conscious of costs, Grif said this was cheaper than living in Cambridge! To recall world events at that time it is interesting to note that during this trip Grif saw his first airplane and the first dirigible — the Graf Zeppelin. At the time the newspapers were also full of the discovery of the North Pole by Peary and the controversy with Cook.

Grif graduated from Cambridge on 25 June 1909. After paying £17, Taylor was eligible for the degree of B.A. (research) from Cambridge. Since he did not own the appropriate black clothes required for graduation, he borrowed Wright's coat, Simpson's vest, and Kleeman's hood for the occasion and had his photograph taken in his borrowed finery.

October 1909 marked the beginning of Taylor's third year at Cambridge and there were many changes. Simpson did not return, and Laby had obtained a job in New Zealand. Early in November Shackleton gave a lecture at Cambridge which was attended by a large crowd since this was the period during which the English were fascinated by polar exploration. Taylor liked Shackleton's style of lecturing but did not think much of the fact that he hardly mentioned any of the men on the expedition. This was the first time Grif seemed interested in polar exploration, but it is doubtful that he ever thought of it in connection with himself. He must soon think of what he should do after Cambridge. On October 6, Taylor received a letter from Professor David stating:

would like to hear your plans for the future. Do you contemplate returning to Australia? There is a possibility of a position of Physicist to the Meteorological bureau of the Commonwealth. Let me know if there is any chance of your being a candidate for such a position (14).

Taylor was not sure what the job entailed and wrote to David,

If it consists of a careful scientific study of the physical controls governing life and industry in Australia, then there is hardly any position in the world I should better like to apply for . . . If however, the work is mainly meteorological, I have had too little experience (15).

However, on December 11 another exciting prospect arose for Taylor, one that would change his life. He was invited by Dr. Arthur Hutchinson, a university demonstrator in mineralogy, to attend a dinner in the Old Combination room at St. John's College, the very formal annual dinner of the Cambridge Philosophical Society. The menu of that dinner, printed in gold on white, (now in the Fisher Rare Book Library, University of Toronto) was preserved by Taylor with the notation, "The dinner that sent me to the Antarctic."

The dinner was attended by many famous men, among them the son of Charles Darwin, Sir George Darwin, who was the Plumian Professor of astronomy and experimental philosophy at Cambridge. During the evening, Hutchinson and Wright were discussing Scott's forthcoming Antarctic expedition and Wright stated that he would go if Taylor would. Marr asked Taylor if he would like to go with Scott as English geologist and that he (Marr) considered him "just the man." He said he had already discussed the matter with Dr. E.A. Wilson, Scott's scientific advisor, who, he said, would phone Taylor the next day to sound him out.

References

1. Griffith Taylor. Private Diary, 1907.
2. National Library, Canberra, MS 1003/1/150.
3. National Library, Canberra, MS 1003/1/153.
4. National Library, Canberra, MS 1003/1/151.
5. Letter from Taylor to Davis, dated Dec. 16, 1907 quoted in George Tomkins. "Griffith Taylor and Canadian Geography," Unpublished Ph.D. thesis, University of Washington, 1965. p. 186.
6. Letter from Davis to Taylor in Tomkins, p. 19.
7. Taylor, Griffith: "Journeyman at Cambridge," p. 71.
8. Taylor, Griffith: "Journeyman at Cambridge," p. 67.
9. Taylor, Griffith: "Journeyman at Cambridge," p. 169.
10. Taylor, Griffith: *Journeyman Taylor*, p. 63.
11. Tomkins, p. 21.
12. Taylor, G: *Australia in its Physiographic and Economic Aspects* (A. J. Herbertson ed.). The Clarendon Press, Oxford, 1911, p. 3.
13. National Library, Canberra, MS 1003/1/155.
14. National Library, Canberra, MS 1003/2/30.
15. National Library, Canberra, MS 1003/2/31.

CHAPTER 3

Antarctic Preparation

Because Taylor's role in the Scott expedition is little known to modern geographers and because much new information was available in the Taylor papers in Canberra, the Scott expedition story is told here from Taylor's point of view. To anyone growing up in the first half of the Twentieth Century, Scott of the Antarctic was a household word. Every schoolboy or girl knew the tragic story by heart; how Scott and his four gallant companions struggled to reach the South Pole only to find that they had been beaten to their goal by the Norwegian Amundsen, and how all died on the return journey just a few miles short of a food depot.

To the generation born after 1950 Scott is not well known. The Second World War and the moon explorations provided a new group of heroes. It is, however, interesting that books about Scott and the tragic expedition of 1910-12 are still appearing: *Scott of the Antarctic* in 1977, *Scott and Amundsen* in 1979 and *Captain Oates* in 1982.

In the early years of the Twentieth Century there were few parts of the earth remaining to be explored. The North Pole had been reached in 1908 by Peary and Cook, although some controversy existed as to which, if either, of the two contenders actually reached the North Pole. The South Pole was the goal of the explorers of the day, especially of English explorers, aided and encouraged by the Royal Geographical Society and its President, Sir Clements Markham. Markham saw Polar exploration as a nursery for seamen, and one of his protegés was Robert Falcon Scott, a young naval commander. Markham was instrumental in getting funding for Scott's first Antarctic expedition, in the *Discovery*, in 1902. Two members of that expedition were A.E. Wilson and Ernest Shackleton. "Uncle Bill" Wilson was to be Scott's greatest friend and supporter, and Shackleton his rival and enemy. The expedition was not an unqualified success. The ship was frozen in the ice and the expedition reached only 82° 17'S, but the book that Scott wrote, *The Voyage of the Discovery*, was a resounding success and paved the way for Scott's second expedition.

Shackleton led an Antarctic expedition of his own in 1907 and achieved the furthest south — within 97 miles of the Pole, 360 miles beyond Scott's furthest south. This was the expedition of which Edgeworth David and Douglas Mawson, both friends of Taylor's, were members. Another member was Raymond Priestley, the English geologist who was later to become Grif's brother-in-law. In June 1909, Shackleton returned to London to a hero's welcome. The Shackleton expedition excited the English public to the thought that the South Pole must be discovered by an Englishman. In a speech in London in June 1909, Scott said that he must:

go forth in search of the object and thank Shackleton for nobly showing the way . . . (1).

Scott finally announced his plans for his second expedition on 10 September 1909, and an expedition office at 36 Victoria Street was rented.

Perhaps his decision to go for the Pole was due partly to Kathleen, his bride of a few months. Born Kathleen Bruce, the daughter of Rev. Lloyd Bruce, the Canon of York, she belonged to the advance guard of feminists in the early years of the Twentieth Century. She had studied art in Paris and, in Rodin's studio, met and formed a close friendship with the American dancer, Isadora Duncan. She was a beautiful woman, tall and blue-eyed with an olive complexion, and had the rare quality called presence, and an elemental vitality that was both obvious and elusive. Kathleen wrote Scott on 11 July 1908

> Write and tell me that you shall go to the Pole. Oh dear me, what's the use of having energy and enterprise if a little thing like that can't be done. . . . It's got to be done, so hurry up and don't leave a stone unturned (2).

She and Scott were married in September 1908 in the Chapel Royal at Hampton Court, and she immediately began to work hard at advancing his career. She knew a good many important people in the Navy and in the upper echelons of London society, and she was determined that Scott would be the first to the Pole.

She was very helpful in getting financial assistance for the expedition while Scott, with the help of Wilson, began to gather the scientific crew. Wilson was given the task of interviewing the prospective members. Thousands of applications for places on the expedition were received and were carefully screened by Wilson. Many of the scientists chosen were from Cambridge, and Taylor was one of them. It happened in the following way.

After the momentous dinner at St. John's on December 11, Taylor, as agreed, met Wilson at the Cavendish Laboratory and heard about the proposed research aspects of the expedition. Wilson gave Taylor a letter of introduction to Scott, but Taylor did not immediately go to London to see Scott, since Christmas vacation was approaching and he was planning another European trip. Four of the young Australians at Cambridge, Suvain, Glassen, Lusky and Taylor, eager to escape England's cloudy skies for some sunshine, left for a cycling holiday in the south of France. One of the experiences Taylor remembers about his trip was that passing through the Alps he was able to ride his bicycle for some forty km over an ice field and

> Got a wrong impression of the ease of riding on snow. In the Antarctic . . . tried another cycle on snow and nearly came to an untimely end (3).

Wilson wrote Taylor on January 9 to "call at the office, 36 Victoria St. Monday afternoon, where you will meet Captain Scott. He has all your papers." Taylor duly called upon Scott and was a little worried.

Swells in hop hats and spats were there and I was shocked to hear that they were future members of the expedition. However, in the South they were just as untidy as any of us. Scott was just as I had expected him to be, a sturdy, clean shaven naval officer with plenty of humour and plenty of decision (4).

Scott informed Taylor that his idea was to have three geologists on the expedition, one of them being his old sledge mate, and Taylor's friend, Douglas Mawson. He also told Taylor that he was going to try for the Pole along the route he had used before.

Scott was obviously pleased with the interview and Wilson was instructed to inquire about Taylor's physical capacities. Taylor wrote him:

I have never had a serious day's illness as far as I remember. My father is over sixty and is now inspecting mines in the backwoods of Tasmania. A few years ago he was in the interior of Borneo on the same business, so I hope I shall stand the Antarctic work fairly well, if heredity accounts . . . I have tramped through Samoa and Fiji and done 400 miles of hiking in the Swiss Alps . . . I write this to show that I am not unused to roughing it (5).

Obviously Taylor was in a quandary. He wanted to go to the Antarctic with Scott, but he wanted a job to come back to. Concerning the negotiations regarding his appointment to the Antarctic expedition, Taylor noted on these private letters now in the National Library of Australia: "I hope the details will be kept confidential until after my death" (signed G.T. July 6, 1961).

It is interesting that Taylor believed that someone would write a biography of him and perhaps he was embarrassed by these private letters. They show Taylor as eager to make the best deal for himself, both in the Antarctic and afterwards in his job in Australia. Similar correspondence probably took place in similar situations for many scientists. Grif was at least honest in showing himself to the biographer, warts and all.

In January David cabled him from Australia advising him to apply for the Weather Service position. Taylor kept his options open. He applied for the Australian position, at the same time consulting with Wilson and Scott with regard to Antarctic matters and visiting the expedition ship the Terra Nova in Tilbury. He also wanted more time in the Alps and suggested in a letter to Wilson in January:

I had a talk with the Secretary of the 1851 Commission and he thinks that if Captain Scott would write a note to him, to the effect that it would be advantageous that I spend the next few months studying Alpine topography as modified by ice action, the Commissioner would readily permit me to change my plan of work (6).

Professor David was not convinced that Taylor should accompany Scott. The evidence was in a letter from Wilson to Taylor, January 23:

Yesterday I got a letter from David. He made no mention of you, but he mentioned several others whom of course we feel we should consider if only in common courtesy as his nominees. Probably in withholding your name he felt he had something better for you. . . . We shall stand by the wire which I sent you this morning (the offer to take Taylor as senior geologist) . . . as I understand you are as keen as ever to go with us and that you will do all you can for the good of the expedition as well as your own credit wherever you may be stationed when it comes to finally settling places by Scott. I want you to send me as inclusive an idea as you can of what you particularly look forward to working at (7).

A letter from Scott to Taylor January 24:

I have seen Mawson and his opinion of you entirely satisfies me as to your suitability for the expedition. I therefore write to formally accept your candidature. I am sure that you will perform the work in the right spirit and easily surmount all the small difficulties which are bound to arise from time to time (8).

Again, Wilson to Taylor January 26:

Supposing David decides against your proposal of coming with us? From your letter, I understand you have left the decision in his hands. When do you expect to hear? We have to make up our minds that we will accept you if you apply but we cannot run the risk of losing you in a month or so and then find it necessary to fill your place. I cannot consider myself tied to your appointment unless you consider yourself tied also. I committed myself by my wire to you on Sunday but you withheld your decision. That of course liberates me if I wish, but I would prefer that you accept the billet and come with us. I hope you will come (9).

Cables flew back and forth between Taylor and David. David convinced the Weather Bureau to appoint Taylor and he would work for them until November, when he would join the Scott expedition in New Zealand and would be in their employ while in the Antarctic. In a letter from Wilson February 9:

I expect to see Captain Scott on Friday and will get answers to questions raised in your last letter. Will you let me have a list of anything that you consider necessary in the way of scientific outfit. I will ask Scott about 1) your proposed visit to Switzerland, 2) cost of return fare, 3) proposal you made of going out before the *Terra Nova* (10).

And again, February 11 from Wilson:

The letter you wished Scott to write to the Society of the '51 Commission has been sent. You may count on £10 from the expedition fund to cover your travelling expenses to Switzerland (11).

Things were falling into place. Taylor was very pleased to receive a cable on 15 February, 1910, from the Commonwealth of Australia.

Offer Griffith Taylor, Emmanuel College, Cambridge professional position Meteorological Office, salary to commence £310, duty Shackleton records, no insuperable objection if he wishes to accompany expedition Scott. I shall be glad if you will let me know as early as possible whether you accept the appointment as I understand it is desired to make it immediately (12).

Meanwhile, letters flew between Taylor and Wilson and indicated that not only was Taylor taken on as senior geologist, but that Scott would pay for his trip to Switzerland. The above correspondence depicts Taylor as money grabbing. He was certainly concerned about his future. All his life he had had to be careful of money, and knew that, unlike many of his wealthy Cambridge friends, he had only his own intelligence to get him a place in the world.

Scott was keen to have Mawson join the expedition because of his Antarctic experience. Mawson visited Taylor in February in Cambridge and met his friends, showed them his Antarctic pictures and gave a lecture at the Research Students' Club. Mawson was a great success with the Cambridge students but was undecided about joining the Scott expedition. In a letter to Taylor February 15 he stated:

My movements are too involved even for me to understand. I am almost getting up an expedition of my own. Scott will not do certain work that ought to be done, I quite agree with him that to do such would be to detract from his chances of the Pole and because of that I am not pressing the matter any further. I certainly think he is missing the main possibilities of scientific work in the Antarctic by travelling over Shackleton's old route. However he must beat the Yankees. I may proclaim my expedition shortly. In the meantime the geologists of Scott's expedition are yourself, Thompson and myself. If I draw out I get somebody in my place. . . . Have had long discussion with Scott at his office and home (13).

Soon after another letter (no date):

I have not seen Scott yet. I have had enough Antarctica unless very good offer. Shackleton particularly does not want me to go with Scott. He has something on Strictly private [underlining is Mawson's].

And again

I have just called on Scott and made an appointment to see him. He referred to you. I told him you were a good man. I guess you will be able to go if you want. I shall not go unless I reckon he offers me something very good. I have had experience enough for a lifetime. If I do join Scott, Shackleton will fume no end (14).

This exchange of letters does strengthen the notion that Shackleton and Scott were enemies. Shackleton was indeed planning another Antarctic expedition of his own, one that eventually took place in 1914.

Mawson told Taylor of the prowess in walking possessed by Antarctic explorers. In order to impress Scott with their stamina, Taylor and Wright decided to walk the 50 miles from Cambridge to London one cold February day. They started off at 5:45 a.m. with a supply of chocolate and hard boiled eggs. They covered 26 miles in the first six hours but by the time they entered the London suburbs they began to feel the blisters on their feet. At 5:45 p.m. they had reached St. Paul's Road in Islington where they dropped the hard boiled eggs in favour of tea and toast. They had averaged 14.4 minutes per mile in the non-stop effort, and although Wright appeared to suffer no ill effects, Taylor could hardly stand on his feet the following day.

Taylor was also eager to have his friend Charles Wright join the expedition. At meetings with Scott in February, he pointed out how useful Wright's special training in Canadian surveys and in physics in Cambridge would be in the Antarctic. Scott sent for Wright and in an hour or so he was engaged as physicist for the study of ice in a land still undergoing an ice age. Wright felt that he owed his position on the expedition to Taylor, as he wrote many years later:

Griffith Taylor and I were research students together at Cambridge. Grif was a friend of Douglas (later Sir Douglas) Mawson who had accompanied David to the South Magnetic Pole during the Shackleton expedition of 1907-9. . . . I was doing some research on penetrating radiation which I thought might be quite different in the Antarctic. I naturally at once applied for the post of physicist. I was promptly rejected. Grif Taylor then persuaded me to walk with him to London next day to see Captain Scott and Wilson. . . . The upshot was that I was accepted by Scott on Wilson's advice (15).

By March 3, Wilson had informed Taylor that Mawson had refused the offer of a place in the expedition. Taylor, however, had almost everything he had requested, two months in the Alps because of Scott's financial generosity, permission to return to Australia to his new job at the Weather Bureau, then some weeks in the New Zealand Alps before joining the *Terra Nova* in November.

With fellow geology student Vernon, Taylor set out for the Alps in March. He admitted that he never had the same travelling companion twice, since they usually said "once was enough." Again this was a walking tour — first to Berlin, then up the Rhine to Switzerland. Before returning to England, Grif visited

Florence and Rome and spent a few days with the glaciologist Nussbaum at Bern.

Taylor had only a week to prepare for the Antarctic before leaving England for Australia. In London he visited Douglas Mawson who gave him a ticket to Albert Hall to see Peary presented with a medal. Taylor recalled that on that occasion he met Captain Bartlett, the Newfoundlander who had just returned from Greenland with Peary, and who also received a medal. This was the same Captain Bartlett who was later to experience the awful adventures in the Beaufort Sea with Stefansson. Taylor remembered that Bartlett thanked the donors with a very loud voice and that Peary dropped his medal, a medal that Taylor discovered later had been designed by Kathleen Scott.

Taylor was invited to dine with the Scotts before leaving England and was enchanted by Kathleen Scott who was a brilliant conversationalist. Taylor stated that they

> discussed politics, and militarism, a subject upon which Scott and his
> wife did not see eye to eye (16).

He was impressed that she was also a keen walker and had done long tramps in Switzerland, and she was impressed with the tale of Taylor and Wright and their 50-mile walk from Cambridge to London. Taylor remained an admirer of Kathleen Scott all his life, asking her advice later during his courting days and persuading her to design the engagement ring for his wife-to-be.

On 20 June 1909, Taylor boarded the steamship *Orontes* for Melbourne to take up his job in the Weather Bureau. He was the first scientist to be appointed with training in a science other than meteorology so felt impelled to learn something of meteorology on the voyage to Australia. Taylor never did like the daily forecasting which appeared in every important paper in Australia, and which was the main work of the Bureau. As part of his job with the Weather Bureau, he was also asked to collate Professor David's meteorological notes taken on the Shackleton Antarctic expedition, a task he did not enjoy. He spent some time consulting with David as to the research he would be doing in the Antarctic.

At the University of Sydney a room was filled with David's Antarctic specimens from the 1907 Expedition. Here Grif first met Raymond Priestley who had also been on the Shackleton expedition, and was working on David's data with Alan Thompson who had been engaged as one of the geologists on the Scott expedition. However Thompson, a graduate of Oxford, developed lung trouble at the last moment and his position on the Expedition was offered by Scott to Raymond Priestley. Priestley accepted the offer and by so doing certainly changed Griffith Taylor's life since, on their return from the Antarctic, Priestley introduced Grif to his sister Doris who subsequently became Grif's wife.

Grif had one further request concerning the Expedition. Ever conscious of money matters, he wished to be paid his regular salary from the Weather Bureau while in the Antarctic, but also to receive remuneration for his services as Senior Geologist. In a letter from the Department of Home Affairs dated August 5, he was granted the former but:

> it will be necessary to obtain Executive approval for you to receive remuneration for your services as Senior Geologist and this will be sought at an early date (17).

This approval finally came on December 2 from Dr. Hunt, the Commonwealth Meteorologist:

> permission is granted to Mr. Thomas Griffith Taylor, physiographer in the Meteorological Bureau to take up the duties of Senior Geologist and to receive remuneration therefore in connection with the British Antarctic expedition (18).

Grif spent the months before going to the Antarctic on surveys for the New Federal Capital in the Canberra region. Canberra at that time consisted of an old church built in 1823, a parsonage, and a post office occupying an apartment of a house in the shadow of Mt. Ainslie. The surveyors camped in tents pitched approximately where the Prime Minister's Lodge now stands. Taylor covered most of the area by bicycle. He did a rough topographic survey which he employed later to make a large relief model used in the actual designing of the capital. In a letter to Professor Marr at Cambridge Taylor wrote:

> Our politics are very funny. The two papers in Melbourne are bitterly opposed to a "bush capital," for at present all Government is from Melbourne, though later it must be from a new city in New South Wales — but over a hundred miles from Sydney! When they read my report showing that both Canberra and Dalgety are on the belt of lowest rainfall in Eastern Australia . . . and are on a long low valley extending 200 miles south from near Yass, and quite liable to seismic shocks . . . they may feel somewhat concerned. However there's a rainfall of 60 inches in one corner of the Territory, and it's a beautiful situation with the large River Murrumbidgee flowing through it. We had fifteen senators to inspect the site, and four nearly got drowned (19).

Finally on November 4 the *Terra Nova*, with Scott in command, arrived in Lyttleton, New Zealand. While the ship was undergoing repair, Scott agreed that Taylor, with Debenham and Wright, should spend a couple of weeks in the Mt. Cook region of New Zealand seeing as much of ice eroded landscape as possible. Taylor learned a great deal from this field work, for the glacial features represented a stage between what he had seen in Europe and what he was to see in the Antarctic. Grif asked his sister Dorothy to come along on the trip, since he always enjoyed her company and she was an excellent hiker. On the trip they practised skiing which Grif had never done before. Again he proved to be no athlete, achieving some remarkable contortions with entangled legs and skis. Taylor, ever ingenious, invented a method of skiing with Dorothy on the backs of his skis, somewhat, he said, after the fashion that the Emperor Penguin carries its chick.

Dorothy proved herself an excellent hiker who could keep up with the men. It was Dorothy who made a sledging flag for Frank Debenham which he took with him to the Antarctic. She was a feminist, and probably because of her influence, Grif also was a champion of women's rights. In a letter to Grif while he was in the Antarctic, Dorothy said:

> I would have gone myself (to the Antarctic) with half a chance. I suppose it will be some time before feminine exploration parties are organized in those regions (20).

After the two weeks in the New Zealand Alps the party, including Dorothy, made its way to Lyttleton for their rendezvous with the *Terra Nova* and the rest of the expedition. There Taylor received a letter from Scott, written on October 10 while Scott was in South Africa before boarding the *Terra Nova*. In it, Scott told Taylor the plans for his Antarctic duties, especially his plan that Taylor make a sledging trip soon after the arrival in the Antarctic:

> Your letter is in my hands, gives great pleasure. You have indeed kept the Antarctic flag flying — well done — we are lost in admiration of your journalistic talents. We sail on Saturday; I want to get to know the people on board so am coming with the ship, Wilson goes by mail, will fix everything in Melbourne. I think you will be very pleased with the spirit on board. I have never seen a happier ship's company. I feel whatever our success we shall make a record for contentment and good comradeship . . . as far as I can see every suggestion you make is sound and workable. Naturally you have freedom to select your own position and I am glad that you have decided to make south as leading geologist. I should like you to see all that can be seen. I think that great use can be made by you of the coming season. You can have a little party to go west in February, March, April next, if you like — but we will discuss all this when we meet (21).

On the *Terra Nova* en route to Melbourne, Scott did not know that Amundsen was also on his way south. The Norwegian explorer had announced his intentions of an Arctic expedition, but after leaving Norway in the *Fram* announced his change in plans and his intentions to try to be the first to reach the South Pole. On October 12, when the *Terra Nova* reached Melbourne, Scott was given a cablegram from Amundsen which read:

> Beg leave to inform you Fram proceeding Antarctica, Amundsen (22).

Despite Mawson's misgivings, Scott had organized a scientific expedition, and only one part of his plans was the proposed dash to the South Pole. Now he knew that he was involved in a race which he did not want and the idea of which upset him. On the way south, he was to convey to his men his fear that the Norwegians might win the race to the Pole.

Taylor with Debenham and Wright boarded the *Terra Nova* in Lyttleton. Grif felt that he had his affairs in order. He was ready to go. The Antarctic and the greatest adventure of his life lay ahead. His sister Dorothy waved farewell to him from the dock in Lyttleton, when the *Terra Nova* sailed south on 30 November 1910. Grif sent his last letters to his parents. In none of his letters did Taylor ever admit the possibility that he might not return from the Antarctic. However, he was a realist and knew that there was such a possibility. He wrote to his father:

> If I have bad luck and do not get back, I wish any salary owing to me (250 per annum from Scott and 310 per annum from Commonwealth) be divided equally between Mater and Dorothy. If it reaches noble proportions (say 800 or so), they might give 100 to the Varsity for a small annual prize in Economic Physiography. But I trust the Varsity will not get any such endowment for 10 years at least when I may be a millionaire (23).

Grif celebrated his 30th birthday en route to the Antarctic. He was ambitious enough to want some measure of acclaim from his Antarctic adventure. He was prepared to work hard and he did, both physically and mentally. He certainly wrote a prodigious amount during his months on the Antarctic continent, probably more than any other member of the expedition. His sledging journals, his diaries, and his letters are still exciting to read. They show a rather naive young man, with a good sense of humour, one who was willing to help his friends and colleagues and to learn as much as he could from the experience. He had some near catastrophes but no indication of fear or even pessimism appears in his journals. He seemed to have had an immense store of self confidence and a belief that he could surmount every obstacle that the Antarctic put in his way. He was ready to test himself against that most challenging of all the continents.

References

1. Huntford, Roland: *Scott and Amundsen*. Hodder and Staughton, London, Sydney, Auckland, Toronto, 1979, p. 247.
2. Huxley, Elspeth: *Scott of the Antarctic*. Weidenfield and Nicolsen, 1977, p. 168.
3. Taylor, Griffith: "Journeyman at Cambridge," p. 176.
4. Taylor, Griffith: "Journeyman at Cambridge," p. 186.
5. Taylor, Griffith: "Journeyman at Cambridge," p. 186.
6. Taylor, Griffith: "Journeyman at Cambridge," p. 187.
7. National Library, Canberra, MS 1003/3/21.
8. National Library, Canberra, MS 1003/2/23.
9. National Library, Canberra, MS 1003/2/24.
10. National Library, Canberra, MS 1003/2/26.
11. National Library, Canberra, MS 1003/2/27.
12. National Library, Canberra, MS 1003/2/29.

13. National Library, Canberra, MS 1003/2/140.
14. National Library, Canberra, MS 1003/2/141.
15. Wright, Sir Charles. "Foreword" in Edward Wilson: *Diary of the 'Terra Nova' Expedition to the Antarctic 1910-1912* (edited by E.G.R. King). Blandford Press, London 1972, p. XII..
16. Taylor, Griffith: *Journeyman Taylor*, p. 85.
17. National Library, Canberra, MS 1003/2/44.
18. National Library, Canberra, MS 1003/2/48.
19. Taylor, Griffith: "Journeyman at Cambridge," p. 216.
20. National Library, Canberra, MS 1003/2/6.
21. National Library, Canberra, MS 1003/2/45.
22. Griffith Taylor. Private Diary, 1910.
23. National Library, Canberra, MS 1003/2/46.

CHAPTER 4

Grif in the Antarctic

The ship that took Grif to the Antarctic, the *Terra Nova*, was a wood barque built in 1884 by A. Stephen and Sons, Dundee. It was 187 feet long and had a gross weight of 764 tons. Purchased by the Scott expedition for £12,000, the ship had 20 years experience in the Arctic and Antarctic ice. The ship carried three masts, and was officially a Royal Yacht which meant that she could fly the white ensign, a privilege accorded to certain favoured vessels. She sailed from England to South Africa under the command of Navy Lieutenant E.R.G.R. Evans. Captain Scott then took command of the ship for the voyage to Lyttleton, New Zealand. There the provisions, the 19 Siberian ponies, 34 sledge dogs as well as the motor sledges, the scientific equipment, the disassembled house that was to be their headquarters, the 65 people and their gear, and coal were fitted in every spare space available.

Thirty-five people were to be disembarked on the Antarctic continent, members of the "Shore Party." This included 7 navy men and 12 scientific staff, most of whom Taylor had met before leaving England. On board ship they soon got to know each other, and soon all acquired nick-names. Under Captain Scott who was usually called "The Owner," was the second in command, "Teddy" Evans. Teddy Evans seems to have been an enigmatic character in all the accounts of the Expedition. He had hoped to mount an Antarctic expedition of his own, then transferred his support to Scott at the price of his position as second in command. He wanted desperately to be a member of the Pole Party, but Scott decided against it. Because of this, he survived, and after Scott's death became the official leader of the expedition. He rose to the rank of Vice Admiral, Commander-in-Chief of the Royal Australian Navy and was raised to the peerage as Lord Mountevans in 1946.

Lieutenant Victor Campbell, called "The Wicked Mate," was a very popular member of the expedition and was chosen by Scott to be the leader of the so called "Northern Party," which underwent unbelievable hardships that next winter. The story was well told by Priestley in *Antarctic Adventure*.

Captain Lawrence Oates was a captain of the 6th Inniskillin Dragoons and the only Army man on the expedition. He too was a member of the Pole Party, and his name is familiar to all who know the Scott story as the tragic figure who went out alone to die, and whose body was never found. Oates was the subject of a recent book on the Scott expedition, *Captain Oates, Soldier and Explorer*, in which he is presented as the English gentleman typical of his age, who loved his country, and did what he considered to be his duty, even to giving his life to help save his companions. He did not always agree with Scott, but from the book it is obvious that Oates admired Scott and that the admiration was mutual.

37

Lieutenant Henry Bowers, only 26 years old, was a Scot, an officer in the Indian Royal Marine and a great favourite of all the expedition. The shortest (5'4") of all the members, he had flaming red hair and a very prominent nose, so was affectionately nicknamed "Birdie." He was intensely loyal to Scott who praised him as a "perfect treasure." In a last minute change of plan he was chosen by Scott as the fifth member of the team who would make the final dash to the Pole. Many people have speculated about Scott's reasons for taking Bowers: his navigating ability, his toughness, his irrepressible cheerfulness and optimism, and most important, his loyalty to his leader. Cherry-Garrard described him as "one of the two or three greatest friends of my life. He was transparently simple, straightforward and unselfish. For him, difficulties simply did not exist" (1).

The chief of the scientific staff was Dr. E.A. Wilson, called "Uncle Bill" by everyone on the expedition. Scott looked to him for moral support as well as scientific advice, and the scientists and navy men liked and respected him. He had been with Scott on the 1902 expedition, and although he had been trained as a medical doctor, Wilson's role in the expedition was that of artist as well as scientific leader. Many of his exquisite water colour drawings of the Antarctic landscape are preserved at the Scott Polar Research Institute and have been reproduced in a beautiful book published in 1972 for the Institute (Edward Wilson, *Diary of the Terra Nova Expedition to the Antarctic 1910-12*, H.G.R. King, editor). In the foreword of this book, Charles Wright, then 84 years old, recalled that the man who most influenced his life was Edward Adrian Wilson.

> Affectionately known to all of us on Scott's last expedition as Dr. Bill. Scott was the mind of the expedition and Wilson its heart. . . . Undoubtedly Dr. Bill's most important function on the expedition was as mentor and advisor to Captain Scott. Some of the younger members, including myself, used him as our go-between to Scott (2).

As a doctor as well as Scott's friend, Wilson was understandably chosen as a member of the Pole Party and died with Scott in that last camp only a few short miles from One Ton Depot.

Scott said of him "Words fail me when I talk of Bill Wilson. I believe he really is the finest character I ever met" (3). Cherry questioned

> What made him so loved? Because he never for a moment thought of himself. He truly believed that circumstances do not matter, are nothing, but that the response of the spirit that meets them is everything. He had immense self control and patience; behind that calmness and gentleness was a strong and decided personality. In such a world, violent, angry and tired, Wilson set a standard of faith and work (4).

The men whom Taylor knew best and wrote about in his own book of the expedition, *With Scott: The Silver Lining*, were the scientists. There were two other geologists — Frank Debenham, "Deb," whom Taylor had grown up with in Sydney and who was to be his sledging mate, and Raymond Priestley, who had been on Shackleton's expedition and was to become Taylor's brother-in-law. Charles "Silas" Wright, who made the famous hike from Cambridge to London with Grif, was the physicist-glaciologist on the expedition.

George Simpson, Grif's friend from Cambridge, was the meteorologist, and because of his perpetual good humour was called "Sunny Jim." The biologist Edward Nelson, not a particular friend of Taylor's, was extremely right wing in his ideas, and Taylor, being rather a socialist, had great arguments with him.

A particular friend of Grif's was Apsley Cherry-Garrard who was the only Oxford man on the expedition. Cherry, who came from a wealthy family, was so keen about the Antarctic that he had paid £1,000 for the privilege of joining the expedition. "Cherry" became famous as the editor of the *South Polar Times*, the newspaper with three editions published by the expedition during the winter of 1911. Cherry was the person sent out with the dogs to meet Scott's party on the return from the pole. After waiting for a time at One Ton Depot, not knowing that the three survivors desperately needed help only 11 miles south, he returned to the base camp. He remained for the second year in the Antarctic, and was a member of Atkinson's search party which finally found Scott's tent and the bodies of Scott and his two companions. Cherry felt partly responsible for the tragedy for the remainder of his life, and it bothered him so much that he suffered a mental breakdown. One of the best books written about the expedition was Cherry's *The Worst Journey in the World*, published only in 1922 after Cherry had returned from the First World War.

Herbert Ponting was the official photographer of the expedition and Grif was not too fond of him, resenting the fact that Scott almost made him rather than Grif the leader of the "Western Party." Ponting's beautiful pictures of the Antarctic, many of which were published in *The Great White South*, are classics to this day. Cecil Meares, in charge of the dogs, and Bernard Day, in charge of the motor sledges, did not appear very frequently in Taylor's journals.

Tryggve Gran, strangely enough, was a Norwegian member of the expedition. Although only 22 years old when the expedition began and with a passion for polar travel, he had attempted to organize an Antarctic expedition himself in 1909. However, when Scott came to Norway in March 1910 to test his motor sledges, the famous Arctic explorer Nansen persuaded him to take Gran as a ski instructor. Gran became a great friend of Grif's and was one of the four members of Grif's Western Party. His usual nickname was "Trigger." Taylor himself was usually called "Grif," but sometimes "Keir Hardie" because of his socialist views.

On December 2, just a few days out of Lyttleton, the ship experienced a full gale and although Taylor played down the danger, it was almost the end of the expedition. As Taylor recalled:

> The ship was hove to for two days and though we novices could see well enough that things were very lively we did not know how grave a risk we were passing through. . . . The seas were incessantly washing over the waist where the pumps are placed at the foot of the main mast and burying the deck under several feet of water (5).

39

The pumps became clogged and the bilge was feet deep in water, so the command was given to bail out the ship with buckets, a rather unique experience with a ship of that size. For two days, in two-hour shifts, the men bailed. Luckily the gale died down. It was an experience Taylor said he never wished to repeat but fortunately the ship was saved — and the expedition. The gale had begun on Taylor's 30th birthday and he noted in his diary "the storm which nearly sank us was making too much of a simple birthday" (6).

Taylor wrote letters daily to Dorothy and to his mother and father while on board the *Terra Nova*. These letters, which were delivered when the ship returned to civilization in March, are preserved in the National Library at Canberra, along with letters which Dorothy wrote to Grif and kept for him to read on his return. About the storm, she wrote that they were

> worried sick at the news of the storm at sea, and "bailing out." Mother thinks you capable of the most romantic fibs just to ease her mind (7).

On board ship there was time for fun and games as well as the preparations for the Antarctic. Debenham played the flute and Nelson a mandolin. Scott played bridge with the officers. Lillie, a biologist on the expedition, did caricatures of some of the men. The caricatures are preserved in the Scott Polar Research Institute and a clever one of Grif is seen in Figure 2. He laughed at the caricature, but was a little hurt. Dorothy, in a letter to Grif in April 1911 sympathized:

> I went to bed in a blue fit of melancholy, all because you did not like your caricature. Well anyway, it is better to have big uglinesses that can be enlarged, than little uglinesses that if they are exaggerated in pictures, save the drawing all together. I suppose it was your chin and your forehead peaks they chose to poke fun at. I am not sure your face won't make you more friends when you come home famous than if you were regularly handsome (8).

On board ship, there was time also to talk to "the Owner" about the scientific work to be done in the Antarctic. Scott was very interested in the scientists' problems. He was well aware of the pressing need for comprehensive surveys as a means of ultimately producing detailed and accurate maps of the region and the bulk of this task fell to the two geologists, Taylor and Debenham (9).

Scott informed Taylor that he was to be a member of the first "Western Party" to leave shortly after arrival in the Antarctic to do a geological exploration of Victoria Land. Taylor wanted very much to be the leader of this party, and resented Scott's choice of Ponting:

> I wasn't frightfully pleased and pointed out it was practically a glacier investigation and that I had three years on such work . . . it would seem queer if the chief scientist of the trip were under the charge of a photographer even if he has climbed many peaks and travelled everywhere (10).

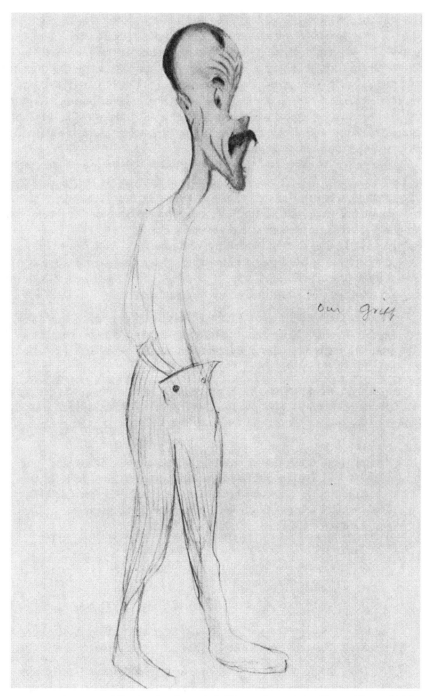

Figure 2. Caricature of Taylor by Dennis Lillie on board the *Terra Nova*, 1910. SPRI S4/24/3

It was the first time — but certainly not the last — that Taylor argued with Scott. Taylor quoted Scott as saying, " 'You are about 26, aren't you?' and I replied, 'No sir, I'm over 30.' I didn't feel it necessary to add 'but only by four days.' 'Oh,' he said, 'in that case Ponting won't mind your being in command.' " As it turned out, Ponting was not made a member of the Western Party, and Grif was put in charge. Without doubt Taylor's significant contribution to Antarctic exploration and geological and geomorphological study was the result of his leadership of this and a second geological party, since he chose the actual areas traversed and the work to be done.

By December 9 the ship had entered the zone of pack ice and on December 10 crossed the Antarctic Circle. The ship was delayed in the pack ice until December 30, a frustrating delay for Scott since he now knew that Amundsen was also on his way to the South Pole, and Tryggve Gran said to Taylor about Amundsen, "He's just the man to do what he desires" (11).

Typically, Taylor kept busy writing while on the *Terra Nova*. He had an arrangement with a Melbourne newspaper, the *Argus*, to do a series of six articles about the expedition. These, of course, would have to be finished before the ship returned to civilization, and Grif calculated:

> 3200 words = 2 columns = 1 article. Now each page of this journal equals roughly 700 words . . . a little more than a penny a word or a pound a page. I wouldn't give that for them. I wonder if I can do it (12).

He had to obtain clearance for these articles from Scott who was very careful that none of his scientists scooped his own reports of the expedition. Finally on January 3 Scott gave his permission in writing (13):

> Dear Taylor:
> Having regard to the condition of the ships articles and our discussion in Sydney, I give you permission to write articles for the Australian press to be sent home in the ship in 1911, provided that these articles are not published in any form except in Australian Daily Newspapers.
>
> Yours sincerely,
>
> R. Scott.

Grif managed to complete the articles and they were duly published and read with interest in Australia, as Dorothy reported in one of her letters.

> Mrs. Harris tells me she read all your articles with much interest but Mrs. Boulton says the articles are hard to understand, being too scientific for the ordinary reader to appreciate. This is exactly the opposite of what everyone else tells us (14).

Grif also loved writing poetry and penned a little poem called "Life's Round in the Antarctic." He was very fond of this poem and used it as an introduction to his Antarctic lectures in later years.

> Big floes have little floes all around about them
> And all the yellow diatoms couldn't do without them
> Forty million shrimplets feed upon the latter
> And the shrimps make the penguins and the seals and whales much fatter
>
> Along comes the Orca and calls them down below
> While up above the afterguard attacks them on the floe
> A bold explorer tumbles down and stoves the mushy pack in
> He's crumpled up between the floes and so they get their whack in
>
> And there's no doubt he soon becomes a patent fertilizer
> Invigorating diatoms, altho' he's none the wiser
> So the protoplasm passes on its never ceasing round
> Like a huge recurring decimal, to which no end is found (15).

The *Terra Nova* was still in the pack on December 25, so Christmas was celebrated on board with great festivities. The wardroom was hung with all the sledging flags that the Expedition members had brought south with them — another tradition of Polar travel. Grif's flag was oblong with a Union Jack and a map of Australia, and the shields of Emmanuel College and Sydney University. His motto was *Expergiscamini* (meaning "Get a move on," according to Grif). Scott's flag had the St. George's cross and Wilson's showed a lion with the motto *Res non verba*. Several of these flags can be seen today at the Scott Polar Research Institute at Cambridge. Taylor recalled the activities.

> The service was read by Captain Scott and differed little from the ordinary Church of England service, except by the insertion of two special collects. Then some gifts of tobacco and sweets were distributed to all on board. Christmas dinner was turtle soup, penguin stew, roast beef, mince pies, plum pudding. Afterwards songs and banjo music ended the festivities (16).

Finally, on 31 December 1910 land was sighted:

> Late in the evening of the last day of the year, the officer of the watch reported, "Land in sight". . . . On the starboard bow . . . extended a range of mountains in a vast panorama. There were two widely separated peaks rising in solitary splendour . . . even grander owing to the clothing of snow from top to bottom (17).

The ship finally reached Cape Crozier by January 4 and Taylor saw the awesome sight of Mt. Erebus rising 13,000 feet in the Antarctic sky. Photographer Ponting took a picture of Taylor and Wright exploring a grotto in

Figure 3. Taylor and Wright explore iceberg. Jan. 5, 1911. *Terra Nova* in distance. Ponting photograph SPRI D79/27/88

a huge iceberg (Fig. 3) By January 6 the *Terra Nova* had anchored and unloading began — hard work for each man, hauling 200 lb. loads all day from the ship to the site on Cape Evans. Meanwhile their winter head-quarters was being assembled by the seamen, a house 50 by 25 feet, and the expedition had moved all its gear to its new home by January 10th. In his journal, Taylor described in detail the appearance of the hut. It was arranged in typical navy style. Near the entrance were the quarters assigned to the seamen and cooks. A large galley-stove was placed on the right, and behind this the rows of tins of food. To the left were the wire mattresses of the seamen, supported on iron frames. The wardroom where the 16 officers lived occupied two-thirds of the hut. A long table extended down the middle. The right and left side were divided into cubicles — on the left those of Oates, Meares, Bowers, Atkinson and Cherry-Garrard; on the right the three compartments for the scientists, one for Debenham, Gran and Taylor (Fig. 5), one for Nelson and Day, and one for Simpson and Wright. This was to be their home for the six months of darkness — 17 square feet each. Half of the left side was for Scott, with his own cubicle, and one for Evans and Wilson. There was a darkroom, stove and even a pianola, taken from the officers quarters of the *Terra Nova!*

Taylor did not have long to become accustomed to life at Cape Evans, since Scott handed him his letter of instruction on January 26 (18).

Letter of Instruction to Griffith Taylor, Esq.

'Terra Nova'
Jan. 26th 1911

Dear Taylor:

I propose to disembark a sledge party of which you will have charge on the sea ice of McMurdo Sound as near the Ferrar Glacier as possible.

Your companions will be Messrs. Debenham, Wright and Petty Officer Evans.

You will have two sledges with food and equipment for 8 weeks. The object of your journey will be the geological exploration of the region between the Dry Valley and the Koettlitz Glacier.

Your movements must depend to some extent on the breaking of the sea ice. Your best and safest plan appears to be to carry all your provision up the Ferrar Glacier to a point in the medial moraine abreast of Descent Pass and to make a depot at that point. With a fortnight's food you could then continue the ascent to the junction of the Dry Valley Glacier and descend the valley of that Glacier. On returning to your Depot you will be in a position to observe the extent of the open water and you can either descend the glacier and pass to the East around Butter Point or climb Descent Pass descending by the Blue Glacier or by one of the more Southerly foothill glaciers and thus continue the examination of the Koettlitz Glacier area.

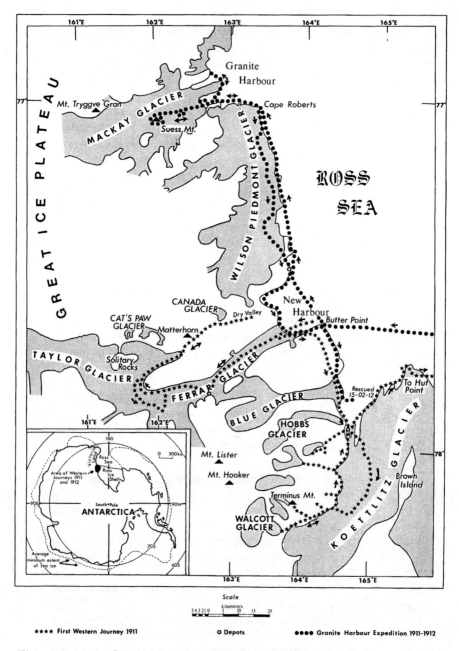

Figure 4. Map of Taylor's Antarctic Journeys 1911 and 1912 (redrawn from map in *With Scott: The Silver Lining* by Griffith Taylor.)

46

On completion of your work you should cross to Hut Point being careful not to camp near the open water. Supplies of biscuits and other provision will be found at Hut Point but should be used sparingly — [this last phrase crossed out by Scott] remaining from the discovery Expedition and seals will certainly be found near Pram Point. I regard it as practically certain that Cape Evans can be safely reached over the new sea ice before the third week in March provided that the party keeps well within the bays.

The safest course would be to climb the ridges behind Arrival Heights, descend to the sea ice beyond Castle Rock, continue on the sea ice to a point one or two miles from the end of Glacier Tongue and from thence to the South Side of Cape Evans.

Wishing you the best of luck [This added in pencil].

Yours sincerely,

R. Scott

[This added in pencil as a P.S.]:

It is very probable that you will see some sections of the Depot Party near Castle Rock or East of it on the Barrier. If so you should communicate.

The letter identifies Taylor's sledging companions as Debenham, Wright, and Seaman "Taff" Evans. Evans was a Welshman, and considered to be very strong. He was chosen by Scott as a member of the Pole party. No one will ever really know why Evans broke first on the return from the Pole, tragically delaying the team. However, on this earlier sledging trip with Taylor, he was a strong member and earned compliments from all three scientists.

The purpose of the journey was the geological exploration of the region between the Dry Valley and the Koettlitz Glacier (see Map Fig 4). Taylor was to study the physiography and glaciation, Debenham the geology, and Wright the forms of ice structure. Taylor described his work as:

the bearing of geology on scenery — in other words how has the land surface been affected by the flow of glaciers, by the action of wind, frost, water and ice? How do the resulting features differ from those observed in more temperate regions where water plays such an important part and ice erosion is absent (19).

On January 27, the ship carried Taylor and his party to the western side of McMurdo Sound, a distance of about 30 miles. The total load for the eight-week trip was a heavy one, about 260 lbs. per person, and man hauling was to be the means of transportation. The weights were the following:

2 sledges and sledge runners	171 lbs.
food for 8 weeks	630 "
tools, tents, etc.	130 "
instruments, cameras, etc.	65 "
4 personal bags	50 "
Total	1,046 lbs.

Taylor was evidently a very good leader, but he was also lucky in that no major problems were encountered — from the weather, the terrain or the men. The area they were assigned had been briefly explored during Scott's Discovery expedition, but Taylor's party was to examine the area of the Ferrar Glacier and the nearby Dry Valley in more detail. It was the kind of experience that Taylor loved. They were exploring unexplored territory and everything was new and exciting. Actually no student of glaciology or topography, except Edgeworth David, had ever visited Antarctica before this time.

They spent a week in that interesting area of Antarctica — the Dry Valley, a twenty mile area free from ice or snow. They studied the snout of the Taylor glacier, and examined its terminal moraine. A drainage lake some two miles long occupied the valley at the snout, and this lake Taylor named after his old friend Professor Bonney of Cambridge. Several tributary glaciers Taylor also named after his geology friends — Sollas, Marr, Suess, and this toponomy was later adopted by Scott. Taylor's first impression of the Dry Valley was given in his sledging journal:

> Imagine a valley four miles wide, 3000 ft. deep and 25 miles long without a patch of snow and this in the Antarctic in latitude 77½° S (20).

Taylor's sledging journals during this period are filled with beautiful and detailed sketch diagrams of the topography. Taylor gave the name Taylor Glacier to this arm of the Ferrar Glacier. He was pleased and honoured that Scott later confirmed the name of the glacier — and the Dry Valley — in his honour. However, this honour was not without argument, as was seen in a letter several years later from H.T. Ferrar. Ferrar was a geologist in Scott's 1901-04 expedition, and had ascended with Scott the glacier which was subsequently named after him. He had also roughly surveyed the great Koettlitz glacier, a task which Taylor and his colleagues repeated in much greater detail. As Ferrar pointed out in the letter below, Taylor decided that the North Fork of the Ferrar Glacier was a separate glacier and gave the name Taylor to this feature. In his letter to Taylor dated 27 September 1913, Ferrar wrote:

> The other day I saw a proof sheet of your map which I understand is to be published in the narrative of Scott's Second Antarctic Expedition. You have omitted the names North Fork and East Fork which have appeared on Admiralty charts and displaced the name Ferrar with your own. As your action is contrary to the customs of

geographic practice, besides being somewhat in bad taste, I venture to draw your attention to it before the map is finally published (21).

However, the Taylor names were adopted by the Admiralty, and the glacier and dry valley are still called after him.

In preparing for the trip, Taylor allowed each man to take some reading material. He described in his journal the books the members of his party carried with them:

> Debenham took a copy of Browning, Taylor Tennyson and three small German books, Wright took two mathematical books, both in German and Seaman Evans a novel and a "Red Magazine". In the evenings, we discussed literature. Evans had read many popular works and was far superior in this respect to any of the other seamen . . . He had read some of Kipling's poems and had no use for them . . . Especially did he delight in the works of the French writer whose name he anglicized as Dumm-ass! (22)

A few excerpts from his diary give an idea of Grif's evocative style of writing and the evident good spirit and friendship of the explorers.

> As we could not take the sledge beyond the glacier, we packed up the tent and sleeping bags and carried them down towards the sea. Wright carried his pack in the Canadian method by a "tump-line" round his forehead.

> He took the theodolite. Evans wrapped his goods and tent round the tent poles and carried them like a standard over his shoulder. Debenham and I took the food. I found as usual the Italian method of carrying a harp — a strap over the right shoulder — suited my convenience best. Debenham copied an Australian swagman with a smaller bundle in front neatly balancing a roll on his back.

> — Next morning before rising Wright remarked on the severity of his exercise the day before, which had left him so bathed in perspiration that he felt clammy all night. On examining his sleeping-place however, he found that something had blocked the stream by the tent and its icy current had been flowing under his bag most of the night. With the temperature ten below freezing his hydropathic treatment was by no means appreciated by him!

> — We had much difficulty guiding the sledges and they capsized several times. Every now and then the sledge runners would jam sending a jar through one's frame so this unpleasant experience became known as a "jam-jar" (23).

Cherry-Garrard described Grif's appearance on his sledging journeys:

> Thus old Grif on a sledge journey might have notebooks protruding from every pocket and hung about his person a sundial, a prismatic

compass, a sheath knife, a pair of binoculars, a geological hammer, chronometer, pedometer, camera, aneroid and other items of surveying gear, as well as his goggles and mitts (24) (Fig. 6).

On March 2 when the exploration work was completed, Taylor and his party started out for Hut Point, the campsite used by Scott in 1902 as his headquarters and later by Shackleton:

> The summer was over now and we were getting 50 degrees of frost in the nights. The weather was gloomy, the sun rarely appearing till it had sunk below the level of the pall of stratus (25).

The last few days before reaching Hut Point were very miserable, with blizzards, high winds and fog. The sleeping bags were three times their normal weight. The weather was very cold and they had been sledging for six weeks. Taylor's diary records their condition:

> March 10 . . . a rotten night . . . there is no joy in us although sounding merry . . . a long argument arose as to course. Evans felt frost bite in toes.

> [And March 12:] rotten night, slept about 4½ hours, sore ear, cold knees, everything wet, helmet a mass of ice, and so wrapped my head in windproof pants . . . we tried dancing to warm feet. Played cards, sang, changed socks . . . We can't see a hundred feet anywhere (26).

Probably because of Grif's good humour (imagine dancing under such conditions!) and his correct decisions as to the route to Hut Point in spite of the fact that his maps were in error, they survived. Shackleton's hut was reached on March 13. They found Scott with Wilson, Atkinson, Cherry-Garrard, Bowers and Keohane already camped. Bowers described their arrival thus:

> For days their doings were the topic of conversation. Taylor especially is seldom at a loss for conversation and his remarks are generally original if sometimes crude. Most of us were glad to listen when the discussions in which he was a leading figure raged around the blubber stove (27).

Grif spent the next month until mid-April in the 1902 hut. He considered it one of the most interesting spots in the Antarctic. As he wrote many years later:

> It is the locality where the Ross Ice Shelf presses on Ross Island, and where, if a ship is lucky, she can reach the fixed ice to unload her stores for exploration most easily. Our expedition made much use of it, though it was 15 miles south of Cape Evans. But more significant perhaps is the fact that hundreds of folk have visited it since. Dozens of huts and labs are sited near it. The American base in the I.G.Y. work was in the shallow valley a few hundred yards to the east of the old hut, and right under Observation Hill. On the latter is the high

wooden cross which records the tragic end of the 1910 expedition. A mile or so east again on the Ross Ice Barrier itself is the New Zealand headquarters, where Hillary started his journey to the Pole. It is likely to be as busy in the next few years, for modern ice breakers can get through the six-foot pack ice now. No longer will the expeditions have to wait till the pack ice goes out naturally, about the end of January, as heretofore (28).

During this time Taylor came most in contact with Scott since he slept next to him on the bare wooden floor. He enjoyed the month at Hut Point:

Scott told me to carry on with the meteorology while Bowers was away on a depot trip. Wright had not had enough sledging and went with Birdie Bowers. Next day Meares got up early and lit the fire. Keohane and I were cooks. I cut the seal-meat into blocks with my dagger. It went into the "hoosh" (soup) with porridge, raisins, herbs and pepper. Then I made the cocoa. We found a box of Shackleton's big whole-meal biscuits. They were delicious toasted and buttered (29).

In a day or two, the men had swung into a routine, and time passed not unpleasantly, for there were a thousand jobs to do. Grif did the meteorological readings, mended his sleeping bag, fixed his shoes, took his turn as cook and when the weather permitted, went off to get seals. The activities of the geologists seemed to have been contagious, and Bowers was the keenest of the pseudoscientists who was always bringing rock specimens to Debenham or Taylor. "Here you are," Birdie would say of a particularly uninteresting block. "Here's a gabbroid nodule impaled in basalt with feldspar and olivine rampant " (30). It was the sort of wit that Taylor enjoyed. During the month Grif often went sketching with Bill Wilson and marvelled at the wealth of color with low sunlight falling on the expanse of snow and ice. His diary records:

Over Mount Discovery there were bands of stratus, white over the black lava, and dark over the sky. To the south were wide expanses of pale yellow tints. To the north appeared beautiful yellow-green tints shading to yellow-grey on the east. In the sky was a grey green and a brighter orange band, against which stood up the 13000 ft. purple band of Mount Lister (31).

Inside the hut, there were long discussions. Grif liked arguing with Scott and found him interested in everything, from Mormonism, the medieval ramparts of Aigues Mortes to the pronunciation of ancient Greek. Cherry remembered the days at Hut Point fondly as "some of the happiest in my life. Just enough to eat and keep us warm, no more — no frills or trimmings" (32). Grif recalled those days.

51

Every evening before sleeping, Scott, Wilson, Debenham and I had some sort of a scientific discussion, usually of a local geological problem such as the origin of Castle Rock (33).

For his part, Scott found Taylor:

full of good spirits and anecdote — an addition to the party (34). . . . Taylor's intellect is omnivorous and versatile. His mind is unceasingly active, his grasp wide. Whatever he writes will be of interest, his pen flows well (35).

Taylor usually got on well with Scott. He wrote Dorothy about him and she replied:

I like Scott. You do not gush about him but he always shows up in a favourable light. Yes, I have decided that I like Captain Scott (36).

As time went on, Scott became anxious to get back to Cape Evans since he felt that some calamity might have injured hut, men, and ponies at the base camp. On 29 March, Wright was lowered on the new ice below the hut, and found it was three inches thick, but open water lay off Ross Island all the way to the hut. On the 31 Scott said he thought they could get to Cape Evans by going along the coast beyond Castle Rock and skirting the ice-foot, but on April 7 they were still waiting for the ice to thicken. Taylor's journals record that Scott then asked if anyone wanted to walk around the sea ice to Castle Rock with him and Atkinson, and Taylor volunteered. To his chagrin, Taylor fell in when trying to cross a thinly covered lead. Scott reported:

he had a very scared face for a moment or two whilst we hurried to the rescue, but hauled himself out with his ice axe and walked back to the hut. He had gone in up to the armpits but luckily there was no wind, or 24° of frost would have been serious (37).

Finally on April 11, Scott gave the word to leave, and with eight others, including Grif, left for Cape Evans. They had to cross to the camp on the new ice and it was a rather risky business. Taylor was critical of this decision of Scott's, although the criticism found in his diaries did not appear in *With Scott: The Silver Lining*:

Evans fell in as the Owner jerked around for a crevasse too sharply. Scott said, "Shall we camp here or go on?" Everyone said, "Go on." So he promptly said, "Out tents and we'll have supper first." So we wasted 1½ hours at least and when we'd finished it was pitch dark. I had a long consultation with Scott. I would push on 2 miles through blizzard with compass for it all looked good ice but he won't hear of it and says that I appear to think he's conspiring to take my life or some such jest (38).

Taylor stated that none of them enjoyed the situation. They were camped on new ice and had not the faintest idea how far off the open water lay, and had no food with them. About 3 p.m. they shifted camp onto the ledge Taylor had found at 10 a.m., though he wrote in his journal that this was due to Birdie's suggestion, for he (Taylor)

> had kept a well-calculated silence . . . no one else ever seems to put forward any variations in arrangements (39).

Bowers' version of the story went thus:

> You knew that there was only about 6 or 10 inches of precarious ice between you and the black waters beneath. Altogether I decided that I for one would lie awake in such an insecure camp. At this place the island made a wind buffer and it was positively calm though the blizzard yelled all round. I urged Capt. Scott to camp on this ledge and Taylor fizzled for making for Cape Evans, so Scott needed to ensure Taylor's safety, as he put it, and we made for the ledge. We were two nights there and on the morning of the 13th it took off enough for us to head home (40).

Scott had announced that they would take food sufficient for only one lunch for the 16-mile trek to Cape Evans — a statement that caused Taylor to confide to his diary, "But what if we have to camp two days on the Glacier Tongue?" Taylor considered the trip unnecessary in view of the risk since they had plenty of seal meat at Hut Point and could have waited longer for the ice to be safe. He had cause to be alarmed, since it was under exactly the same conditions, in 1916, that several members of the abortive Shackleton expedition also tried to cross the pack ice to Cape Evans and were never seen again. It was assumed that they were drowned in the vicinity of Glacier Tongue. Grif described that night as follows:

> That night we had a strong blizzard and looking out in the morning, we saw that the whole sound was free from ice. If it had been half a day earlier, it would have meant the loss of half the expedition (41).

They finally set off at 8:15 the next morning to complete the remaining few-mile-hike to Cape Evans. They were all glad when they finally reached camp and Ponting recorded the return with a photograph which shows Taylor with a beard. This was the only time during his lifetime that Taylor sported a beard and because it was so criticized (he confided to his diary), he typically kept it most of the winter.

In Taylor's journal there is a page dated April 1 and marked "private" which is rather revealing. It begins "Pal's birthday. Good luck to her and to all of us." The rest of the page is in shorthand. It is a shorthand that must have been private between Grif and Dorothy since it contains some undecipherable symbols. However, enough can be deciphered to indicate that there certainly was some dissatisfaction among the scientists concerning Scott's leadership.

> Last night owing to the absence of the Owner, we had a general discussion dealing with sedition and conspiracy. There is strong

53

uniformity of opinion as to the misdeeds of our leader. . . . Ponting is sore due to the way he has been treated in regard to photographs. . . . They wasted time at the Hut which could have been used in going South. The motor sledge was lost by the Owner. . . . This last trip home was suicidal as all are agreed. He jibed at carrying a tent and only allowed one meal of hoosh. . . (42).

It certainly is not surprising that under such conditions, there could be criticism of their leader by the men. It seems incredible that they got along so well. Thus it is quite understandable that Taylor's criticism of Scott did not appear in his published accounts of the expedition. Basically, Taylor liked Scott, and when he died a hero's death, Taylor rightly decided not to publicize the disagreement.

In April the long Antarctic night began and the Expedition was fairly well confined to quarters for six months. In later years, Taylor was often asked what they found to do during this slack period, but would reply that they never felt time heavy on their hands, and said that they got on very well together probably because of Scott's foresight in choosing congenial friends for the expedition members. He described how they spent their days thus:

Let us consider the routine of an average day in the hut during the winter. Since we never saw the sun, what time did we keep? It was rather curious. We were on the 170° meridian; so that our time was actually twelve hours and forty minutes earlier than Greenwich. However we did not bother about the forty minutes, and our clock in the hut recorded Greenwich time. Needless to say we had several chronometers for accurate work in surveying, and most of us carried watches. Several times our men would visit one of the distant huts, and sleep there. Then later they couldn't decide whether their watches showed noon or midnight, and would tramp back demanding breakfast, when we were turning in for the "night".

In the hut men would turn in about nine or ten, and the night watchman would take over till eight next day. Each of us was on watch once a fortnight. The Messdeck slept in, and much enjoyed scolding an officer, when he fell over something, and woke them up. I usually heated up some ice and so got enough hot water for a bath. Then I wrote up my diary, or worked out something comic (so I hoped) for our South Polar Times. Our chief job was to see there was no risk of fire, and to go out every hour to see if there was an aurora display or not. Our duty was unpleasant if a bliz was "on". If we saw from the graph on the "blizzometer" that nothing was registering, we took a whisk-brush, and crawled on the the ridge of the roof. We found the inlet pipe of the blizzometer was choked with snow, so it could not work. We cleaned out the pipe, meanwhile usually getting our clothes full of snow, and then descended to see the blizzometer pen behaving properly. An hour or so later we might have to repeat the operation (43).

54

Figure 5. In winter quarters — Cape Evans. May 18, 1911. Debenham, Gran and Taylor. Ponting photograph SPRI P79/27/270

Another duty was to keep the galley-stove going with coal, take out the ashes and waken the cook. Taylor found himself getting very sleepy at the end of his watch and often Wilson got up early to take part of Grif's watch, although always stating that he needed to do some painting. With his usual kindness, Wilson also copied some of Taylor's sketches for him and spent hours coaching him in drawing.

One of the highlights of the winter, at least for Grif, was the series of evening lectures, three each week, organized by Scott and called by him "Univeritas Antarctica." In this respect, Scott was unlike Shackleton who never showed any interest in the scientific work of his colleagues. Scott was a naval officer, but had an exceptional grasp of the physical sciences. He presided at the head of the big table and attendance was optional, but the fifteen officers and scientists always attended. All were asked to speak on their specialty, and all but Cherry-Garrard did so. The Seamen were invited and came to the first two lectures, that of Wilson on Antarctic birds, and Simpson on halos and auroras, but the third, Taylor's lecture on physiography, was too much for them, as Taylor stated in his journal, and they stopped attending. Oates, who was in charge of the horses, talked about horsemanship, Ponting about photography, and Scott about the Ross Ice Shelf. Nelson, the biologist, chose as his topic, "The Origin of Life," Wright spoke on radioactivity, Simpson on meteorology, and Atkinson, the doctor, on scurvy. Of course, at this time, the cause of scurvy was still not known, since nothing was known of vitamins. However, "Uncle Bill" Wilson knew of the importance of fresh meat and insisted they eat fresh seal meat before they were given the tinned meat they had brought from England. Grif loved to lecture and described his experiences thus:

> My first lecture was given on the 5th May. I had made a dozen diagrams, which were displayed on Clissold's pudding board. We ran a tube across to the table from our cubicle, and so had a fine acetylene light on the sketches. Cherry drew a rude sketch of the lecturer and pinned it on the lamp shade. I talked about topography at Lake George and Canberra, and explained peneplains and the effect of uplift on small streams. Deb criticised the physiography technique, and the Owner egged him on! But Bill came to my rescue, and said the onus was on the geologists to try and disprove these new scientific ideas. A good time was had by all; for Sunny Jim said he started half-asleep, but was quite awakened by the discussions (44).

Scott was very impressed with Taylor's lectures stating "Taylor gave an introductory lesson on his remarkably fascinating subject, modern physiography" and the next morning told Taylor he had dreamt of his lecture saying:

> How could I live so long in the world and not know something of so fascinating a subject. I must enter a protest against the use of the word "glaciated" by geologists and physiologists. To them a "glaciated" land is one which appears to have been shaped by former ice action. The meaning I attach to the phrase and one which I believe is more commonly correct is that it describes a land at present wholly or partly covered with ice and snow. I hold the latter is the obvious meaning and the former results from a piracy committed in very recent times (45).

Taylor also lectured on the Beardmore Glacier, which he had never seen but he had Shackleton's expedition account with him and had read Professor David's journals. Of special interest to him was the fact that his own special fossils the *Archeocyathinae* had been found there. Grif even had a specimen of the fossil-bearing green marble to exhibit. Scott enjoyed Taylor's lectures and wrote in his journal:

> Taylor gave a most interesting lecture on the physiographic features of the region traversed by his party in the autumn. His mind is very luminous and clear and he treated the subject with a breadth of view which was delightful (46).

In the evenings, Grif loved the arguments or "cags" he had with the other scientists. Cherry described the evening arguments as follows:

56

Scott sat at the head of the table. If you felt talkative you might always find a listener in Debenham. If inclined to listen yourself, it was only necessary to sit near Taylor or Nelson. . . . There was never any want of conversation (47).

There was a very definite difference in outlook among the men. The staunch liberals, or leftists were Taylor, Debenham and Gran. Wright and Simpson also called themselves liberals. Nelson was extremely conservative and Ponting and Cherry-Garrard were also conservatives. Taylor believed that Wilson was a liberal but he, with Scott and Teddy Evans, kept away from the "cags." One evening the subject of "Votes for Women" came up. Debenham and Taylor tried to persuade the conservative group:

> that women, being rather more important than men as regards to the population of the world, did at least deserve to have the small say in affairs resulting from the vote (48).

A "cag" with Gran about the Celsius and Fahrenheit scales is interesting for climatologists. Taylor said he had devised:

> Taylor's natural and rational scale in which zero equals -40° F, below which it is damned uncomfortable and 100° F is the other point — with similar effects on man. Divide into 1000 parts — don't worry about decimals. After all, it is the effect on man that matters (49).

The other activity which took a good deal of time and made for lots of fun was the publication of a paper, *The South Polar Times*, to continue the tradition begun on Scott's earlier expedition. Cherry-Garrard who had brought a typewriter with him was appointed the editor. The contributions were to be non-scientific and anonymous. Taylor certainly contributed more than his share of copy for the *S. P. T.* — about one third of the three numbers published. The copy produced in the hut, Taylor mentioned many years later, eventually occupied a position of honour on a special stand in the British Museum. Raymond Priestley many years later described the magazine as one "of more than ordinary merit . . . one of the outstanding literary productions of the Expedition" (50).

These original hand written or typed articles, now in the archives of the Scott Polar Research Institute were presented by Mrs. Angela Cherry-Garrard in 1959 (51). Of Taylor's contribution to the newspaper, Cherry wrote:

> He was a most valued contributor to the S.P.T. and his prose and poetry both had a bite which was never equalled by any other of our amateur journalists (52).

The articles are unsigned, but the poem reproduced below can be easily recognized as Taylor's

Polar Wireless

When the Southern blizzard surges from the white plains of the Barrier.

57

Covering all with deadly snow-wreaths, blotting out both land and
sea.
Can it break the magic cables linking us to every region
Where we spent our days of study, days of youth and revelry?

Half the world is our possession: naught can curb imagination.
Though we're wrapped in folds of deerskin camped amid a field of
ice.
By the blessed help of Fancy, still we're free to wander gaily.
Through the wooded lanes of England — true explorer's paradise!

By the happy help of fancy we can leave the land of glaciers;
Hear the tolling from old Tom Tower, or the chimes from
Cambridge Arches.
Since the thrill of Skier's prowess on the slopes of Holman's Kol
Once again can feel the tump-line as we cross the muskeg marshes.

We can clothe the slopes of Terror with the sward of Kosciusko.*
When a thousand steers are grazing mid the tarns and moraines
green.
See the land of Cherryblossom and the maidens of Japan
Or the peaks of Himalaya hung above the Indian plains.

Lightly fades the lonely Igloo, merges in the college gray.
Where the Proctor and his Bulldogs hold their oft disputed sway.
Thus from the Lonelands to the Homelands all our thoughts are
speeding forth.
Faster far than wire or wireless: on Stretched Wings toward the
North (53).

*(Taylor had noted for his friends unfamiliar with Australia that
   "Kosciusko is an old glaciated region with tree covered moraines.")

An article that Taylor wrote for *The South Polar Times* called "Valhalla"
much impressed Scott. Not knowing the author, Scott wrote:

An article entitled Valhalla appears to me to be altogether on a
different level. It purports to describe the arrival of some of our party
at the gates proverbially guarded by St. Peter. The humour is really
delicious and nowhere at all forced. In the jokes of a small
community, it is rare to recognize one which would appeal to an
outsider, but some of the happier witticisms of this article seem to me
fit for wider circulation than our journal enjoys at present. Above all
there is distinct literary merit in it. . . . I unhesitatingly attribute this
effort to Taylor (54).

Taylor was of course very pleased by Scott's posthumous praise and he wished
the Valhalla article to be published in his last book Journeyman at Cambridge.

Since this book was never published, the article is reproduced here, since Scott seemed to think it was fit for wider circulation. It was the kind of humorous writing that Taylor enjoyed. He kept the manuscript all his life and it is now part of the National Library material in Canberra.

Valhalla. 2000 A.D. A celestial Medley

Dramatis Personae in order of appearance:
Jimson, whose rapid footsteps
    often sounded in the night.............................Simpson
Trigoran, our Norwegian ski expert..................Tryggve Gran
Neddy, our very active surveyor
    and second in command..........................Edward Evans
Turkey, our most good-natured,
    red-haired Lieutenant..............................Birdie Bowers
Etonspride, our military mate
    in charge of horses................................Captain Oates
Ratch, our medico, who was busy with
    improved blubber stoves...........................Dr. Atkinson
Charrard, our youngest mate from Oxford,
    helped Wilson....................................Cherry-Garrard
Jasper, our mineralogist from
    the Blue Mountains (Sydney).........................Debenham
Phizzy, the writer, who wandered about
    observing topography.....................................Taylor
Carolus, my Canadian mate from
    the Cavendish Lab (Physics)..............................Wright
Great Artist, used a sledge loaded with
    various cameras...Ponting

As the sun rose above the Sapphire Mountains, the Golden Gates of Valhalla swung open, ready to receive the heroes who might happen to be due from their stay in Purgatory (or lower). It was early in the day, and no one usually arrived until much later, for heroes are notoriously fond of their sleeping bags.

But soon, echoing through the silent porch, came the "flap-flap" of a new-comer, whose solid footsteps made each regenerate burglar turn in his sleep and dream of stalwart policemen. With head bending low the new arrival muttered, "Dear, dear! Here I've left the nether regions to get the first complete temperature record, and my thermometer is not working." Here he poured some of the liquid contents of the tube into the palm of his hand, and tasted it. "It's not like the alcohol I used to imbibe in my misguided youth. I doubt I've filled it with kerosene. Dear, dear! I wonder if I can get at the Medical Comforts up here?" And off he flapped around the next corner.

Soon two more applicants arrived at the Golden Gate. "Not allowed to bring in heavy baggage," said Peter.

"Dot is not baggage vot me and Neddy av got: dat is a teodolite," explained the laden speaker; and his companion added, "Oh, I say, you know, think how awfully jolly it will be to have an accurate survey of Valhalla. I've never see one of any description. That's what I've come up here for."

"Sorry," said Peter, "No surveys admissible. We'd be having companies floated to exploit the Golden Streets if they knew how to get here."

They entered somewhat disconsolately, the more so as the taller hero was abruptly ordered to hand over two pieces of plank — one down each trouser leg — with which he proposed to ski his way into the hearts of the Houris.

Peter looked out of his lodge window, and saw in the distance more company approaching. In the vanguard, with head up and chest well out, trotted a sturdy hero with a crimson crest. Volubly he queried:

"May I be permitted to enquire, that is to say, ascertain, if certain individuals with whom I am acquainted, to be explicit and with circumlocution, Mr. Jimson, F.R.S., and the renowned Scandinavian, Herr Trigoran, have perambulated this way for their matutinal constitutional?"

Here the speaker stood at gaze, like an improved Napoleon at Saint Helena.

"Oh stow that, Turkey," came from behind. "Let's get on in time for breakfast," and the objector (who was addressed as Etonspride) pushed forward with a grim look of determination on his visage that boded ill for any who came between him and his prey.

The pair moved forward and sighted Jimson trotting round, profoundly disgusted with the haloes of the Saints. "Hello, Jimson. Splendid Day," cried Turkey.

"What, what!" interjected the perturbed scientist.

"I entirely disagree with you. I fully believe that previous records of the weather of Valhalla were very negligently taken. My observations of the last few hours make me feel sure that its climate is much the same as that which we have just left down below. Where's Ratch and Charrard and all the rest?"

Ratch is behind improving his patent Hellfire Radiators. He's been as merry as a grig in the lower regions, carving up corpses and preparing for the comparatively cold time up here. I wonder how he will blarney Peter to let in the stoves. As for Charrard he's with the Director. They are attending the angelic moults, and studying variation in wing feathers.

Here Etonspride interjected: "There's two of our precious scientists fooling about over by the Sapphire Hills. Jasper's chipping off unauthorized crystals by the bag here. I don't see the use of them. You can't ride 'em, eat 'em, or sell 'em here. As for Phizzy he's gabbling German as usual, and he's so loaded with gadgets he can hardly move. I heard him say some rot about the topography from here to Hades being well-matured. So's my appetite. I'm off."

"Hi! Wait a bit you fellows," came from the gateway, "Just wait a minute. I want you to 'pont' right there, while I get a picture of your entry into Valhalla. I can't get this fellow to let in my apparatus, though I've packed it neatly in a Pantechnicon."

They looked back and saw the intellectual brow of the great artist gleaming with the reflected glory of the Golden Gates, and falling into studiously unstudied attitudes they 'ponted' to their utmost ability.

"It's a pity Carolus heard there was no ice up here," murmured Turkey when the ordeal was over. "He wouldn't take his ticket-of-leave, and is stopping down below to study the Conductivity of Electricity by bodies undergoing Combustion. Splendid fellow."

Here seeing a restaurant . . . 'they all went into the shop'.

Scott was pleased with the literary and academic efforts of the explorers but worried about the effect of inaction on the physical condition of his men. Somehow, he thought of the idea of playing football.

Taylor is another backslider in the exercise line and is not looking well. If we can get these people to run about at football, all will be well (55).

Several games were played and, as Taylor reported:

Would have been hilarious to watch, although there were no spectators. It was too dark to see the performers, the ground was usually slick ice, half the players had never played before, and two couldn't speak English. The teams were called "Gentlemen" and "No Gentlemen" and most of the players suffered some injury (56).

Grif himself could not walk after the first game and Debenham got a severe case of football knee in the last game. This had the more serious consequence of delaying the departure of Grif's sledging party for at least two weeks.

A great occasion was made of Midwinter Day, June 22. The hut was hung again with the sledging flags and they had a great feast with champagne, and speeches. Most of the speeches began with, "Captain Scott, Scientists and Gentlemen," so Grif brought down the house by stating, "Captain Scott, Gentlemen and non-scientists." Taylor reported that:

Charles Wright, who obviously was no public speaker said: "I have no remarks to make sir, in addition to those stated," and Birdie said he couldn't make a funny speech so he was going to show us something funny. Therewith entered four of the Seamen with a unique Xmas tree. It was built of a ski-stick draped with bunting with penguin-feather foliage, hung over with candles and candied fruit. The gifts were from Mrs. Wilson's sister. Birdie's contribution was magnificent!

Then later,

... a few of the seamen became rather merry by this time, and a set of lancers was not a great success, my partner finding the floor unsteady. . . . We all turned in before 2 a.m. and so ended our Midwinter Feast (57).

On June 27 the famous, or infamous, Midwinter Expedition left. Wilson, Bowers and Cherry-Garrard went to visit the Cape Crozier rookery to study the habits of the Emperor Penguin during the nesting season in darkness, in the middle of the Antarctic winter. Cherry-Garrard described this expedition in his book, *The Worst Journey in the World*, a book considered to be one of the most moving ever written on polar travel. Grif wrote later that he would never forget the return of the Cape Crozier party.

They looked inhuman. . . They didn't need to tell us what a hell they had been through, all the time, for the whole five weeks and a day. Their tent blew away. . . They could get down only once to the Emperor penguins nesting on a shelf. . . It took them 2 hours to crawl down, and then they found only a hundred penguins instead of the thousand they expected. . . The temperature was down to 77° below zero. Their sleeping bags froze stiff and they couldn't roll them up (58).

The long winter darkness went on, and by August most of the writers had lost their early enthusiasm for writing. Scott was an exception since he wrote an hour or two every day. Among the scientists Gran and Taylor were the most voluminous writers. More typical was Wright's journal that went something like this:

Aug. 1 — went up the ramp with G.T.
" 2 — ditto
" 3 — ditto

Taylor suggested to Wright that he should fill in his blank days with "Did not go up the ramp with G.T." (59).

Scott insisted on observing religious services each Sunday. Usually the scientists and navy men had to recite the Psalms in turn with Scott. Years later Debenham recalled some remarks of Grif's on one such occasion.

I was next to Grif and a little too close to Scott to quite hide the muttered comments on the verse. When Scott came to the phrase "and the little hills skipped like rams", it was too much for Grif's realistic soul and everyone could hear his "Damn nonsense! the psalmist was no geologist." Scott gave him a stern look (60).

In August, when Simpson, who was the meteorologist of the expedition, went on a sledging trip with Scott, Taylor was left in charge of the weather observations. He described his duties:

1. When I hear the automatic signal, I have to fly around and mark all the recording instruments to show exactly 8 o'clock on their charts.
2. I read the large standard barometer and its attached thermometer.
3. Change the chronometer papers and put ink on the pens for the blizzometer, thermograph, barograph and wind velocity charts.
4. Wind up the various clocks — once a week, on Monday.
5. Stagger up to the top of Wind Vane Hill . . . at a definite minute I read the anemometer figures alongside the anemometer cups.
6. Then I press four times on a button alongside and this is electrically transmitted to the record in the hut, and so gives a datum each day on that record.
7. I walk near to the screen and read the 3 thermometers — present, maximum and minimum. Then I readjust the 2 latter and read again.
8. By this time 3 minutes have elapsed and I walk a few paces to the anemometer and read the latter figures again.
9. Read the wind direction and note the steam-cloud direction on Erebus.
10. Change the blue paper in the sunshine recorder and clean the glass sphere. This is an awful job, for the frost crystals cling like glue to the 5 inch glass ball and have to be melted off by rubbing with the bare hands. A slow and painful job at -40° (61).

The sun finally returned in August, and Scott asked Taylor and Debenham to do a detailed topographic survey of the site at Cape Evans. They improvised a plane table from a telescope tripod and a drawing board, and the survey took several weeks — not a pleasant task in -40° weather!

An experience that Grif had that September was one that was typical of him — riding a bicycle in the Antarctic! He had ridden a bicycle on a glacier in Switzerland during his Cambridge days and persuaded Scott to accept a bicycle as a gift from a New Zealand firm to take to the Antarctic for short trips around head-quarters. On September 8, he had Scott's permission to go to Turk's Head, eight miles away, and be back in time for dinner. Grif found the bicycling hard going. His boots sank very little into the hard snow but the wheels of the bicycle made a two-inch rut and he had to push the bicycle for half the distance. Getting back was the problem. He became exhausted, and stopped to rest, then found

63

himself getting very cold in the forty-below-zero weather. When he was nearly done in, he luckily was met by Wright who was out walking and had come to investigate what he thought was a very large penguin, and they had almost reached the hut when Taylor collapsed. Wright went on to bring a sledge for Grif but he managed to make it on his own,

> I made a vow that the first bicycle ride in the Antarctic would be my last, and have every intention of keeping that vow (62).

Scott was not too pleased with Grif's escapade.

> He is a person who goes full bore at everything that interests him without a thought of what has to be done after, or how he is going to get back, a trait which is good enough except for the half dozen people who have to go and nurse him home again (63).

When Grif suggested to Scott that he would have to put it down to enthusiasm Scott replied

> Enthusiasm is all right in its place, but not when it means taking unnecessary risks. I expect more sense from one of my leaders (64).

However, in general, Scott was pleased with the scientists. In a letter to J.J. Kinsey, 28 October 1911, he wrote:

> On the whole, I am greatly pleased with the work done so far. If not journalistically exciting, it is far more scientifically interesting than that of our previous Expedition. We shall have an enormous mass of scientific data. Taylor, a remarkable character, has done some remarkable work in his own line (65).

Spring was now approaching and everyone was busy getting their sledging gear in order for the coming season — Scott and the support parties for the "Pole" trip, Campbell for the "Northern" party and Grif for the "Western" party.

On October 21, Scott gave Taylor his sledging orders for his big trip — the Granite Harbour expedition, called in later publications the "Western Party." The party included Taylor, as leader, Debenham, Gran and Seaman Forde, and the purpose was to do a geological exploration of the coast of Victoria Land. Originally they were to leave before the departure of the Pole party but because of the football injury to Debenham's knee they were delayed until early November. Taylor was a little disturbed by Scott's arrangements for them to be picked up by the ship.

> The method of our relief by the ship seemed rather comic. We were first of all to find Granite Harbour and then recognize a 5000 ft. bluff. . . . Here we were to await Captain Pennell (in the Terra Nova) in mid-January. No one on the ship had seen Granite Harbour (66).

As Taylor was to find out, the harbour turned out to be a dozen miles wrong longitude and the only bluff was 1650 feet rather than 5000 feet in altitude. Also,

Figure 6. Taylor in his sledging gear. April 13, 1911 Ponting photograph. SPR1
P79/27/255

Scott told Taylor he could spare no dogs or ponies for them since they were not racing against time:

> He also said quite reasonably that we need not take all our food on the sledges from Cape Evans since we could get sealmeat as ours was Coastal survey work. I think we all preferred pemmican but we had to bag in a supply of sealmeat when we could get seals (67).

Because of the delay due to Debenham's knee, Taylor was at the base camp on 30 October 1911 to bid farewell to the Pole Party. Grif recorded in his diary that Scott marched off first, Oates next, then Wilson and Taff Evans. Bowers was the last away. Many years later when he was retired in Australia, Grif confided to the writer D'Arcy Niland his thoughts of the Pole Party:

> I ran to the end of the cape and watched the little polar cavalcade, already strung out into remote units, rapidly fade into the lonely white waste to the southward. . . Nine hundred miles they had to go, and five of them were doomed. Their route lay over the Great Ice Barrier, up the Beardmore Glacier, across the awful no-man's land of the Summit Plateau (68).

The tragic story of the Southern Party was not known until 1912 when Atkinson's search party found the frozen bodies of Scott, Wilson and Bowers. The bodies of Oates and Evans were never found. Scott's journals were published with some editing by Leonard Huxley as *Scott's Last Expedition* in 1913 and the English speaking world learned the story from Scott's own words. Who of that generation did not thrill at Scott's words penned at the South Pole when they found that the Norwegians had reached there a month previously?

> Great God! This is an awful place and trouble enough to have laboured to it without the reward of priority (69).

Scott became a hero to the world at large. After the publication of *Scott's Last Expedition* in 1913 almost all of the other scientific members of the party also wrote their stories. Cherry-Garrard's book appeared in 1922 and his analysis of Scott's character is revealing:

> He was eager to accept suggestions if they were workable. Essentially an attractive personality with strong likes and dislikes, he excelled in making his followers his friends by a few words of sympathy or praise. I have never known anybody, man or woman, who could be so attractive when he chose. His was a subtle character, full of lights and shades. He was certainly the most dominating character in our not uninteresting community. But few who knew him realized how shy and reserved the man was, and it was partly for this reason that he so often laid himself open to misunderstanding. Add to this that he was sensitive, femininely sensitive, to a degree which might be considered a fault. Temperamentally he was a weak man and might

very easily have been an irritable autocrat. As it was he had moods and depressions which might last for weeks. He cried more easily than any man I have ever known. What pulled Scott through was character and a sense of justice although he had little sense of humour and was a bad judge of men. Scott was the strongest combination of a strong mind in a strong body that I have ever known (70).

Grif was not critical of Scott in *With Scott: The Silver Lining* but his private papers showed criticisms and later in his life he voiced some of them. In a newspaper interview in 1962 in Sydney he confided to the journalist:

Why the party comprised five has never been clear to me. We were organized in teams of four; four to a sledge, four in a tent, our rations made up for four men for a week. The original plan had been to take only four men. Some hold that Oates was given a place as a reward for his splendid management of the pack-animals, but then Oates was already one of the four in Scott's sledge-team and therefore a natural starter. It was Bowers who was with the second sledge-team, under Evans, and he was retained when, under the rule of four, he should have returned with the three others of the last supporting party (71).

The recently published, lengthy, and well documented book, *Scott and Amundsen*, is very critical of Scott and it aroused a storm of protest in England. Scott and his gallant companions have a position in the hearts of the English-speaking world that is difficult to change. Cherry-Garrard explained it thus:

To me, and perhaps to you, the interest in this story is the men rather than what they did or failed to do. It is a story about human minds, which stretch beyond the furthest horizons. Does it really matter whether Amundsen or Scott was first at the Pole? Their story is a human story told magnificently by Scott (72).

References

1. Cherry-Garrard, Apsley: *The Worst Journey in the World*. Chatto and Windus, London, 1922, p. 205.
2. Wilson, E.D: *Diary of the Terra Nova Expedition to the Antarctic 1910-1912* (edited by H.G.R. King). Blandford Press, London, 1972, p. 2.
3. *Scott's Last Expedition*. Smith Elder & Co. London, 1913, Vol. 1, pp. 432-33.
4. Cherry-Garrard, Apsley: *The Worst Journey in the World*. p. 597.
5. Taylor, Griffith: *With Scott: The Silver Lining*. William Clowes and Sons, London, 1914, p. 40.
6. Griffith Taylor. Private Diary, 1910.
7. National Library, Canberra, MS 1003/2/6.
8. National Library, Canberra, MS 1003/2/8.
9. Hanley, Wayne: "Mapping Antarctica — The Difficult Years," *The Globe*, Journal of the Australian Map Curator's Circle, 9, 1978, p. 28.
10. Griffith Taylor. Private Diary, 1910.
11. Taylor, Griffith: "Journeyman at Cambridge," p. 117.
12. Griffith Taylor. Private Diary, 1910.
13. National Library, Canberra, MS 1003/2/6.

14. National Library, Canberra, MS 1003/2/8.
15. Taylor, Griffith: *With Scott: The Silver Lining*, p.84.
16. Taylor, Griffith: *With Scott: The Silver Lining*, p. 78.
17. Taylor, Griffith: *With Scott: The Silver Lining*, p. 79.
18. National Library, Canberra, MS 1003/2/14.
19. Taylor, Griffith: *With Scott: The Silver Lining*, p. 120.
20. Hanley, Wayne: "Mapping Antarctica — The Difficult Years," p. 91.
21. National Library, Canberra, MS 1003/2/199.
22. Taylor, Griffith: *With Scott: The Silver Lining*, p.151.
23. Griffith Taylor. Private Diary, 1911.
24. Cherry-Garrard, Apsley: *The Worst Journey in the World*. p. 308.
25. Taylor, Griffith: *With Scott: The Silver Lining*, p. 174.
26. Griffith Taylor. Private Diary, 1911.
27. Cherry-Garrard, Apsley: *The Worst Journey in the World*. p.163.
28. Taylor, Griffith: "Journeyman at Cambridge," p.189.
29. Taylor, Griffith: "Journeyman at Cambridge," p. 235.
30. Taylor, Griffith: *With Scott: The Silver Lining*, p. 199.
31. Griffith Taylor. Private Diary, 1911.
32. Cherry-Garrard, Apsley: *The Worst Journey in the World*. p. 177.
33. Griffith Taylor. Private Diary, 1911.
34. *Scott's Last Expedition*, p. 204.
35. *Scott's Last Expedition*, p. 261.
36. National Library, Canberra, MS 1003/2/6.
37. *Scott's Last Expedition*, p. 219.
38. National Library, Canberra, MS 1003/2/59.
39. National Library, Canberra, MS 1003/2/59.
40. Cherry-Garrard, Apsley: *The Worst Journey in the World*. p. 175.
41. Taylor, Griffith: "Journeyman at Cambridge," p. 240.
42. Griffith Taylor. Private Diary, 1911.
43. Taylor, Griffith: "Journeyman at Cambridge," p. 248.
44. Taylor, Griffith: "Journeyman at Cambridge," p. 256.
45. *Scott's Last Expedition*, Vol. 1, p. 263.
46. *Scott's Last Expedition*, p. 332.
47. Cherry-Garrard, Apsley: *The Worst Journey in the World*. p. 195.
48. Taylor, Griffith: "Journeyman at Cambridge," p. 258.
49. National Library, Canberra, MS 1003/2/178.
50. Priestley, Raymond: "Griffith Taylor" in *Frontiers and Men*, a volume in memory of Griffith Taylor (edited by John Andrews). F.W. Cheshire Co. Melbourne, Canberra, Sydney, 1966, p. 3.
51. Scott Polar Research Institute, Cambridge, SP 121, MS 505/5.
52. Cherry-Garrard, Apsley: *The Worst Journey in the World*. p. 307.
53. SPRI, Cambridge, SP 121, MS 505/5.
54. *Scott's Last Expedition*, Vol. 1, p. 330.
55. *Scott's Last Expedition*, Vol. 1, p. 335.
56. Griffith Taylor. Private Diary, 1911.
57. Taylor, Griffith: *With Scott: The Silver Lining*, pp. 268-269.
58. Griffith Taylor, as told to D'Arcy Niland in *Walkabout* (Sydney, Australia), Vol. 28, no. 10, October 1962.
59. Taylor, Griffith: *With Scott: The Silver Lining*, p. 289.
60. The Polar Record "Obituary to Grif Taylor." Vol. 12, pp. 76-81, 1964-65, pp. 230-231.
61. Taylor, Griffith: *With Scott: The Silver Lining*, p. 306.
62. Taylor, Griffith: *With Scott: The Silver Lining*, p. 316.
63. Wilson, Edward: *Diary of the Terra Nova. Expedition to the Antarctic 1910-1912*, p. 175.
64. Niland D'Arcy in *Walkabout*, Vol. 28, no. 10, October 1962.
65. Pound, Reginald: *Scott of the Antarctic*. Cassell and Co. London, 1966, p. 263.
66. Taylor, Griffith: *With Scott: The Silver Lining*, p. 321.
67. Taylor, Griffith: "Journeyman at Cambridge," p. 264.
68. Niland D'Arcy in *Walkabout*, 1962.
69. "Scott's Last Expedition." Review in *The Times London, Literary Supplement*, November 6, 1913, p. 502.
70. Cherry-Garrard, Apsley: *The Worst Journey in the World*. pp. 200-202.
71. Niland D'Arcy in *Walkabout*, 1962.
72. Cherry-Garrard, Apsley: *The Worst Journey in the World*. p. 545

CHAPTER 5

Taylor's Contribution to the Scott Expedition

Taylor wrote his farewell letter to his family on November 13 and mentioned the possibility that he himself might not return from the Expedition that Scott had asked him to lead:

> I feel that it would be such awful luck to have had such a fine time and not get back to retrospect it, that I'm bound to see you all in April next. . . (1).

The account of the Granite Harbour expedition from which quotes appear below was written by Taylor two months later while the party was marooned on Cape Roberts waiting to be picked up by Captain Pennell in the *Terra Nova*. Because of the problems Taylor's party encountered in trying to rendezvous with the *Terra Nova*, the journal was left at Cape Roberts and was found by Campbell's Northern party on their trek to head-quarters the next spring. Campbell's party had undergone unbelievable hardships, having survived an Antarctic winter without adequate clothing or shelter, an experience described by Raymond Priestley, who was a member of Campbell's team, in his book *Antarctic Adventure*. It was Raymond Priestley who took Grif's journal back to England and handed it to him at the Priestley home in Tewkesbury in 1913. Scott, to whom the narrative was addressed, of course never saw it. The journal was given to the Department of Geography at the University of New England in Armidale by Taylor in 1960.

The first few entries of the journal quoted below show Taylor's detailed writing style under very trying conditions, and the trials of Antarctic sledging.

> The objects of our journey may be summarised (vide my Instructions) as comprising "the Geological Exploration of the coast of Victoria Land." It was intended that we should leave Cape Evans about October 21st, but owing to an unfortunate accident to Debenham the date of our departure was still uncertain when the Southern Party left us.
>
> On the 6th November after considerable discussion with Dr. Simpson we decided that as Debenham could not safely do anything for a week, the best procedure was for the able members to push across to Butter Point (30 miles) with the bulk of the material to be transported from Cape Evans. Nelson very kindly volunteered to help us.

We moved off on the 7th with two sledges — the smaller carrying our sleeping bags and camp equipment, and the larger some 600 lbs. of food and gear.

The surface was very heavy and we found we could only drag the two sledges along at about one mile an hour. The snow drifts across our path due to the late blizzards were so difficult to negotiate that I note "they nearly dislocate one's pelvis". We therefore had to start relaying even this early, with only half our load.

By midday we were 4½ miles from the hut and halted for our lunch camp — also our supper camp. For in ten minutes it was blizzing strongly and we had considerable difficulty in pitching the tent. Luckily Forde's hand was so much improved that he could help greatly.

The drift snow was very thick and piled up to the peak of the tent to windward and the sledges were covered a foot deep under the snow. We had arranged to turn back on Thursday night so as to be back at the hut on Friday night but now our chances seemed very slim of so doing.

8/11/11

Next morning it was still very thick to the west but the blizzard had stopped. The surface was however surprisingly little changed, and in fact a little better than before; so that we did rather better than a mile an hour. I fount it paid well to follow a circuitous path rather than try to cross a snowdrift. The weather soon cleared up.

At lunch time we had done over three miles and it was curious how clearly Butter Point appeared. We could see cracks in the ice face though we were a long twenty miles away. During the afternoon we finished seven more stages reaching 12½ miles. Hard pulling after eleven hours had given us eight miles of progress.

9/11/11

We were favoured by a fine morning and the surface was of harder snow so that I hoped to get close to Butter Point during the day. However we had to camp at 4 p.m.; for a blizzard came up and there was no possibility of moving further. We were almost twenty miles from the hut.

10/11/11

This day — which was to be spent returning from Butter Point saw us held up by a strong blizzard so that we could do nothing but lie in our bags and wait.

11/11/11

(Saturday) As we were overdue on our return I left the heavy sledge well flagged here — still nine miles from the depot at Butter

Point — and we pushed off for Cape Evans. We started at 4:30 a.m. and had an awful surface, so that with a practically empty nine foot sledge it was quite heavy pulling at times. However we reached the hut at 4:30 p.m. We found that Debenham had been hobbling about the last day or two and thought he could walk alongside the sledge by Monday. Nelson again came to rescue and suggested that he and Anton help us to Butter Point and return with a small sledge. I was glad to accept his help — as Simpson agreed.

During the next two days the weather was bad, and the Western Mountains were rarely visible. It was advantageous from one point of view to wait, but on the other hand Professor David was of the opinion that Dec. 8th was late enough to be on the sea ice to the west. As at this time I felt it would be impossible to get to Granite Harbour even by the 8th, it was obvious that we must move off immediately or run grave risk of not reaching Granite Harbour at all.

14th Nov.

We are ready and waiting but the weather was most unpromising. However we got off at 3:30 p.m. as soon as the other side of the Sound loomed up through the clouds. I realised from our first relay that we could not manage three sledges over the soft snow, and therefore we took across for our own use only one large sledge, the small nine foot sledge being handed over to our convoy, Nelson and Anton. I also left four weeks' provisions at Cape Evans — for it was now 24 days later than the date on which Captain Scott's instructions re provisions were based.

This afternoon we had the pleasure of crossing a mile or so of clear sea ice — over which the sledge was blown by the dying blizzard — with Debenham resting on the cargo! This absence of snow was due to the presence of the long line of bergs and of Inaccessible Island, but we never met any more bare ice during the whole of our trip that was of any assistance to us (2).

As on the previous trip Taylor proved to be a good leader, and his good humour helped the four to avoid any serious arguments. At first there were problems with Debenham's knee, and he could pull very little weight. By November 20, however, when they reached Cape Bernacchi Debenham improved and began his plane table survey, which he carried out throughout the whole journey, producing the most detailed map of any part of Victoria Land. As Hanley pointed out, the ability to determine latitude and longitude accurately was a skill that was essential to their very survival. Hanley reminds us that:

When matched against contemporary survey equipment, that used by Taylor and Debenham must be regarded as simple and perhaps primitive. . . . The two main instruments used in combination were the plane-table and the theodolite (3).

Debenham usually manned the plane-table and Taylor the theodolite.

> With the plane-table, Debenham carried out a unique detailed survey of the coast line, not only showing the outlines of the land, but also all the physiographic features. With the theodolite, I was able by observations on the sun to determine the latitude and longitude of the main stations of our survey (4).

The Western party had to man-haul their sledges, which with food and equipment weighed about 1200 pounds each. Ever inventive, Taylor rigged some sails for the sledges, and with the wind behind them, they accomplished 6½ miles by 7 p.m. instead of the 4½ miles by 9 p.m. that would have been possible by man-hauling alone. He also found that temperatures were so high that daytime sledging was agonizingly slow, so changed to night marching, when the surface was frozen and harder. This was something which Amundsen also did, as seemed only common sense.

Food was very important as it always is on such expeditions, and descriptions of the meals occupied a good deal of space in Taylor's journals. They killed seals for their hoosh, Taylor killing his first with an ice axe and cutting it up under Forde's direction. Unfortunately, Grif cut his right hand several times cutting up the seals, and several of the cuts refused to heal. He tried all the pills in their medicine chest and Gran lanced the fingers with the result that they swelled to twice their normal size. Even this inconvenience did not stop Grif from writing in his journal — and sketching with his left hand. He said that toward the end of his trip he could read his left-hand writing, but no one else could. His journals are filled with excellent pencil sketches of the Antarctic scenery. Grif had a great facility in this regard. He could look at a landscape and, picking out the most salient features, make it come alive for the viewer.

In November, while they were exploring the south coast of Granite Harbour near a cape they named "Cape Geology" (see map, Fig. 5). Taylor decided that some sort of shelter, other than tents, would help to conserve their fuel. So they erected Granite House, named for the building in Jules Verne's *The Secret of the Island,* choosing a sheltered site enclosed on three sides by ledges and building up the walls using large boulders. A sledge on top covered by sealskins formed a roof. The western party lived in their "Granite House" for two months, until they left for the rendezvous with Pennell in the *Terra Nova.* It was not the most comfortable of residences, as Taylor reported. It was smoky and drafty but in it he and Gran planted a small garden — of kale — which sprouted! Doubtless it was the first garden in the Antarctic.

They celebrated their second Christmas in the Antarctic with a feast of skua eggs with Christmas pudding and caramels. Taylor had received from Scott a copy of the detailed and lengthy instructions that he had given Pennell regarding the return of Taylor's and Campbell's parties. Scott had written in October 1911:

> I assume that you arrive at the rendezvous, Granite Harbour, on or about Jan. 15th and pick up the Western Geological party as

arranged. . . In case the Party should be absent, it is well to quote Taylor's plan in brief.

To Nov. 10 — exploring along coast north of Granite Harbour.

Nov. 14-28 — exploring coast and inland south of Granite Harbour.

Dec. 8-Jan. 8 — exploring inland of Granite Harbour region.

Taylor will make every effort to return to Granite Harbour in time to meet you, and should the Party be absent, you may assume that it has probably been delayed inland. On the chance that it may have been cut off, you may proceed to search the coast in a southerly direction if ice conditions permit.

The time occupied in the search must be left to your judgement, observing that the Party will reach Granite Harbour with sufficient provisions to last till April 1912 and should be able to work its way back to the depot. . . . Should the party be recovered at once, as is most probable, I wish you to take it to Evans Coves and land it without delay. . . . I imagine this landing will be effected about Jan. 18 or 19 and the party should be instructed to be prepared to be reembarked on Feb. 15th (5).

Grif noted on his copy of the above letter that the ship could carry out none of the instructions about Campbell's party or his own Western party, owing to the unprecedented barrier of pack-ice in early 1912.

Taylor also noted in his diary that the Discovery map was obviously quite incorrect, stating:

Our chief guide was Professor David's (written) account. From the times of his daily marches we expected to reach Granite Harbour earlier than the rough chart indicated . . . we found that the Harbour was twelve miles nearer than we had reason to expect. Indeed the error in the maps made me doubtful if we were in Granite Harbour at all (6).

Taylor assessed the situation and decided that they had best move about 14 km. eastward to Cape Roberts, where they could be seen by the *Terra Nova*. They left their 271 kg. of geographical and biological specimens on the roof sledge at Granite House with all the other equipment they could spare, to be picked up later, and took only essential supplies with them for the trip to Cape Roberts.

Two years later, in 1913, Tryggve Gran with a six man party picked up the sledge with the precious specimens. Other items left by Taylor's party, including a sled and two books — Grif's *The Secret of the Island* by Jules Verne, and Deb's *Tales of Mystery and Imagination* by Edgar Allan Poe — were found perfectly preserved in November 1959 by a U.S. geological party led by Robert Nichols of Tufts College. He sent the books to Dr. Thomas Jones, Director of Antarctic Programs, National Research Foundation, who sent them to their original owners.

Since then the Granite House area has been visited several times by Antarctic scientists and in 1983 Ursula Marvin wrote an article in the *Antarctic Journal of the United States* about her visit to the area in 1982:

> We found we could still match stone for stone almost all of the blocks and boulders in Taylor's original picture of 1911. . . . but Granite House itself still stands, as a granite edifice should. It's heartening to know that it is among the structures being documented by New Zealand specialists in the preservation of historic huts (7).

I am sure that Grif would be pleased to know that his "Granite House" is being preserved as a historic site. However, that 12th day of January in 1911 they were pleased to leave their Granite House to the skua gulls and go to Cape Roberts and the rendezvous with Pennell. They began watching for th Terra Nova early in January, and often saw mirages — sometimes three *Terra Novas*! Debenham did a detailed plane-table survey and he and Grif played chess with cardboard "men" on the back of the plane-table. There was not much else to do but wait for the ship.

January 20 was Gran's 23rd birthday, and Taylor wrote him a poem in lieu of a present. The first verse is given here:

> O Tryggve Gran, O Tryggve Gran
> I would thou wert a moral man
> And yet since we
> (The other three)
> Are just as moral as can be
> A "soupçon de diablerie"
> Improves our little company (8).

Gran was the last survivor of the Scott expedition. He died in 1980 at the age of 91, and this poem by Taylor was quoted in his obituary in the *Geographical Magazine* in March 1980.

Taylor was just writing the last line of the poem when Gran yelled "ship ho". He had finally sighted the *Terra Nova* — but Taylor's party was unable to board the ship, about 20 miles away across the broken floes. They awaited rescue camped on the cape, with no shelter from the wind. Rations had to be cut down by half:

> We now had 3 or 4 biscuits a day, butter every other day, chocolate, one stick, pemmican, one eighth, sugar and tea, two thirds a day. However, we had plenty of seal meat and as we were not working, we required much less food (9).

On the first of February, Taylor held a council meeting and re-read Scott's instructions. Things were becoming a little dicey. It looked as if the ship would never reach them at Cape Roberts, but with luck they might cross the Piedmont glacier to Cape Bernacchi where the ship might be able to get in. Also they had only two weeks of food left. On February 4, Taylor wrote a letter to Pennell which they all signed, and made a depot on the highest point of the cape with a flagpole. They took nothing with them but the clothes they stood up in, a few extra clothes and instruments. They had some 30 miles of badly crevassed country to cross, and then 30 miles of coast largely over moraine and rock:

> We turned our backs finally on Cape Roberts on the 5th. Our flag waved bravely and below us the cairn covering the food left there by Scott's orders. . . . In the next spring, six desperate men sledging southward (Campbell's northern party) found the first news of the main party. Our depot possibly saved Browning's life. Brave old flag! It hangs in Tewkesbury in Priestley's home (10).

Grif's depot did indeed save Browning's life, since he was so ill he could no longer eat the seal blubber, the only food available. Grif's flag along with his narrative for Captain Scott was taken by Raymond Priestley, who was one of Campbell's party, and finally arrived safely at the Priestley home in Tewkesbury.

The next few days were literally hell. For three days Grif did not even write in his journal, thinking that no one would be reading it. They crossed awful crevasses, falling in repeatedly and also succumbing to snow blindness.

> In the afternoon my eyes gave out. I put bandages on the right eye and gave up the lead to Debenham. . . . Deb treated me for snow-blindness. The zinc sulphate may truthfully be described as an eye-opener but later the cocaine in the mixture calms things down. . . . Though everything appeared double for many hours (11).

On February 8, they reached Cape Bernacchi where they hoped Pennell could reach them. But there was no sign of the *Terra Nova*. They had to decide whether to keep to the coast or head back to Cape Evans. Taylor advised going inland but on February 13 Gran again sighted the ship. They were finally picked up at the Koettlitz Glacier near the Dailey Islands a month later than the date fixed by Scott.

For Taylor the most wonderful thing about being on the *Terra Nova* was a hot bath and clean clothes. Grif said that the explorers all looked like Adelie penguins since they had white circles around the eyes where the blubber soot had not accumulated (Fig. 7). There was also a whole pillow-case full of mail from home. Taylor was pleased to find that his mail included a copy of his first book, *Australia in its Physiographic and Economic Aspects*, published by Oxford University Press. However, the happy mood did not last long.

> But for the blizzard which now struck the ship, driving her far to the north, we would have been back in the hut within a couple of hours or so. Pennell decided to relieve Campbell's northern party, now at Evans Coves some 200 miles to the north. This however was found impossible because of the new pack which prevented the ships getting close to the shore (12).

Figure 7. The Western Geological party after rescue: on board *Terra Nova*. Ponting photograph SPR1 P79/27/549

A second and third attempt to reach Campbell's party also failed, so Pennell finally landed his passengers at Cape Evans on February 25. Grif went ashore after a five-month absence to pick up his gear and return to the ship for the voyage home. Simpson, Teddy Evans (who was ill with scurvy), Ponting, Lillie and several of the seamen also returned to civilization with the *Terra Nova*.

The rest of the Expedition's scientists remained at Cape Evans, and since Evans had been invalided home, Campbell became the officer in command. Cherry-Garrard admitted that they missed Grif.

> His gear took up more room than was strictly his share and his mind also filled up a considerable amount of space. He always bulked large, and when he returned to the Australian government, which had lent him for the first two sledging seasons, he left a noticeable gap in our company (13).

On board the *Terra Nova*, Simpson and Taylor discussed the meteorological data they had gathered during the expedition. Simpson was on leave from the Meteorological Bureau of India, and was returning to Simla to take up his duties. He was later knighted and became director of the Meteorological Service in Great Britain. He and Grif kept in touch throughout the rest of their lives.

Grif wrote up his notes and wrote letters to his chums. On March 4, he wrote to Debenham, who was staying another year in the Antarctic:

Hard luck for Campbell. We did a sort of "blanket stitch" route round the Pack and couldn't get in anywhere. If we hadn't pushed off from C. Roberts, we'd be there yet I do believe.

Good Luck to you old man. Be cautious when sledging. It pays every time. If the Pole is won I believe you'll have a pleasant winter. If not, Gott Ihnen hilft (14).

Huntford in his book *Scott and Amundsen* interpreted this German phrase, "God help you," as proof that Grif did not like Scott. Perhaps this is correct. Perhaps not. Grif liked sprinkling his writing with German phrases.

While the *Terra Nova* was steaming towards Wellington, a series of tragedies was taking place on the continent they had left. By March 21, Scott and his two remaining companions, Wilson and Bowers, had reached their last camp just 11 miles south of One Ton Depot where food and fuel awaited them. In the north, at Hell's Gate, near Evans Coves, Campbell and his party, in a hole in the snow, waited out the long winter night. After eight months of uneasy existence, they finally made it back to Cape Evans. At the main head-quarters, Nelson, Debenham, Wright and Gran were spending a second winter under very different conditions from the winter before, while 14 miles south in the old Discovery hut was a party including Atkinson and Cherry-Garrard. In a letter to Grif in 1913 Cherry wrote:

Dear Old Grif. . . . It's been a hairy year. Atch. has done jolly well in command and Atch & Deb have been splendid. We had an awful time at Hut Pt in the end of March and April. Then open water at C Evans all the winter. Hurricane winds, June and July were one long blizzard and we seldom got out. For myself I had a breakdown when we got in with the dogs, continual sick headaches through the winter, but we will all get a rest now I hope. I know I must (15).

The next spring, on 12 November 1912, a search party under the leadership of Dr. Atkinson, with Wright and Cherry-Garrard, found the tent and the bodies of Scott, Wilson and Bowers, and brought back to civilization the journals which have become famous. Cherry described the scene:

We have found them — to say it has been a ghastly day cannot express it — it is too bad for words. Scott lay in the centre, Bill on his left, with his head towards the door, and Birdie on his right, lying with his feet towards the door. They got to this point on March 21 and on the 29th it was all over. Atkinson read the lesson from the Burial service from Corinthians. Perhaps it has never been read in a more magnificent cathedral and under more impressive circumstances — for it is a grave which kings must envy. That scene can never leave my memory. It is all too horrible — I am almost afraid to go to sleep now (16).

All of this of course was not known aboard the *Terra Nova*, which finally made contact with civilization on April 1st when it arrived at Akaroa harbour in New Zealand. Two men in a launch came by the ship and called out to them,

> Why didn't you get back sooner? Amundsen got the Pole in a sardine tin on the 14th December (17).

This was the first news any of the expedition had had of Amundsen, and the returning explorers at first thought it a poor April Fool's joke. They still did not know Scott's fate, of course, and on board ship they reasoned

> Scott will have reached the Pole about January 16. When he sees the tent and flag there (Amundsen's) he will get a most unpleasant shock. Amundsen started eleven days before Scott and was 80 miles nearer (18).

Grif had to wait almost a year, until February 1913, before hearing the news of Scott's party. He and Simpson left the *Terra Nova* where they had embarked — at Lyttleton, New Zealand — and Taylor was back in Australia on 7 April 1912. Grif was glad to be returning to civilization, but would always remember his Antarctic experience. His best friends would always be his polar colleagues — Debenham, Wright and Priestley. And he would never forget Bill Wilson, whose character had made such an impression on all the young scientists and after whom Grif would nick-name his first son. He had survived the expedition and the adventure of a lifetime. He summed up his experiences thus:

> I shall in all probability never again see the Antarctic but my advice to any volunteer who has that opportunity offered to him, is to take it. Especially is this the case if he is a scientist or writer, for the present tendencies of modern life are all opposed to the multiplication of such experiences. Only in Polar Lands is to be found the joy of a real return to the primitive in association with the best types of strenuous youth. There, if anywhere, is life worth while and effort sure of recognition (19).

The amount of work that Grif and his colleagues had accomplished was phenomenal. Taylor's interest was always in physiography and especially in the way in which the surface of the land had been affected by the ice, as well as by wind, frost and water. Debenham was more interested in geology and collected and identified rocks in each locality. Their detailed surveys were remarkable, especially in view of the fact that they were done with plane-table and theodolite and they obtained the altitude of the peaks with considerable accuracy. The final package produced by Taylor and Debenham was unique and marked the beginning of the modern era of description of the Antarctic continent. It was a great step forward in the mapping of the Antarctic continent — not to be surpassed until the age of aerial photography.

They also attempted to determine the rate of flow of the Ferrar and Mackay glaciers by placing stakes and making sightings of them. Sightings a month later

Figure 8. Five Antarctic explorers from Australia, Taylor, Mawson, Davis, David, Stillwell, 1912. National Library of Australia. MS 1003/2/144

showed the stake had moved 82 feet, and Taylor deduced that the glacier was advancing about a yard a day. Because of this, the coastline in this area varied greatly from year to year and this fact was the cause of an argument between Scott and Taylor concerning the coast at the mouth of the Ferrar Glacier. Scott said it was a bay in 1903. Taylor insisted a tongue jutted out into the sea in 1910. They were probably both right. Grif wrote many years later:

We had our successes. We surveyed Granite Harbour, we found Devonian fish-plate fossils, and we discovered the Gomphocephalus, the largest antarctic animal living wholly on land — a bluish spring-tail insect a millimeter long. It had never been seen before... We were almost at the end of our tether when the *Terra Nova* picked us up in February (20).

With his sketches, his journal notes, and his plane-table surveys, Taylor was able to produce several extremely detailed three-dimensional relief diagrams of the coastal mountain area. Taylor was to make good use of his work in the Antarctic, first in the official account of the Expedition, then in his book *With Scott: The Silver Lining* and in a thesis for which he was awarded his doctorate from the University of Melbourne several years later.

He developed a theory, possibly the first, to explain the build of the Antarctic continent, pointing out the close similarity of the two southern continents, Australia and Antarctica. He pointed out that in Australia the structure consists of the low western Shield, the series of plateaux and horsts which forms the so-called Great Dividing Range, the deep downfold of the Tasman Sea, and to the east the high "Young" fold mountains of New Zealand. Grif developed the theory that in the Antarctic there were also the same four elements of structure: low shield, line of horsts, downfold, and young mountains (21).

Certainly Taylor had proven himself an asset to the expedition. Scott had praised him and Cherry-Garrard said of him:

When his pen was still (rarely) his tongue wagged and the arguments he led would begin. The hut below Mt. Erebus was a merrier place for his presence. . . . He would throw himself into his curtained bunk with a show of ferocity whenever he was bored or emerge from it to take part in some argument which was troubling the mess table. A demon note-taker, he had books protruding from every pocket on sledge journeys. . . . His gaunt, untamed appearance was atoned for by a halo of good fellowship (22).

After Scott's death, Commander Evans was given command of the expedition and he also was aware o. Grif's good qualities. In his own book on the Scott expedition, *South with Scott*, Evans mused on the prospect of organizing a polar expedition of his own.

If that great good fortune should come my way. I shall telegraph Grif, and ask him to be my "Uncle Bill" and to help me as Wilson helped Scott (23).

Many years later, fellow Australian Hanley wrote of Grif's work in the Antarctic.

It must be realized that these men were of a different breed, and of a different era, thrilled to be able to participate in what amounted to real adventure, treading paths not previously trod and privileged to be among the few who had by that time been given the opportunity to apply their scientific knowledge to the last and perhaps the greatest continent (24).

References

1. National Library, Canberra, MS 1003/9/1590.
2. Hanley, Wayne: Journal of part of the Second Western Geological Expedition to Granite Harbour (November 1911-February 1912) in *The Griffith Taylor Collection*. University of New England, Armidale NSW. Department of Geography Research Series in Applied Geography, 1978, pp. 143-144.
3. Hanley, Wayne: "Mapping Antarctica — The Difficult Years," p. 30.
4. Hanley, Wayne: "Mapping Antarctica — The Difficult Years," p. 31.
5. Hanley, Wayne: *The Griffith Taylor Collection*, pp. 206-207.
6. Griffith Taylor. Private Diary, 1912.
7. Marvin, Ursula: "Granite House: 1911-1981," *Antarctic Journal of the United States*. National Science Foundation. Vol. 18, March, 1983, p. 19.
8. Taylor, Griffith: *With Scott: The Silver Lining*, p. 401.
9. Taylor, Griffith: *With Scott: The Silver Lining*, p. 403.
10. Taylor, Griffith: *With Scott: The Silver Lining*, p. 406.
11. Griffith Taylor. Private Diary, 1912.
12. Taylor, Griffith: *Journeyman Taylor*, p. 119.
13. Cherry-Garrard, Apsley: *The Worst Journey in the World*. p. 308.
14. National Library, Canberra, MS 1003/280/26.
15. National Library, Canberra, MS 1003/2/230.
16. Cherry-Garrard, Apsley: *The Worst Journey in the World*. p. 485.
17. Taylor, Griffith: *With Scott: The Silver Lining*, p. 434.
18. Taylor, Griffith: *With Scott: The Silver Lining*, p. 434.
19. Griffith Taylor. Private Diary, 1912.
20. Taylor, Griffith: Quoted in Niland, D'Arcy in *Walkabout*, 1962.
21. Taylor, Griffith: "Journeyman at Cambridge," p. 266.
22. Cherry-Garrard, Apsley: *The Worst Journey in the World*. p. 480.
23. Taylor, Griffith: *Journeyman Taylor*, p. 130.
24. Hanley, Wayne: "Mapping Antarctica — The Difficult Years," pp. 27-35

CHAPTER 6

England Again 1912-14

A week after his return from the Antarctic, Taylor was invited by Professor David to meet and have lunch with Amundsen, just back from his conquest of the Pole. It must have been a strange meeting for Grif, who like the rest of the world did not yet know what had happened to Scott. The luncheon was duly reported in the Sydney *Morning Herald* (11 April 1912), and Grif pasted the clipping in his diary of that date, with no comment.

> A private luncheon of exceptional interest took place at the Hotel Australia yesterday when representatives of no less than four Antarctic expeditions gathered — Captain Amundsen, the discoverer of the South Pole, Professor David who accompanied the Shackleton expedition, Captain Davis of the Aurora, relief vessel to the Mawson expedition, and Mr. Griffith Taylor who has just returned from braving the blizzards in company with Captain Scott (1) (Fig. 8).

The next four months were anti-climactic for Taylor after his Antarctic experiences. Back in Melbourne at his job with the Bureau of Meteorology, he wrote an account of the climate and weather of Australia for a military handbook. This was the beginning of his work on the climate of Australia and subsequent writings over the next decade constituted the first thorough systematic study of Australian climate, and established Taylor as the outstanding world authority on this topic, giving him an international reputation as a climatologist.

In September 1912, Grif again became involved in the geological survey of the new Federal Territory. One of his jobs was to see if there were suitable supplies of building stone, limestone and brick clays. Grif wrote a letter about Canberra to Scott for him to read on his expected return from the Pole:

> It is not often that a city is planned on such a grand scale before a trench is dug... A Federal University and other magnificent buildings will cover this empty plain in twenty years (2).

Scott of course never received this letter but Grif's prophecy would come true: not in 20 years, because of the intervention of two world wars, but in 40 years. In March 1913, Grif was present at the impressive ceremony when it was christened Canberra, a name Grif himself had suggested in a report to the Federal Government.

On 10 February 1913, the *Terra Nova* arrived in New Zealand with the news of Scott's death — news that shook the world. In his diary of 11 February 1913,

Taylor wrote one sentence "Heard of Scott's death." There is nothing more and no indication in any of Taylor's papers of his assessment of Scott or how the tragedy affected him. There was a memorial service for Scott on February 14 in Sydney which Grif attended, but it was not until the end of the month that he heard from Tryggve Gran the whole tragic story.

> They were on the Barrier, hoping to find what had happened to Scott. Gran saw two sticks when they came about 160 miles south of the hut, on Nov. 12, 1912. Wright went along and saw it was the sledge mast. Bowers and Wilson were wrapped up in their bags. Uncle Bill had a smile on his face. Poor Scott had crawled out of his bag Gran thought, so as to end things quickly. They then marched still further south, and found a camera and theodolite near where Oates died, but could not find his body (3).

There is among the Taylor letters a letter from Wright dated 15 February 1913, which could be interpreted in different ways.

> Can you not keep David quiet? It is a damn pity Evans has got this fool idea of keeping quiet about things.

Perhaps this can be interpreted as an order from Evans, now the official leader of the Expedition, to the other members of the BAE to keep silent about the problems with Scott. Scott had thought Teddy Evans

> a well meaning little man, but not at all fitted to be second-in-command, as I was foolish enough to name him (4).

However Evans remained loyal to Scott throughout his life. After accompanying the Pole Party up the Beardmore Glacier, and not being chosen for the final team, Evans became very ill on the return trip and almost died. He returned to England in 1911 on the *Terra Nova*. He lived a more abundant life than he ever dreamed of, becoming Commander-in-Chief of the Royal Australian Navy and raised to the peerage as Lord Mountevans. He often admitted in later life that he had more of his share of luck and, unlike Scott, that Providence had served him well.

Commander Evans suggested to the Meteorological Bureau that Taylor be given a year's leave of absence to go to Cambridge to write up his Antarctic research and Taylor was very pleased when they agreed. Evans had arranged rooms at the Royal Geographical Society for the Antarctic scientists to collate their field surveys. Evans himself gave the official account of the Antarctic Expedition in London in May, and Grif described it thus:

> Winston Churchill occupied the chair, and a number of suffragettes interrupted him when he rose to speak "You have peace abroad," they shouted, "but not at home." After the ejection of 5 men and a woman, Evans was accorded an attentive hearing (5).

Figure 9. Debenham, Priestley and Taylor leaving Buckingham Palace after receiving Polar Medals from the King. July 26, 1913 (Photo from Bill Taylor)

There were also dinners and honours in abundance for the famous explorers. The most impressive was in July 1913 when the remaining members of the Scott team were awarded the Polar Medal by the King. Taylor was not overly impressed by the ceremony:

> I regret to say that I was not properly impressed with the opportunity to meet the King and receive the Polar Medal. There were so many of us, and the proceedings did verge on the comic. We were informed that we had to wear morning-coats and spats and other frills which none of us possessed. So there was a great rally round of relatives and friends in this connection. Some Priestley folk at Gloucester — whom I had never met — provided the essential garb. I bagged a top-hat that Ray had desired. I think I bought the spats — and never wore them again (Fig. 9).
>
> Since the medal was for scientific work, and since so many Cambridge scientists were concerned, I think it in place to describe the ceremony in this not-too-high-brow journal. The expedition met at Caxton Hall under Teddy Evans, and I think there were 55 in all. Here we awaited the telephone call from Buckingham Palace, where the scientists assembled in the outer audience-chamber. Soon we heard the tramp, tramp, of the 30 seamen, led by Lieutenant Rennick. They formed up in two lines. Then three aides appeared armed with lists, and we were all checked voluminously, and they lined us up also. Since Simpson was in India I took the lead of this group. Lady Scott and the other widows were seated nearby. The "shark-hook episode" interested me. An officer appeared and transfixed each of us with this support for the medal.
>
> About 11:30 the folding doors were opened a wee way, and Lady Scott had a short talk with the King, and the other ladies followed. Mrs. Wilson was asked about some of Bill's pictures presented to His Majesty. Teddy went in next, and all of the rest of the 50 followed in line. We gave our cards, which were read out by Prince Louis. I thought the King seemed a bit bored, and he was taller than I thought. He took the medal from a cushion, hung it on the hook, and Debenham said I made a graceful bow, but forgot to walk out backwards. I was rather keen on the sharkhook as a memento, but a flunkey carefully removed it as we left the chamber. However the King was so busy giving "Marie" Nelson his medal that he did not spot my misdemeanor, and I was not charged with Lèse-majesté. We then went back to Caxton Hall, and there on 26th July 1913 Evans disbanded the Expedition (6).

The BAE had officially ended, but it was not forgotten by the British public. Scott had written in his diary during his last days

But if we have been willing to give our lives to this enterprise, which is
for the honour of our country, I appeal to our countrymen to see that
those who depend on us are properly cared for (7).

There was a public appeal for a memorial fund to honour Captain Scott and
£75,000 was raised. Of this, £34,000 went to the widows and relatives of the men
lost on the Expedition, £500 to pay the deficit, £17,500 for publication of results,
including some salaries for scientists for some months, and £18,000 for a
memorial. Much of the latter helped to found the Scott Polar Institute in
Cambridge of which Debenham was Director for twenty years.

Kathleen Scott was granted the rank, style and precedence that would have
been hers had her husband lived to be made a Knight Commander of the Order
of the Bath, as the King had intended. Lady Scott kept in touch with the
members of the Expedition and their wives and families and was active in the
affairs of the Scott Polar Research Institute. It was she who did the lovely
sculpture that stands in front of the S.P.R.I. to typify Antarctic exploration,
entitled "Stretched wings toward the south," her husband's motto.

Along with Priestley, Wright and Debenham, Taylor began work on the
Expedition results, a task which kept them busy for several months. Grif's
official account of the Expedition ran to 35,000 words, and he was also writing
an article for the *Geographical Journal* as well as his own account of the
Expedition, which he named *With Scott: The Silver Lining*.

He bought a motor bike, and when he had time off, went to see the Priestleys
in Tewkesbury where the senior Priestley was Headmaster of the Grammar
School. His Antarctic friend, Raymond, had entered Christ's College
Cambridge, but left in 1914 when war broke out, to serve with the Royal
Engineers. He ultimately became Vice Chancellor of Melbourne University in
Australia, then Vice Chancellor of the University of Birmingham, England. In
1949 he was knighted, as was Charles Wright, the only members of the
Expedition to be so honoured!

Grif considered Tewkesbury on the Avon River, not far from Gloucester, a
lovely corner of England. The attraction there was not only Raymond, but
Raymond's attractive youngest sister Doris whom he had met when she had
come to London to see the King present the Polar medals. Doris at the time was
18 years old, and was secretary to her brother Herbert, who was a Professor of
Botany at Leeds University.

It was obviously love at first sight, and October 1913 saw Grif at Tewkesbury
trying to persuade Doris to marry him (Fig. 10). There was some opposition,
especially from her brother Herbert, who considered Doris too young to make
up her own mind. In a letter to Grif, dated October 7, Herbert wrote:

I think it desirable that we should know where we are, particularly
for Doris' sake. She is very young, in many ways younger than her
age and it was because she was so obviously doubtful what to do and
distressed that I offered to write for both yesterday to her obvious

relief. It is not playing the game on your part, to press for a decision and I think you will only succeed in completely upsetting her peace of mind. You will have to rest content at present with knowing that she is certainly fond of you but feels herself too young to decide her future. As an elder brother I have had to study the genus sister, and I want at least the chance of talking to you before you continue your own plan of campaign. I think it is really unnecessary to say that you will have to be very gentle with her. One word more. Later I should support your case very heartily though I think it would be unnecessary (8).

However, Doris obviously was not too young to decide, and the engagement was announced in Tewkesbury that month, although the marriage did not take place until the next July in Melbourne. About the same time Grif's friend Charles Wright became engaged to Doris' sister Edith. Taylor was a little envious of Wright when the latter was appointed Lecturer in Surveying at Cambridge, since his future seemed more secure than Grif's.

Among the friends congratulating Grif on his engagement was Professor Herbertson from Oxford. Grif had visited him several times on his return to England and they were collaborating on several books. Taylor contributed articles on Australia and Antarctica to the Oxford series on the British Empire of which Herbertson was the editor. Herbertson wrote to his young friend:

I think you are a very lucky beggar. One piece of advice I'll venture on. Always consult her about all that is important, and take her advice for she will probably be wiser than you, wise though you are (9).

The story of Doris' engagement ring is an interesting one, one Taylor was fond of telling and since it concerns the Antarctic, it will be given here:

Among the rock specimens brought back by Shackleton's party from the top of the Beardmore Glacier. . . was a small piece of green marble which Professor David thought contained fossil fragments. This specimen was handed to me . . . on examining it under the microscope, I found evidence of my Cambrian Archeocyathinae, a not unimportant discovery, upon which I contributed a short paper to Shackleton's scientific memoirs. A piece of this marble, resembling a split pea in size and shape I have on my watch chain. Thus it went back to the Antarctic. On my return to London, I showed it to Lady Scott, mentioning that I thought of incorporating it in Doris' engagement ring. The suggestion interested Lady Scott who advised a border of Saxon design round a central D a device executed by an artistic jeweller, without in the least spoiling the smooth surface produced by the blizzards of the Plateau (10).

Grif got on very well with Lady Scott, and she obviously liked the young scientist. In a letter to him (dated only 1913, 174 Buckingham Palace Rd.) she wrote:

Dear Mr. Taylor:

Ever so many thanks for sending the photographs. Could the stone be cut as a D and a band of tiny pearls or diamonds around it and could the date or something nice be engraved on the inside. I didn't have an engagement ring and my wedding ring cost 17/6. I shall certainly come again. You made me feel very happy to be with you (11).

The ring was made with the "D" outlined in small pearls, and was very dainty and charming. In the centre, of course, was the Archeocyathinae. Lady Scott invited Grif for lunch, and asked him to pose for a sculpture she was doing of Bill Wilson, as Grif was about Wilson's height and weight. He wrote about this and other Antarctic matters to Cherry-Garrard, whose beautiful family estate near St. Albans, Lamer Park, he visited many times. Grif was very impressed with the lovely mansion, which had been in the family since Elizabeth's day. He wrote to Cherry that September:

Figure 10. Taylor at the Priestley home in Tewkesbury. Courting Doris. 1914. (Photo from Bill Taylor)

Dear Cherry 16/8/13

The other day I spent the p.m. with Lady Scott — mostly posing for a statue to Uncle Bill; in which as regards gloves and belt and blouse, I suppose I do as well as another. However we discussed many things. Inter Alia S.P.T. [South Polar Times]. She says R.S. is willing to publish it. She asked me to help you get it ready for the press. This was her suggestion, but I should like to be associated with its production for obvious reasons. She approves — as you did — with the idea of an explanation introduction or appendix. As perhaps most of the farfetched skits and puns emanated from this very pen (now a — worrying you), I may be of special value to the harassed editor? I've just sent to Lady Scott a pretty complete account of the Owner's lecture on the Ross Barrier, of which I amassed 8 pp. of foolscap notes. They are giving us 24 photos in the book for the W. Geol. Party, and I've chosen nearly all of them. I shall be here till the 23rd I think and then return to London. I wrote today to your mother (12).

Grif enjoyed his weekend visits with Cherry but, most of the time Evans kept the members of the Expedition at their task of writing their accounts, and in October 1913, the two volumes of *Scott's Last Expedition* were published by Smith and Elder. Volume I contained Scott's actual *Journal*, and Volume 2 the reports of the journeys and scientific work of members of the expedition. The preface to the first volume was written by Sir Clements Markham who was the father of the Expedition, and the work was "arranged" by Leonard Huxley.

In a review of Scott's work in *The Times Literary Supplement*, Thursday, 6 November 1913, the reviewer mentions Scott's great interest in the scientific achievements of his men, and he specifically mentions Taylor and his work in that area between geology and geography that Grif called physiography.

His comments on Mr. Griffith Taylor's physiographical lectures may be taken as instance as bearing upon a branch of investigation which in certain features is new. To Scott's mind the branch presented itself thus "These modern physiographers set out to explain the forms of land erosion on broad common sense lines, heedless of geological support — an interesting memorandum upon that disputed frontier between the realms of geography and geology."

In discussing Volume 2 the reviewer states:

The Western Journeys are described by Mr. Griffith Taylor whose pen is that of a readier writer than others of his colleagues. He contributes in a later chapter, a Résumé of the Physiography and Glacial Geology of Victoria Land, and in his hands the physiographical system of describing the areas which he visited affords a verbal picture of them at once explicit and scientifically

90

reasoned. He has ably filled an important part in the preparation of the volume.

Grif as usual was making the most of his time in England. He was finishing his book, *With Scott: The Silver Lining* and he was also preparing for two lectures which he was asked to deliver in January to the Royal Geographical Society, one concerning the founding of Canberra, the other on the Glacial Geology of Antarctica. He was also busy arranging his future. He felt that his position in Australia was not very clear:

> I was officially described as Acting Commonwealth Geologist in a Government publication. I had no desire to continue doing purely meteorological research in Melbourne, and the geological work at Canberra was drawing to a close. However the war broke out in 1914, before anything definite about a geological survey was arranged and it was six years before I could shift into the geographical work which I loved (13).

He knew he must soon return to Australia. He hoped that on the return trip, he could do some lecturing and thought about the United States. This idea was squelched by Evans.

> With regard to America. I am afraid I cannot acquiesce in your lecturing there as I am going over in March on a tour of my own, lecturing in the big towns, so must keep that field clear until I have finished (14).

Money was obviously important to Grif especially now that he was planning to be married, as can be seen in Evans' remarks:

> You received 2½ times as much as the average naval officer, although you served half the time they did. Please treat this as confidential or I will have to contend with a terrific moan from Ponting who tries to claim the lecture rights for the whole world. Why don't you go out via South Africa. There is good business there (15).

Again in a letter to Grif, December 11/13:

> My dear Grif. What I suggest re your lecture tour is that you should demand ⅔ of the profits on your lectures. These terms have been adopted by Shackleton, Scott, Amundsen, Nansen etc. and seem to be a fair contract ... Your suggestion of South Africa is very good (16).

Obviously, Ponting was also having trouble with Evans about his Antarctic lectures. In a letter to Grif, dated 13 January 1914, Ponting complained:

> For 6 months I have been totally unable to exploit the right which Scott gave me to lecture, as Evans has taken the cream of everything

and I could get no one to back me. I should not like to see Evans kill the golden goose and so long as he is willing that others as well as he should benefit, all will be well. . . I do not want Evans to see this letter but I shall be grateful if you will let him know what you think and that what I ask is fair (17).

Taylor had requested permission from Ponting to use some of his pictures. He and Ponting had never gotten along very well and Ponting replied rather curtly in a letter dated January 9:

If you will only come to me in the right way, you will find that I shall be willing to help you all I can. Let me ask you how you and Deb. and Priestley would like it if I claimed the right to all your specimens without even being consulted. The cases are nearly parallel (18).

However, things were worked out and Taylor did a South African tour before returning to Australia. While still in London, on 12 January 1914, Grif gave a lecture on the founding of Canberra at the Royal Geographical Society. Lord Curzon was in the chair. Grif's lecture was well received and his subsequent article on Canberra was a thorough study of the physiography and history of the Australian Capital Territory. Again on January 15 he lectured at the Royal Geographical Society on the Glacial Geology of Antarctica, and both Professor David and Ernest Shackleton were in the audience. He had worked hard on this lecture, and the outline is preserved in the Canberra papers. He dealt with the problems connected with the shape of the continent, the climatic effect on the surrounding area, and detailed descriptions of the physiography of the Ferrar outlet glacier, and his theories of glacial erosion in the Antarctic.

Grif had been in England less than two years and he had finished an amazing amount of writing. His articles on Antarctic physiography were very well received and he had also completed several papers on the climate of Australia. Of special interest to geographers was the publication of his first book with geography in the title. His association with Herbertson in Oxford had resulted in several publications that show a broadening of Grif's interest. He wrote in 1914 of "Physical Features and their Effect on Settlement," the first time human factors had been included in his physiographic writings. The work in England resulted in nine publications in 1914, five of them books.

Grif left England in early 1914. He was a pacifist, so with Europe preparing for war, he was happy to leave England and return to Australia to continue his scientific work.

References
1. Griffith Taylor. Private Diary, 1912.
2. Griffith Taylor. Private Diary, 1912.
3. Taylor, Griffith: "Journeyman at Cambridge," p. 286.
4. Pound, Reginald: *Scott of the Antarctic*, p. 263.
5. Taylor, Griffith: *Journeyman Taylor*, p. 128.
6. Taylor, Griffith: "Journeyman at Cambridge," p. 291.

7. *Scott's Last Expedition*, Vol 1., p. 605.
8. National Library, Canberra, MS 1003/4/1.
9. Taylor, Griffith: "Journeyman at Cambridge," p. 299.
10. Taylor, Griffith: *Journeyman Taylor*, p. 131.
11. Letter, Lady Scott to Griffith Taylor, SPRI 2/190.
12. National Library, Canberra, MS 1003/559/134-3.
13. Taylor, Griffith: "Journeyman at Cambridge," p. 301.
14. National Library, Canberra, MS 1003/2/270.
15. National Library, Canberra, MS 1003/2/271.
16. National Library, Canberra, MS 1003/2/272.
17. National Library, Canberra, MS 1003/2/193.
18. National Library, Canberra, MS 1003/2/194.

CHAPTER 7

Grif Begins Career in Australia

On board ship, Grif enjoyed himself. He played in amateur theatricals, wrote letters to his family, played bridge and wrote up his Antarctic material for *Silver Lining*. He stopped in South Africa where he visited Capetown, Kimberley, Pretoria, Johannesburg, Bloemfontien, and Durban and although he did not make much money lecturing on the Antarctic, he saw a good deal of South Africa. Most of the month of March was spent on board the ship from South Africa to Melbourne. During these months, the first away from Doris since they had become engaged, he wrote long letters to her every day.

The letters in early 1914 were the only love letters in the Canberra files and they reveal a very different Grif from the scientist and the ambitious lecturer. On the first page of the collection, Grif had written in 1961,

> I don't suppose my letters to Miss Priestley will have any scientific value. Do not publish any personal details until five years after my death (1).

These letters show the "private" Grif, at the same time romantic yet philosophical. In his diary he wrote of Doris, "She is staunch and true and industrious and honest and pretty and active and clerical and Priestleyish and housewifely and matey." She was the one love of his life. On February 18th he wrote:

> Ma Chérie: On the road to Mandalay. I believe in people marrying who have similar tastes to a large degree — similar upbringing and similar friends — and so I think, Liebe, that you'll find that I suit. I know you'll say what you think I want. I was afraid you wouldn't at first. Always do so, dearest, especially at first while I forget that I'm not in command. It's rather terrifying at times to think that I've got almost everything I wanted since I graduated. . . Philosophy is religion for a scientist (Gad, that's a hot idea!) The true aim of life is to leave the world happier than when you found it. Here's a schedule of life's rules:
> 1) Work — because life is short and precious
> 2) Be jolly, because it lubricates the social wagon
> 3) Put yourself in the other man's place
> 4) Be content with the best rank in your own circle in life (2).

Grif certainly believed in the first three of these rules, and practised them in his own life. In July Doris arrived from England and on 8 July 1914, she and Grif were married in Queen's College Chapel at the University of Melbourne. It was a rather unusual ceremony since Professor David's wife, herself a well known liberated woman, gave the bride away.

While Taylor was back at the Weather Bureau, surely an anticlimax after the exciting year in Britain, he began thinking of a University post and discussed this with his superior, Hunt. The chair he wished for at the University of Melbourne was in Meteorology and Atlas and Geodetic Surveys, but with the outbreak of war in July 1914, the position never materialized and Grif was very disappointed.

However, that year he finally finished *Silver Lining*, with some 200,000 words, his longest book. He wished to improve his rough sketches and found David Low, a young artist who was later to become quite famous as a satirist with *The Sydney Bulletin*. He wrote on June 19:

> Dear Mr. Low: I have been hoping to send you the sketches for those drawings we discussed. But the position I was expecting to gain is not yet available so money isn't very plentiful. I enclose seven rough sketches. . .If you can do them at about a £ each (only not much more) go on with them (3).

Low did an excellent job of the sketches and they duly appeared in *Silver Lining*.

Also in 1914, Taylor's book *A Geography of Australasia* was published. It was very factual and included information on Australia, Tasmania, Papua, Fiji, the Solomons and New Zealand. Like much of his early work, it was edited by Herbertson and as a textbook for secondary school reflected Herbertson's interest in promoting geography at this level.

With the outbreak of war, Grif was given the job of teaching meteorology at the flying school at Laverton. There was little available material on Australian meteorology and even less equipment, so that in his inaugural lecture on winds, Grif used a flying helmet to represent the globe. Grif was busy during 1915 with the flying school but managed to finish a book on *Climate Control of Australian Production* for the Commonwealth Weather Service, an attempt to show the correlation between crops and rainfall. In this work, his use of the term "desert" was strongly objected to in Western Australia and began a controversy that was to rage for 14 years.

The number of Grif's publications increased during these years. In 1916 another book appeared, *The World and Australia*, published by Oxford University Press with Herbertson as editor, and finally in March *With Scott: The Silver Lining* was published, as Scott's account was, by Smith Elder and Co. The price was 18s. The review in the *London Morning Post* was very favourable.

> His chronicle of the works and days of the Terra Nova brotherhood will fascinate even those who regard the most majestical of the sciences (if we except astronomy) as a cold dreary business of stones and barriers. There is not a page without some pleasant touch of human interest, and whether consciously or unconsciously Dr. Taylor never suffers us to forget the weird, brooding, inhuman

wilderness which like Egdon Heath in Mr. Thomas Hardy's quaint novel is really the protagonist in the Antarctic play. Here then, is one of the best half-dozen stories of exploration and the explorer's life, and we are sure it will be read and remembered (4).

The *New York Post* said "his narrative shares the simple healthy humour of high spirits" (5) and in 1923 Caroline Oates, the mother of Titus Oates, wrote to Grif that she had just finished "yet another reading of your interesting book *With Scott: The Silver Lining* . . . I feel almost to have seen the Antarctic" (6). Reading Grif's book 70 years after the event generates the same feeling that Mrs. Oates had — a feeling that you were there. It is a newsy, chatty, chronological account of Taylor's personal experiences and views of the Expedition. Although it does not pretend to be a scientific account, there is a good deal of scientific information to be gained.

At the same time, Taylor had been negotiating with the University of Sydney concerning requirements for a doctoral degree and he was finally successful in March 1916 in being awarded the D.Sc. from that University for his thesis on "The Facies of the Southern Antarctic Littoral."

As far as their family life was concerned, Grif and Doris felt that time was going by and they were eager to start a family. They were happy to learn that they were to become parents in August and Grif became philosophical at the idea. Most of his notes in his personal diaries are cryptic items about lectures, books, and financial matters, but on March 10th he wrote:

> Man evolves to something higher
> Having ascended from amoeba
> Yet it is his children born
> Before his death, which carry on the
> Evolution to something better. Hence the
> Deeds before one dies are the factor determining
> Our after life. So shall a strenuous liver
> Ascend higher (7).

In Grif's diary for 28 August 1916, is the statement "Son Born" and the facts that the baby arrived at 6:03 and that he weighed 8½ pounds and had "blue lips, dark hair and big hands and feet, especially a big toe." Grif's diary that year was dotted with comments about Bill, "Bill slept 8 hours," "Bill smiled," "Bill gained 1/12 lbs in 1 week," "Bill holds head up." On December 1st, he was christened Griffith Priestley after both sides of the family, but from the day he was born, he was called "Bill" by his father in memory of the person Grif had admired most — Dr. Bill Wilson. In a letter the next year to Cherry-Garrard, Grif wrote:

> Mrs. Priestley tells me you are invalided home from the front. I hope you will have recovered when you receive this note. . . My wife is blooming and young G.P. Taylor grows out of his duds between fitting on and completion. . . Tell Mrs. Wilson our young son is always known as Bill after dear old "Uncle Bill" (8) (Fig. 11).

With a family to support, Grif wanted more than ever to have a university position. Before Bill was born, he had applied to the School of Geography at Oxford with no success and in November 1916, he heard of a position as professor of Geology at the University of Otago in Dunedin, New Zealand. He sent off an application, but nothing came of it so he had to be content with his job as instructor to the officers at the flying school. In 1916 he produced for them a brochure on meteorology "Syllabus of Lectures on Meteorology for Aviators" which eventually became the book *Australian Meteorology* published by Oxford Press. When the war finally ended in 1918, he was thanked for his part in the war effort by the Department of Defence. A letter from the Acting Secretary of the Department 15 February 1918, stated:

Figure 11. Bill Taylor, aged 10 months with Doris and Grandfather Taylor. April 1918. (Photo from Bill Taylor)

For the valuable instruction given by you to the students at the Central Flying School, I was directed to convey to you the thanks of the Minister of Defense (9).

During this period Taylor continued his extraordinary volume of writings — a book on *The Australian Environment*, an *Atlas of Contour and Rainfall Maps*, and several papers on the climatic factors influencing settlement in Australia. He wrote a paper entitled "The settlement of tropical Australia" for the Melbourne *Herald* in October 1917 and it was later published in the *Monthly Weather Review*. In this article, as in Taylor's other climatic articles, it is obvious that he realized the importance of rainfall to settlements. He perhaps was the first geographer to use the notion of "homoclimes" to clarify a place's climate. He pointed out that in northern Australia, Townsville had a climate similar to that of Calcutta while Wyndham in the hottest of Australia's climates, had for a homoclime only the extreme tip of India. One of Taylor's first loves was climatology and he published a brilliant series of papers which, as critics later stated, laid the foundations of the scientific study of the Australian geographical environment, work on which all later scholars have built (10).

There was some controversy over Taylor's assumption that the climatic conditions in tropical Australia were a serious impediment to white settlement. Taylor's reply to the criticism was:

As I pointed out there was no use our trying to settle unattractive regions so long as good regions were available. I have said over and over again that one could have a fairly comfortable existence in Antarctica if one liked to pay enough (11).

So Taylor's environmental determinism even at this period did not exclude the possibilist arguments that man could settle in a hostile environment if he were willing to pay the cost.

In 1917 the famous American geographer Ellsworth Huntington wrote to Taylor, beginning an association that was to last thirty years. The first letter referred favourably to Taylor's two articles on the climatic control of Australian production and settlement. Huntington also commented on Grif's excellent use of maps and stated that his "climographs" — a visual representation of the various effects of climate, were the best available.

In 1919 Taylor had three articles published in the *Geographical Review*. In sending his manuscripts to the *Geographical Review*, Grif made a choice that changed his life. He corresponded frequently from 1919 onward with Isaiah Bowman, the director of the American Geographical Society that published the *Review*. Bowman was an outstanding geographer who had the confidence of the President of the United States and who represented that country at the peace conference after the end of the war. Bowman was attracted by the writings of the young Australian and considered him to be one of the ablest geographers of his time. He offered him a job with the Society in 1920 and advised the University of Chicago to offer Taylor a position there in 1928. Bowman was also consulted later by the University of Toronto, which he advised to hire Taylor to begin a department of geography. He was a most influential and important friend to Taylor.

Grif's first article in the *Review* was "Air Routes to Australia." It concerned the future of commercial aviation and the geographical effect of technology on man's future. The second was a rewrite of his previous paper on tropical settlement in Australia. It was the third, however, "Climate Cycles and Evolution" that caught Bowman's fancy and he rightly predicted that it would be a landmark publication.

This last paper showed Grif's burgeoning interest in the geographical distribution of the various races in the world, and in his autobiography he dated this interest from the reading of a book entitled *Climate and Evolution*, by William Diller Matthew, Curator of the Museum of Vertebrate Paleontology in New York. Grif became intrigued with Matthew's theories and began to collect all available anthropological data on the distribution of types of hair, head-breadth, color, stature and plotted them on maps of the world in the form of isopleths. This led to his controversial migration zone theory of race classification.

It included the idea that the more primitive types had migrated from Central Asia, resulting in the fact that relics, skeletons, artifacts, placenames and folk-lore are found in zones outward and strata upward, from the place of origin. Taylor believed that climatic change was the impetus that pushed the races out from the centre. The theory gained a wide audience when it was published in the *Geographical Review*, and attracted notice among world scholars. This paper formed the basis of Taylor's work on *Environment and Race* — his most controversial work and the one that gained him a world-wide reputation. One immediate result was the fact that the International Meteorological Congress in Paris in 1919 appointed Grif to four commissions, more than any other Australian.

Grif was becoming very interested in settlement possibilities in Australia. His memoir on the settlement in tropical Australia earned him the Thompson Gold Medal in 1917, but he continued to make enemies with his statements about the empty heart of Australia. Grif wrote an article on "The Physiographic Control of Australian Exploration," which was published in the *Geographical Journal* in 1919. However, it was the last article of Taylor's to be published in this British journal, a fact that caused him a good deal of distress, and one he never understood.

Increasingly, Grif was becoming restless in his job at the Weather Bureau and yearned to become a full-time University professor. He had heard from Professor David that an associate Professorship in Geography was to be established at Sydney University, a position made possible by a grant from a wealthy pastoralist, Sir Samuel McCaughey. David had urged him to apply for the position. However, as before, Grif was concerned about money since he desperately wanted to enjoy the good things of life and provide a high standard of living for Doris. He wrote to David 29 December 1919:

I am a little anxious about the pay for the proposed Sydney position, for my start in the Government Service was not auspicious. I asked for 500 and was offered 310 to which I cabled a prompt refusal. It's taken 10 years to reach 600 (12).

Grif had another job offer and he used it to obtain what he desired for the Sydney position. Isaiah Bowman as Director of the American Geographical Society offered him a job in New York with the Society. Grif sent the letter from Bowman to Professor David asking his advice, and received this reply on 4 June 1920:

I find it difficult to advise you in the matter. I hope that at the Senate meeting June 7 the matter of the appointment of a lecturer in Geography will be settled. Lecturers will not command a salary of more than £600 pa. Naturally I am extremely keen to secure you for the position... I cannot but think that you would be more comfortable working here with our own British people than in New York as a citizen of USA (13).

Grif meanwhile had replied to Bowman on June 2:

Your major proposition does me great honour but requires careful consideration. I should prefer a University or research position other things being equal. A very important factor is a result of the recent McCaughey bequest of £2M to Sydney University. It is disgraceful that there are no full lecturships in Geography at any Australian University. Professor David is trying to alter this and establish an Associate Professorship at my old Alma Mater. They are good enough to associate my name with this position.

Now as to the N.Y. position, you are naturally not explicit here. I gather (1) the position would be permanent. Does your Society work in with Columbia University? (2) What work do you propose for myself? (14)

However, before the end of June, Grif received an invitation from the Warden of the University of Sydney to join the staff of the University as an Associate Professor of Geography. Grif enjoyed the situation and wrote to Doris that he had received a cable from Bowman offering him $4000 per year with an extra $2000 for five to six months' field work. And in the same letter:

It's a fine lever for the Sydney Senate to chew over on Monday... How will Bill like a Yankee Daddy? Seriously, I like the Americans for prohibition, for Wilson, for treatment of women and for "go". They're ahead of Australians in all these (15).

Finally the University of Sydney offered him £900 a year and he accepted the offer and cabled Bowman to that effect. He also wrote Bowman on July 20:

The Senate of the University of Sydney has a new Associate Professorship in Geography at £900 a year. . . Furthermore, I should not be separated from my wife and family for half the year and she rather dreads the high cost of living in New York and the totally new environment of life in America (16).

It was obvious that Grif felt happy about his new job. At last he was to have a position he considered worthy of his wife and he felt his future was rosy. He was certain that in twenty years he would be knighted, as Professor David had been, and as he intimated in a letter in November to Doris in which he told her of Professor David's knighthood.

Professor Sir Edgeworth David informs me that my school was virtually independent so don't you let Mrs. Professorin Taylor bend the knee to anyone! Not even to Lady David who lectures in Mosman on Prohibition this week. I'm glad he got the knighthood. . . I look forward to our helping the students socially as much as anything. I know the Professorin will shine there. . . What a lot of Ladies you know now. Never mind, there'll be a Lady Taylor within 20 years, so don't you forget (17).

It appeared that Grif felt that he was following in Edgeworth David's footsteps — in geology, in the Antarctic and now in a University post. He desperately wished to be successful and to prove to the Priestleys that he was worthy of their daughter. But the knighthood was to elude him.

On 12 August 1920, Grif was happy to resign from the Weather Service. He set off for Honolulu to attend a Pan Pacific congress by way of Java and Sumatra, since his lectures at Sydney University did not begin until March 1921. He had not much liked his work in the Weather Bureau but it had given him a solid foundation in meteorology and climatology, a foundation which he made good use of in his writings. His textbook on *Australian Meteorology* was published by Oxford in 1920, and was one of Grif's greatest accomplishments, since it presented meteorology in terms of Australian rather than European conditions, and it included the first rainfall maps of Australia. It attracted the attention of all the climatologists of the day.

In 1920, Grif could be said to be a pioneer in the field of geography. From his early interest in geology, he had gradually changed his focus to one more concerned with man-land relationships than strictly with rocks and land forms. His work with the Weather Bureau had forced him to consider climate as a factor influencing land forms and also influencing people, especially curtailing the regions of human settlement. However, his own reading and his curiosity about the world and its people suggested a new focus in his work, the study of the reasons underlying the distribution of races in the world. He was to expand and refine these theories for many years and become famous for his work in this area of man-environment relations.

References

1. National Library, Canberra, MS 1003/15/9/61.
2. National Library, Canberra, MS 1003/105.0.
3. Letter Taylor to David Low, June 19, 1914, University of Sydney, Thomas Fisher Rare Book Library, Griffith Taylor Collection.
4. National Library, Canberra, MS 1003/16/3/16.
5. National Library, Canberra, MS 1003/2/179.
6. National Library, Canberra, MS 1003/3/16 180A — MS 1003/9/215.
7. Griffith Taylor. Private Diary, 1916.
8. Letter from Taylor to Cherry-Garrard, Nov. 17, 1917.
9. National Library, Canberra, MS 1003/122/24A.
10. Aurousseau M: "Obituary Griffith Taylor 1880-1963" *Australian Geographical Studies*, Vol. 2, no. 1, April, 1964, p. 1.
11. Tomkins, George: "Griffith Taylor and Canadian Geography," p. 45.
12. National Library, Canberra, MS 1003/127/27.
13. National Library, Canberra, MS 1003/4/133.
14. National Library, Canberra, MS 1003/127/C.
15. Griffith Taylor. Private Diary, 1920.
16. Letter Taylor to Bowman, July 20, 1920.
17. National Library, Canberra, MS 1003/96E.

CHAPTER 8

The Department in Sydney

Grif returned to Australia at the end of the year to begin his new job. He went househunting in Sydney, while Doris was still in England. The house he chose was at 78 Prince Albert Street in Mosman, and was very posh with eight bedrooms. In January 1921 Doris and Bill returned after their eight-month holiday, and the family moved to their new house. It was nice for Grif and Doris to be near the Taylor grandparents and Bill was left with his grandmother when his parents needed a change.

Grif was happy organizing his new department. He found it a considerable challenge since he had never attended a geographical course of lectures. His background was in geology, but with his practical experience in geology as well as in climatology, he tackled the problem with his typical enthusiasm and self-confidence. He found that students were most impressed by information derived first hand by the professor and he had already tramped over a good portion of the earth's surface. Geography was part of the science faculty, as Grif had requested, and the science student was required to take four subjects during his first year, three in his second and two in his final. There were no special classes for honours students but Grif considered that his graduates should have considerable knowledge of geology and geography, a double major. Although geography was to be a distinct department, it was felt that the course should require a year's study of geology, so the students entered geography in their second year. Grif taught a general introductory course in world geography as well as courses in elementary navigation and climate. For a few years he included a course in anthropology and in 1922 he inaugurated a third year course in Cultural Geography — probably the first geography course to be so named. Laboratories were considered by Grif to be essential for the student's education. He required an assistant and naturally chose his sister Dorothy who had graduated from Sydney University and had been awarded the Physiography Prize in Geology. Dorothy was Grif's assistant for his eight years at Sydney and they were a good team. Dorothy adored her brother and loved the work. The first class had 17 women and 54 men. Sister Nell Stanley was one of the students in those early years and, in 1984, 75 years old, she recalled with great pleasure those years in Sydney and her impressions of Grif:

> He was certainly a many sided man of boundless energy and enthusiasm and a charisma that enthused his students (1).

Dorothy was in charge of the laboratory exercises. Unsure of what was needed, she first used W.M. Davis "Practical Exercises in Physical Geography" but later, with Grif's help, she wrote a laboratory manual called "The Geography

Laboratory." This book of practical exercises Grif used throughout his career for the students beginning geography. The exercises required no expensive equipment but undoubtedly taught the student much practical geography. There were exercises in pace and compass surveying, and building a model of a landscape with layers of coloured cardboard. The construction of a simple block diagram hopefully aided the students in Grif's technique of looking at the landscape and sketching it in three dimensions. Probably none of his students became as proficient in this as Grif himself, but none of them forgot these laboratory exercises.

Grif's developing friendship with Ellsworth Huntington was very important to him. Huntington of Yale University was at the time a well known geographer and it was flattering to Grif to receive a letter from him in March 1920 concerning his "Climate Cycles" article in the *Geographical Review*. Huntington wrote:

> I enjoyed your article. . . I consider it one of those pieces of work which broadens one's horizon's and gives one a great sweep of vision (2).

There was an immediate rapport between the two men which was to last a lifetime. Grif wrote to Huntington on 23 June 1920:

> There are some letters which one always treasures as marks of one's progress in science and your kindly letter about "Climate Cycles" is certainly one of these (3).

However, Huntington did not hesitate to criticize Taylor. On 27 June 1921 he wrote:

> Let me begin by saying that your ideas have set me to thinking as have those of few other geographers. . . I have been genuinely troubled in regard to your future. . . why I have made up my mind to write fully. "Re Cosmic Causes of Climate Change". When I took the matter up with astronomers I received a jolt. . . Men I consulted agreed that you had founded your hypothesis upon astronomical information contrary to fact. . . You had failed to take account of work of other people. . . Although struck by a brilliant idea, you had worked it out most interestingly. . . I am disturbed because so frequently you state as a fact something which is merely a theory. . . When I wrote "Pulse of Asia," I realized that I did just what I accuse you of doing. You need to confer with authorities in these lines (climate, geology etc.). You are a little remote from the main line of scientific work, and have evolved your ideas without criticism or so much personal contact as would come if you were in England or here. . . Isn't there any way that you can plan to come to America for a year? I can think of nothing that I would like better than to have you come here and be a co-worker with me (4).

106

Taylor was no doubt a little upset by this frank criticism by his new friend and tried to explain his problem to Huntington. In a letter dated September 20, he said:

> I should like to have you here to explain some of the difficulties of research work in Australia. In climatology I can safely say that there is no one at all save myself doing genuine research on modern data... I am honoured by your suggestion that I make a visit to Yale (5).

In 1922 Huntington tried to persuade President Angell of Yale to hire Taylor and create a Geographical Faculty at Yale, stating that from the standpoint of scientific research, he (Angell) could do nothing better than to call Professor Taylor and Professor Steven Visher. However, nothing came of the approach.

In January 1921, the *Geographical Review* published another Taylor article "The Evolution and Distribution of Race, Culture and Language." It was a reworking and development of his previous "Climate Cycles and Evolution" and affirmed that the differentiation of races was a result of the marked changes in climate during the Pleistocene age. This paper was a move into anthropology where Taylor attempted to apply the methods he had used in geology and meteorology to the studies of evolution and linguistics. Taylor adapted many of the terms of physical geography to these human phenomena — shatter belt, outlier, eruption. This paper attracted attention because of Taylor's novel techniques. He used an isopleth mapping technique that he had used for rainfall to plot the distribution of languages and other human phenomena. In thus using a geographic method for studying human distributions, he was truly a pioneer.

"The distribution of Future White Settlement" was written in 1922 and also published in the *Geographical Review*. Certainly Taylor found a responsive audience in Bowman at the AGS. Fresh from his peace-making efforts at Versailles with President Wilson, Bowman was most interested in the young Australian's ideas of frontiers of settlement and his world vision. This article was an attempt to expand to a world-wide study Grif's previous theory on white settlement in Australia. It was a landmark paper. It was written clearly and logically and, as always, Grif explained his methods to the reader. He divided the continents into economic regions, based primarily on those of Herbertson; then he tabulated the regions according to what he believed to be the dominant "controls" of temperature, rainfall, location and resources. Using these, he drew an econograph, a four-sided figure which represented the habitability of the region. An ideal region would have 1000 units on Grif's econograph. Britain and North China were found to have 770 units. It was a novel concept and a quite successful attempt to quantify parameters that were not usually quantified. The secret of Taylor's successful writings was that he combined techniques from various disciplines, quantified the unquantifiable and drew maps of things usually thought unmappable. However, Grif was aware that his approach was subjective and that there would be criticism. He stated:

I would remind the reader that the introduction of a similar method of comparing climates by the climograph has led to a number of interesting papers on comparative climatology in which, moreover, useful suggestions for improving this graphic method have been made. The writer hopes for the same happy result from the present paper (6).

In this paper, Grif did not hesitate to predict the future. Based on his tabulations, he predicted a population of 600 million for North America in the next two centuries and 100 million in South America. He also correctly envisaged:

> A vast struggle between higher civilizations with a low birth rate and lower civilizations with a high birth rate seems to be foreshadowed (7).

Grif made much use of Huntington's theories in this paper, especially criteria for the optimum conditions for white settlement, and the correspondence between the two men, and their friendship, flourished.

In 1921, Grif received his first letter from Harlan Barrows at Chicago, dated December 14. Little did Barrows know that Grif would one day be on his faculty in Chicago. This particular letter was to suggest that professors Jones and Platt in his department would like to exchange photographic plates with Taylor. Another interesting letter in the Taylor files was a request from the Thomas Edison company for a message for Edison on the occasion of his 75th birthday from celebrities throughout the world. Grif complied with the request and received a very friendly letter from Mr. Edison:

> As one reaches the higher figures of the yearly stepping stones of life it is one of the compensations of a birthday to be the recipient of friendly greetings and remembrances (8).

Grif liked writing for the newspaper and he loved a good argument. His articles on "The Australian Environment" and "Australian Meteorology" had clearly shown the arid nature of the interior of Australia and had sparked a controversy in the Australian press. One of Grif's antagonists was Dr. Basedow who wrote in *The Argus* criticizing Taylor for being a scientific pessimist about the colonizing of central Australia. Grif replied in an article in *The Argus* (2 April 1921):

> I have read Dr. Basedow's article in which he objects to many of my conclusions as to settlement in Central Australia. Politicians have no right to spend the nation's money on this unprofitable tract where nothing but sparse pastoral occupation is possible (9).

On 20 September 1921 Mr. Hope Robertson, the Acting Director of Education of West Australia, wrote to Grif:

Your geography book was banned from the University and possible pressure will be brought to bear on the Department to have it banned as a teacher's reference book also (10).

On September 28th Taylor wrote a long letter to Hope Robertson complaining of remarks made about his (Taylor's) articles on Western Australia by Catton Grasby. Excerpts from the letter are given below:

I thank you for sending me the leader and cutting from the "West Australian" which embodies some of Mr. Catton Grasby's objections to my writings. It is difficult to reply to a man who uses a special series of definitions for his own State and who objects to the application of scientific deductions made in other regions to his own country... I would ask you as head of the Education Department to form your own opinion of the book irrespective of the views of one or two unwise optimists who seem to wish to stifle scientific discussion of your State's undoubted disabilities. I do not know what text book you will use in place of mine... In conclusion, I am sorry that the University has accepted the views of non-geographical research... Lastly, what object can I possibly have in this alleged labelling either of the arid or tropical lands of West Australia or other States?... I regret that the University is adopting such an unscientific attitude. I enclose a review of the book written by Keith Ward (Government Geologist of South Australia) who is as well acquainted as Mr. Grasby with arid Australia. It gives a different view of the value of this book (11).

Mr. Grasby continued the attack on Grif. It was especially bitter after an article appeared in the London *Times* which quoted Grif's book and stated that the Northwest of Australia was a great sandy desert. The Prime Minister of Australia called the *Times* statements "infamous lies." Grasby wrote in the *West Australian*, 5 November 1921, that Taylor's book was used throughout Australia as a text book and stated:

Why anyone should attempt to defend the teaching of infamous lies is hard to understand. I and others have drawn attention to the matter for years. I directed the attention of the Royal Commission on Education to the fact, but there is nothing in the report to indicate that they took any notice (12).

Taylor wrote to Isaiah Bowman of this controversy over the nature of central Australia and on 3 August 1922 Bowman wrote to Grif that he had received:

a communication from the Department of State respecting an attack on the book by Sir Joseph Carruthers because it misrepresented Australia... I immediately wrote to the Department of State and apprized them of the nature of the controversy raging in Australia itself regarding the possible future of the interior in order that they could call the matter to the attention of the consul at Sydney who had forwarded the item containing quotations from Carruthers (13).

Just as Grif's ideas about the Australian desert were unpopular with politicians and the masses, so also were his deductions of the position of the so-called Yellow Race among the peoples of the world. In 1923 Grif's articles about Asiatic settlement in Northern Australia led to vicious attacks in the press. His statements that the Asiatics were not inferior to the white races and "marriage with Asiatics, why not?" led to newspaper articles entitled "To smear Australia Yellow" and "Counsel for the Yellow Streak" castigating Taylor. A caricature of him with a Mongolian baby appeared in the press. Even the student newspaper at the University of Sydney protested such undesirable principles being propagated in their midst. Taylor loved a good argument but was hurt by these public attacks.

The Australian Association for the Advancement of Science was founded in 1921 and Taylor became a charter member. In 1923 he was elected president of Section E (Geography and History) and his presidential address is interesting as a statement of his views of geography. He defined geography as "the study of environment in its relation to human values"(14). He used a diagram in this speech called the Realm of Geography attributed to and adapted from the American geographer Von Engeln, in which geography was shown as the core science composed of parts of geology, meteorology, history, biology and anthropology. Grif's bias was obvious, since he stated that geology was the chief science basic to geography.

Taylor also stressed the role of geography in nation planning and continued his attack on those politicians and journalists who continued to promote settlement in the desert areas of Australia. This was the period of "Australia Unlimited" and Taylor was aware that his statements of the physical limitations to settlement were not popular. But Grif had the courage of his convictions and continued to talk about the "empty heart of Australia."

In April 1923, Grif learned in a letter from Ellsworth Huntington that he would be visiting Australia in August to attend the Pan Pacific Scientific Congress. Grif was so pleased to know that at last he would meet the geographer he admired probably more than any other. Huntington wrote:

> I am sending you a book by Dixon which I know will interest you. . .
> You will be much pleased I am sure to find that his ideas as to the migration of races agrees in the main with your own. I know you were disappointed that people criticized your theories so much. Perhaps you will be glad to know that I have been studying them once more in connection with Dixon's book and am coming to the conclusion that in the main they are correct. . . I want to reproduce your map of the distribution of races in a book which I am writing entitled "The Character of Races" (15).

Grif wrote to ask him to spend some time at their house in Mosman and Huntington was happy to accept. In a letter to Grif and Doris from Brisbane after his visit, dated September 18, he wrote:

> The seven weeks have been extraordinarily interesting and valuable.
> I would not have believed I could find so many new things to learn. . .
> I have been trying to get some of my ideas as to Australian climate
> into shape. There seems to be a greater degree of adaptation to the
> warm climate than I realized (16).

In May 1923, Bowman had written Taylor that the Council of the AGS had voted him the David Livingstone Centenary Medal for 1923 for his "distinguished work in the geography of Australia" (17). Grif joined the exalted company of other recipients, including Sir Douglas Mawson in 1916 and Theodore Roosevelt in 1917. Grif was duly presented with the beautiful gold medal by Richard Fenneman on behalf of the AGS at the Pan Pacific Congress that summer, and wrote to Dr. Bowman in September to thank him and the Society.

> I am very much delighted with the medal which is a beautiful work of
> art as well as a surprisingly valuable token of good will from your
> Society (18).

On the home front, Grif and Doris were pleased when, on 11 October 1921 a second child, Natalie Joyce, was born. Grif noted in his diary, "baby very vigorous, much hair. Good delivery, quite natural." Natalie was a happy beautiful child, and the apple of her father's eye. Grif's diary in 1923 was filled with entries about his little Natalie and when the Huntingtons came to visit they, too, fell in love with the child whom Ellsworth said reminded him so much of his own daughter (Fig, 12). In a letter to Grif (23 February 1924) he stated:

> Long before I saw you, the similarity of our work and the
> resemblances in the way our minds attack the problems of science
> made me feel that you and I are unusually near together. It is sure
> that there is considerable resemblance between our children
> especially between my Anna and your Natalie (19).

On September 29, in Grif's diary there was a note "Natalie sick. . . bronchitis." They hired a nurse for the little girl when her temperature was consistently 104° and 105° and Grif's diary for October 5 notes "rash out stronger on Natalie." Grif does not say what the diagnosis was, but October 9 saw "no change" and on October 27, she died.

Grif was not a person who showed much emotion, but the death of his little daughter was a blow. Although not a religious man, Grif wrote a touching, religious poem "Natalie," in his diary:

> She is not lost
> She goeth on before
> And to her mother's love and care

Figure 12. The Taylor's daughter Natalie (about age 2); born 1921, died 1924. (Photo from Bill Taylor)

A perfect witness in that life shall bear
And since the arms of this part life below
Is but preparation for a nobler sphere
Take comfort who remain, no dearer soul
E'er entered Heaven than our two years babe.

When Huntington heard the news, he wrote, 5 January 1925, that he felt

sadness about your dear little Natalie, one of the sweetest, brightest dearest little girls I ever knew. I wonder whether we scientists are not losing a good deal by our attitude of doubt as to a future life (20).

The Taylors' sadness at the loss of their little daughter was somewhat lessened on 21 January 1925, when a second son, and last child, was born. Perhaps not surprisingly he was christened David, after the man who was the most influential in Grif's life — Sir Edgeworth David. Again Grif's diary is filled with statistics on the child's development. "Weighs 8 lbs 5 oz at 8 weeks," "Starts smiling."

But life went on and Grif could not keep out of controversy. Bowman wrote to him in January 1924 that the famous explorer Stefansson was coming to Australia and asked Grif's help in showing him around. Bowman said that Stefansson had said to the papers that he was going to see if Australia did not show neglected opportunities of settlement similar to those he had found in the Arctic. . . I tremble to think of the possibilities of mischief that such an attitude implies if he should fall into the wrong hands, or arrive in arid Australia in a period of exceptional rainfall (21).

Stefansson duly arrived in Australia in May and wrote a series of articles about his visit in the Sydney *Morning Herald.* In an article dated 12 August 1924 he wrote:

I want to make it clear that although I consider myself a scientist, I am in this special case writing only as a traveller from a far country. . . I am reporting what I have seen. . . I see no reason to suppose that I shall find myself in important disagreement with the native geographers of Australia (22).

Even Edgeworth David got into the argument (Sydney *Morning Herald,* 13 August 1924):

The recent short visit of. . . Dr. Stefansson into Central Australia has reawakened interest in the controversy which took place lately in your columns as to whether or not Central Australia should be classed as desert. As the result of statements by Dr. Stefansson as to his favourable impressions about Central Australia, and in comparing them with opinions attributed to Prof. Griffith Taylor, the public are likely to be led into the belief that Prof. Taylor has maligned our climate. . . Any impartial Australian who studies these (Taylor's) works, cannot fail to be impressed with their honesty, frankness and ability. . . Stefansson has nowhere been within 50 miles of this main "desert" area (23).

These remarks were made in reply to an article in the same newspaper July 31, which stated:

Reference to the mission of Dr. Stefansson was made in the House of Representatives today by the member for the Northern Territory (Mr. Nelson) who asked whether the P.M. (Mr. Bruce) had noticed Press reports to the effect that Dr. Stefansson had not yet been successful in locating "the alleged desert" in Central Australia and whether, in the interests of Australia, Mr. Bruce would see Prof. Griffith Taylor of Sydney was supplied with a copy of Dr. Stefansson's report. The copy said Mr. Nelson should be accompanied by a word of advice that Prof. Griffith Taylor should desist from his perpetual slander on Central Australia (24).

These criticisms bothered Taylor more than most people realized. He kept all the clippings and they are preserved in the Canberra files. Pasted on the same page as the above reference to the Commonwealth Parliament is a second clipping dated 3 November 1925 beside which Grif had added in pencil "a year later — nemesis." It stated that Mr. Nelson, member for Northern Territory, who was proceeding to Darwin on a motor bicycle was lost in the bush for three days. He was found between Sterling and Barrier Creek in a very low condition, having had nothing but half a pint of water in three days.

Isaiah Bowman tried to cheer Taylor by writing on 24 September 1924:

> I don't want to see you discouraged by a collision with foolish optimists for I have the utmost faith in your methods and your conclusions. I think your work has been of the first order as to quality and brilliance and as you know, we have a special investment of pride and interest in your career as a gold medallist of the Society (25).

Writing was easy for Grif and requests for publications began to increase. In 1925, he was asked to contribute to an Italian encyclopedia and wrote 29 articles on Australia, the Pacific Islands and the Antarctic. In 1926 another article was published in the *Geographical Review* — "The Frontiers of Settlement in Australia."

This article, plus one in *Foreign Affairs* in 1927 entitled "Australia as a Field for Settlement" and one in 1928 for an AGS publication on "Climatic Relation between Antarctic and Australia" showed Taylor as the expert in Australian settlement possibilities and the climatic factors limiting such settlement. His experience in the Weather Bureau stood him in good stead, and he had drawn the first rainfall maps of Australia. He rightly stated that in no other continent are the effects of climate so clearly exhibited as in Australia with its uniform topography and compact structure, thus no other area is so uniquely suited to test the control of climate over settlement. His conclusion "that 42% of the continent of Australia is arid" (26) certainly was not what the government of Australia wanted to hear. His case was clearly argued and Taylor presented maps and statistics that were difficult to refute. So of course he earned the enmity of all the settlement boosters and was continually criticized in the press. At the peak of his enthusiasm for his new geography school and the usefulness of what it could do for his adopted country, he was disowned and vilified. The Sydney newspapers ran a steady campaign against him — arguing that, since Professor Taylor did not seem to like Australia, they wondered why he stayed. Ann Marshall wrote many years later:

> From my later conversations with Grif, and even more from discussions with his devoted and charming wife Doris, it is clear that he was deeply hurt and that the hurt persisted even after he returned to Australia in 1952 — perhaps until he was elected inaugural President of the Institute of Australian Geographers in 1959. His excommunication was not over when he left Australia, and it was not confined to politicians and journalists — a senior Australian geographer, not I admit born in this country but he should have

114

Figure 13. Grif (second from right) at the Great Wall in China with geographers Benson, Wang and Cotton. Peking Nov. 25, 1926. National Library of Australia.

> known better, told me in the 1940s that "it was very unwise of Taylor to emphasise all that desert stuff, washing Australia's dirty linen in public" (27).

In 1926, Grif felt that he had worked hard enough at the University of Sydney that he should be appointed full professor and sent his application for promotion to the Senate. He received an answer on November 3 from W.A. Selle, the registrar:

> . . . inform you that the Senate adopted the following resolution presented by the Committee appointed to consider your application for promotion to full Professorship: "Committee recommends that when funds permit, the Senate should take into consideration, along with other claims, the raising of the Association Professorship of Geography to the status of a full Chair" (28).

He had to be content with that reply and went on with his work. He was pleased to be chosen as a National Research Council delegate to the Pacific Congress to be held in Japan in November 1926. He presented three papers, in three sections of the congress; one on agriculture in Australia, one on glaciation in the southwest Pacific, and one, more controversial, on the Australian aboriginal. He was also invited by the Peking geologists to visit China at the close of the conference. This was Grif's only trip to China and one that he enjoyed immensely (Fig. 13).

There were now a number of graduate geographers in New South Wales and in 1927 the Geographical Society of New South Wales was formed and Grif was elected its first president. Dorothy became one of its first three vice-presidents. The journal of the new society was called *The Australian Geographer* and Grif's only contribution to it was his first presidential address.

Environment and Race, published in 1927, would prove to be more controversial than any other of his works and would make him well known outside the field of geography. This book was an expansion of articles previously published in the *Geographical Review* both in the field of environment and in race distribution and Grif had the encouragement and support of Isaiah Bowman and Ellsworth Huntington. In explaining the scope of the book, Taylor states

> the world problem of today is the adjustment of the nations to the crowding which for the first time in history is affecting the whole earth and this goes hand in hand with a remarkable increase in the aspirations of various backward races (29).

Taylor was the first geographer to write about these problems — problems that were new then but continue to plague society today. Again, Grif was not afraid to tackle large global problems. Indeed he believed that geographers were eminently qualified to do so and world events in the following 50 years certainly showed the truth of Taylor's statements.

In his book, Taylor described his controversial Zones and Strata Theory. In reality, the theory was an adaptation to humans of the paleontologist Matthew's theory of climate and evolution dealing with the original and dispersal of vertebrates.

> One of the main objects of this book is to demonstrate that primitive man, being subject to the same laws as other animals, has evolved and migrated in response to similar stimuli. . . the most primitive races are to be found farthest away from the centre (30).

In his Zones and Strata Theory, Taylor drew on his knowledge of geology, applying the same laws to the migration of peoples. He used an analogy of the evolution of transport in a large city like Sydney, explaining that as one moves farther from the centre of the city one finds more and more primitive methods of transportation. At the same time, if one were to inspect the scrap heaps in the central city, at the bottom would be found evidence of transport from one hundred years ago. Taylor examined each continent with respect to its racial distribution and zones and strata theory and his concluding chapter dealt with the potential white settlement of the world and some forecasts of future populations.

116

The book was reviewed by Ellsworth Huntington in the *Saturday Review*. Huntington criticized Taylor's book but correctly identified his friend's best qualities, that of succinct generalization and his ability to stimulate discussion, and suggested that Taylor was one of those few people who were born to suggest new ideas. He wrote that whatever Taylor wrote was almost sure to bristle with points that challenge controversy, but are well worth considering. Huntington wrote that the book

> has certain highly outstanding qualities: First it is full of meat; second, it is easy to read and highly interesting in the parts where the author gives rein to his powers of generalization, but difficult to follow where he curbs himself and sets down a huge array of detailed facts; third, it displays an extraordinary ability to summarize a vast amount of knowledge in a few paragraphs and especially in diagrams and semi-pictorial maps; fourth, the book teems with conclusions and methods which can easily be criticized; and fifth, it is equally full of ideas which are bound to form the basis of some of the liveliest and most valuable discussions of the next generation. Taylor often seems to be wrong — even his best friends think so — but he is a prophet, and we who criticize are likely to find that in many cases it is we, not he, who are wrong (31).

The book was read by ecologists who were interested in his method of depicting climate conditions by graphs — "climographs" — and who agreed that his fearless discussions of the inevitable consequences of the scanty and erratic rainfall of most of Australia had attracted widespread attention. The reviewer in *Ecology* stated that the book

> will induce stimulating thought. Taylor's E. and R. is a highly original, stimulating, effectively illustrated discussion of important phases of human ecology (32).

Grif sent a copy of his book to H.G. Wells whom he much admired and was very pleased to have this reply from him dated 7 July 1927:

> Spent a delightful evening, reading your book and regretting that I am 60. I cannot hope ever to work in the field you have had the happiness to explore with such vigour. I like your attack on your subject and your diagrams and your ideas which set me thinking and sometimes objecting. I have an incurable objection to an "Alpine" race. I think if it weren't for that, I'd swallow your book whole. If ever I knew why I don't believe in cephalic indices I have forgotten, but I don't believe. I believe heads have "gone square" lots of times all over the world (33).

The book was a popular success. However, some reviewers objected to Taylor's use of the old and badly discredited cephalic index and hair texture while one reviewer had a sneaking feeling all the while that uncongenial facts have been overlooked or neglected (34).

It is probable that the criticisms did not bother Taylor. He loved to expostulate new theories, disregard the facts that did not fit, and let others argue the points. His contributions to science were the new ideas, the generalizations, the world view. His ideas were stimulating not only to geographers, but in the case of racial theories, to anthropologists and journalists.

Grif continued to work hard in the new department at Sydney. The number of students in geography had increased dramatically, and his publication record was outstanding. But he was becoming increasingly frustrated by the lack of staff, poor accommodation and equipment, but most of all the small prospect of an increased salary. Then, in December 1927, Grif's father died. As with most of his private sorrows, Grif did not say much about his father's death in his diaries, but it was one more reason for him to think of leaving Australia.

Perhaps he remembered a letter he had received from his friend Herbert Heaton, an Australian economist who had emigrated to Queen's University in Kingston, Ontario. Heaton had written Grif in 1925:

> Will you let me thank you for the enormous benefit I've got from your work... Last year I learned that Toronto was thinking of establishing a department of geography, and I mentioned your name to the President of Toronto as the most "live" geographer I knew... The Toronto economics men are great friends of mine and they will have a big say in dealing with the matter (35).

Grif remained in regular communication with many influential geographers in the United States. He sounded out Isaiah Bowman about the possibility of a job in the United States and on 11 April 1928 Bowman replied:

> P.S. I shall certainly keep in mind your wish to be nearer this part of the world. There are no major possibilities above the horizon at the moment but they may come into view later (36).

He also asked Huntington about job possibilities and Huntington replied in a letter dated 15 May 1928:

> As to your coming to America, I am going to write Atwood of Clark and one or two others to see whether they want to have you give a course or two during the year 1930-31 [he wrote to Atwood at Clark, Barrows in Chicago, Gray at Harvard, Sauer in California, Russell Smith in Columbia, and Whitbeck in Wisconsin]. I also suggested the possibility you might want to stay in this country. I wish that might happen for it would be a great delight to me to have you here. Your mind, as Woodrow Wilson used to say, goes along with mine and I know that frequent contact with you would be most stimulating. [And again on May 25]: I have received replies from two

of the men to whom I wrote. Barrows of Chicago writes that he is much interested in the idea of having you come to Chicago. He is interested in the possibility that you may wish to stay in this country permanently (37).

Grif was very pleased to hear from Harlan Barrows at Chicago. In a letter dated June 4 Barrows offered him a full professorship at Chicago at an annual salary of $6,000. He added that each member of the staff taught two courses in each of the three of the four quarters, and that in the fourth quarter plus September he would be "off duty." Barrows also mentioned the cost of living:

Chicago is not unlike Sydney. A family of four can live on the same scale. The cost would be $200 more in New York or Cambridge. I would be grateful if you would cable decision and begin lectures January 2/29 (38).

Huntington also wrote to Taylor telling him about the Chicago department. He described Barrows as very tall and impressive and apt to be a little gruff, although capable of inspiring devotion among his associates. Huntington said:

It is really somewhat surprising to me that he seems so eager to have you come when your methods are so different from his. . . I feel that it is a great credit to him that when he knows you tend to be so opposite to him, he should still want you (39).

He mentioned the other members of the Department: Colby, Jones, Whittlesey, Platt. Huntington described Colby as both conceited and shallow, Jones as very pleasant but not very profound as a scientist, Whittlesey something like Jones and Platt as a younger man with fair prospects of achieving something. Huntington's advice was:

I should decidedly advise you to accept the offer — partly because I want you in this country. You will have at Chicago an opportunity you cannot get in Australia. Your presence will give Chicago a scholarly character which it now lacks (40).

Colby also wrote expressing his desire that Taylor should come to Chicago. Bowman urged him to accept but added a word of criticism about Grif's writing and his friend Huntington:

You tend to go too far into theoretical fields. It is with some regret that I see you accepting in what seems to be an uncritical way the loose generalities of my friend E. Huntington. . . who has "almost fierce disdain" for facts. I regard a large part of Huntington's writing as a waste of time to read. Please do not think me presumptuous in offering you thus gratuitously so much advice about yourself. . . my sincere conviction is that you can play a great role in American geography if you start off right. Please take these remarks good naturedly as I am sure you will (41).

It must have been very flattering for Grif to know that three of America's outstanding geographers wished him to accept the Chicago offer. Isaiah Bowman, probably the dean of American geographers at the time, believed that Taylor could play a large role in American geography. Grif was certainly tempted by the Chicago offer but was also interested in a full chair in geography at Sydney University. If the University had offered him the chair, perhaps he would have turned down the Chicago offer. Who can say? As usual, he played a waiting game. He cabled Barrows on June 6:

> Appreciate invitation. Attracted work and colleagues. Sydney authorities remain anxious. Cable decision fortnight. Taylor (42).

Barrows cabled on the 17:

> Offer $6200. Absolute freedom concerning publication results. Research. Members staff elated. Barrows (43).

On July 9 Grif had a meeting with Vice Chancellor Wallace who told Grif he could almost guarantee him a full chair and also a lecturer position. Grif wanted the position of lecturer for Dorothy and told Wallace that she could keep the department going if he (Grif) left. Wallace told Grif not to do anything definite for ten days. Grif waited until July 23 and again saw the Vice Chancellor, who had "done nothing fruitful" as Grif wrote in his diary.

> Full chair and lecturer only what his own commonsense would give
> at end of year. Might as well not have U.S.A. offer. See Doris.
> Decide soon (44).

The next day, July 24, Grif wrote to the Vice Chancellor stating that the next Senate meeting at which the proposal of a full chair for geography would be discussed would not take place until five weeks after he received the Chicago invitation. He said he would "cable them for information on pensions etc. On receiving cable, will decide on course of action" (45).

On July 28, Vice Chancellor Wallace, who obviously was not going to be railroaded into promising Taylor the chair, wrote that he was sorry he was losing Grif's services (46). On July 30, Grif wrote Wallace that he had accepted the Chicago position at an initial salary of £1300 and wished to resign his Sydney position. He could not resist telling Wallace:

> I determined early this year to find a position where my work was
> more appreciated. Nearly a score of my colleagues who were junior
> to me in 1920 have been promoted, the majority to full chairs, and
> quite considerable additions to the staff of other departments have
> been made but no prospect of an adequate staff in geography is
> approved even now. I have only received two months leave in eight
> years and I continue to hope that you will agree to my dating my
> resignation at the end of the year — and to my leaving Sydney early
> in November (47).

At the same time, Grif had tried to obtain a position in Oxford, as can be seen in a letter to him from Professor David, dated 17 July 1928:

> My dear Taylor: The first step will be for me to send a weekend cablegram to the Assistant Secretary to send me out a nomination form and as soon as it arrives to get signatures at this end (eg. Mawson I know would sign) and then send it home for more signatures. I could write at that stage to the 7 men you mention (48).

Nothing came of this attempt at an Oxford position but it does show Professor David's feelings for his student. Throughout his lifetime, David was Grif's mentor and his great booster. When it was obvious that Grif was leaving Australia, David wrote him a farewell letter in October 1928:

> You are a very dear man and I can't tell you how proud I am of having had you as a student in my classes in the good old days. After all, I can only lay a very small claim to the credit of having anything to do with the training of so famous a man. You owe much to Cambridge, much to your parents and upbringing but most of all to your own good self and your indomitable courage, perseverance and devoted service to science and your gifted intelligence tempered by self criticism and a philosophical bent of mind. May you go on and prosper and win more laurels and bring more light into the dark places (49).

Because of the strained relations with the University of Sydney administration, Grif did not leave any of his papers to that university. Rather, before he left Australia in 1928, he presented to the Commonwealth National Library in Canberra many of his books on Australia and much of his Antarctic material.

It was fitting that even while preparing to leave Sydney, Grif was fighting a battle for geography in the secondary schools. Grif firmly believed that geography was a necessity in the education of young people. Modern geography he defined as the study of man's relation to his physical environment. He believed that it was the privilege of the geographer to teach how and why settlement advances, stagnates or retreats, and how climate controls not only man's comforts, but his natural needs.

> It is difficult for one who is a geographer to understand how a curriculum can ignore the paramount importance of these problems (50).

However, Grif was a realist and stated next:

> It is clear that nothing can be added to the curriculum of the school boy unless something is removed. I can see nothing for it but a great diminution in the time given to Latin.

Grif was outspoken in his hatred for Latin. The above and other statements provoked a battle with a Professor of Classics, Fred Todd, and three or four letters from him are preserved in Grif's correspondence. On July 3, Todd wrote:

> In this latest letter you make a number of large assumptions about my deficiencies of knowledge and prejudices. I neither deny nor affirm their correctness. I merely remind you that you had no right, without information, to make any of them. You have never heard me and will never hear me decry another man's studies because I have an ardent belief in the importance of my own (51).

Grif also kept a poem which Todd sent to him:

In Sartorem
De Rebus Sibi Parum Notis Blaterantem

De sutore "supra crepidam ne iudicet" aiunt:
Quid de iudicio, sartor inepte, tuo
Qui te, cum magno blateres clamore furasque
Ipsam semper acu rem tetigisse putas?
"Sutor homo est: Hominis sartor si tertia pars est
Istum haerere in acu terque quaterque decet."

T. Pileus Altus (52)

This poem was a clever pun on Taylor's name. It can be translated as follows:

Against a Tailor Babbling about Matters He Little Understands

> About the cobbler they say, "Let him stick to his last." [Literally, "Let him not make judgements above the sandal."] What about your judgement, silly man, who, when you babble and rave with a lot of noise, always think you have hit the nail on the head. A cobbler is a man: if a tailor is a third part of a man it's proper for him to be repeatedly stuck on a nail.

[signed] T. High Hat (53)

The time came when Taylor was ready to leave Australia and a farewell luncheon was given for him. The Vice Chancellor quoted the university motto "Sedere mens eadem mutato" which, generally translated means "The same mind under a different star." However in his diary, Grif irreverently translated the motto as "Though the heavens fall, I am of the same mind as my great-great-grandfather."

The newspapers interviewed Grif about his resignation and his new position in Chicago. The Sydney *Morning Herald*, 3 August 1928, stated:

> It seems that Prof. Griffith Taylor has accepted the offer of a Chair of Geography at the University of Chicago and that he will be leaving Sydney presently to take up his new work. . . . It would be wrong to assume that the question of pay determined the Sydney professor's

Figure 14. The Taylor family leaving Australia for Chicago 1928. (Photo from Bill Taylor)

consideration of the offer made to him. The honour and advantage of being called to such an important Chair with such great opportunities for both graduate teaching and research work is quite enough in itself to account for Prof. Taylor's decision (54).

Grif's students were sorry to see him go, and a large contingent went to the dockside in Sydney to bid him farewell. Grif and Doris, with their two sons and 23 pieces of luggage, left Australia not to return for almost 25 years (Fig. 14). Grif was excited about his new career, but both he and Doris were apprehensive about living in a northern climate, and Doris dreaded the cold winters she would face in Chicago. All the Taylors loved travelling, and their journey to Chicago took them first to Ceylon, to visit some old friends of Doris, then to England.

While the Taylors were in England, they heard regularly from Dorothy in Sydney. Professor MacDonald Holmes had been appointed to Grif's position and at first got on with Dorothy very well. In a letter 9 December 1928, Dorothy wrote:

Holmes is quite prepared to use such influence as devolves upon him to have me appointed lecturer. I do not think any wiles of Holmes will move our Vice Chancellor. . . he is totally impervious to requests re geography (55).

Things obviously were not going smoothly for geography at the University of Sydney, and the life of the new department was almost extinguished. On 13 March 1929, David wrote to Grif in Chicago:

> The department of geography was very nearly wiped out. The vote of the Senate was very close. . . . Surely we ought never to have lost you. It is a grave calamity to our University (56).

It is interesting to speculate about the real reasons why Taylor left Australia. He loved Australia, always considered himself an Australian, and retired to Australia eventually. But in 1928 at 48 years of age, he perhaps realized that his future was brighter elsewhere. He had made good and powerful friends in the United States. However it was not part of the Commonwealth, and Grif was always an imperialist. He hated to leave his family and Professor David and the lovely city of Sydney. On the other hand he was hurt by the attacks of the press on his empty heart of Australia statements, statements that he found accepted when he returned 25 years later.

He had probably hoped that the threat of leaving would force the University administration to give him the Chair of Geography that he so desired, but it was a threat that did not work. Whatever the reasons, the move to Chicago and the New World greatly changed the course of his career. From being the premier geographer in Australia far from the centres of geographic learning, he acquired an international reputation during his years in Chicago, and his next move to Toronto would further advance his reputation as a world famous geographer.

References

1. Letter to author from Sister Nell Stanley, January 4, 1984.
2. National Library, Canberra, MS 1003/127/6D.
3. National Library, Canberra, MS 1003/127/E2.
4. National Library, Canberra, MS 1003/9/673.
5. National Library, Canberra, MS 1003/9/685.
6. Taylor, Griffith: "The Distribution of Future White Settlement," *Geographical Review*, Vol. 12, 1922, p. 391.
7. Taylor, Griffith: "The Distribution of Future White Settlement," p. 402.
8. University of Toronto. Manuscript Collection 20, Box 16.
9. National Library, Canberra, MS 1003/4/221.
10. National Library, Canberra, MS 1003/9/685.
11. University of Toronto. Manuscript Collection 20, Box 16.
12. University of Toronto. Manuscript Collection 20, Box 16.
13. University of Toronto. Manuscript Collection 20, Box 16.
14. Taylor, Griffith: "Climatic control of Wheat Production in Australia," A.A.A.S., *Report of the 16th meeting*, 1924, pp. 132-38.
15. University of Toronto. Manuscript Collection 20, Box 16.
16. University of Toronto. Manuscript Collection 20, Box 16.
17. University of Toronto. Manuscript Collection 20, Box 16.
18. University of Toronto. Manuscript Collection 20, Box 16
19. National Library, Canberra, MS 1003/9/800.
20. National Library, Canberra, MS 1003/9/801.
21. National Library, Canberra, MS 1003/9/742.
22. National Library, Canberra, MS 1003/4/227.
23. National Library, Canberra, MS 1003/4/228.

24. National Library, Canberra, MS 1003/4/229.
25. National Library, Canberra, MS 1003/9/767.
26. Taylor, Griffith: "The Frontiers of Settlement in Australia," *Geographical Review*, Vol. 16, 1926, p. 25.
27. Marshall, Ann: "Griffith Taylor's Correlative Science," *Australian Geographical Studies*, 12, 1972, p. 192.
28. National Library, Canberra, MS 1003/9/854.
29. Taylor, Griffith: *Environment and Race*. Oxford Press, 1927, p.3.
30. Taylor, Griffith: *Environment and Race*, p. 5.
31. National Library, Canberra, MS 1003/4/44.
32. Ecology, Vol IX, 4, 1928, pp. 527-529.
33. National Library, Canberra, MS 1003/9/983.
34. Review of *Environment and Race*. *The American Anthropologist*, October, 1928, p. 688.
35. Griffith Taylor. Private Diary, 1925.
36. National Library, Canberra, MS 1003/9/930.
37. National Library, Canberra, MS 1003/9/935 and 936.
38. National Library, Canberra, MS 1003/9/959.
39. National Library, Canberra, MS 1003/9/961.
40. National Library, Canberra, MS 1003/9/961.
41. National Library, Canberra, MS 1003/9/962.
42. Griffith Taylor. Private Diary, 1928.
43. Griffith Taylor. Private Diary, 1928.
44. Griffith Taylor. Private Diary, 1928.
45. National Library, Canberra, MS 1003/9/968.
46. National Library, Canberra, MS 1003/9/970.
47. National Library, Canberra, MS 1003/9/972.
48. National Library, Canberra, MS 1003/4/364.
49. National Library, Canberra, MS 1003/4/285.
50. Taylor, Griffith: "Geography in Secondary Schools," unpublished manuscript. University of Toronto. Taylor Collection 20, Box 16.
51. National Library, Canberra, MS 1003/9/939.
52. National Library, Canberra, MS 1003/9/942.
53. Translated from the Latin by Professor William Felver, University of Windsor.
54. National Library, Canberra, MS 1003/4/489.
55. National Library, Canberra, MS 1003/5/27.
56. National Library, Canberra, MS 1003/3/35.

CHAPTER 9

The Chicago Years

Grif spent only seven years at the University of Chicago, but it was a love-hate relationship. He loved being in the mainstream of geographic happenings in a well developed department, meeting all kinds of interesting people, and with the chance to travel and to lecture throughout the New World. But he disliked not being in charge. He was a strong imperialist and really preferred to live under the British flag. From the first days in Chicago, he actively pursued other job opportunities in the British Empire.

Grif's arrival at the Department of Geography in Chicago was noted in the departmental newsletter as a memorable event:

> Dr. Griffith Taylor, the eminent Australian geographer has accepted
> a professorship and will begin his work in the Winter Quarter.
> Professor Taylor needs no introduction as an author . . . his writings
> have made him known in America and Europe no less than in
> Australia as a vigorous writer and original scholar (1).

In addition to Harlan Barrows, Grif's colleagues were Wellington Jones, Charles Colby, Robert Platt, Edith Putman Parker, Henry Leppard and John Morrison. John Paul Goode was Professor Emeritus. Grif had some outstanding students at Chicago, among them Chauncy Harris, Ada Wrigley, Donald Hudson and Gilbert White, all of whom were impressed by Grif's imagination and great energy. However, his only Ph.D. student was John K. Rose who became a life-long friend and in 1964 wrote Grif's obituary for the *Annals of the Association of American Geographers*.

Doris and the boys had stayed in England for a visit while Grif went off to his new job alone. He crossed the Atlantic on the *Mauritania* — the worst crossing the ship had ever made — and landing in New York went to the American Geographic Society offices to see his friend Isaiah Bowman. On January 11th he gave his first lecture at the University of Chicago.

During the first three months in Chicago he lived at the University's very elegant Quadrangle Club. Chicago was a very sociable place and Grif's diary is filled with accounts of dinners and parties at the various professors' houses. The Platts were especially kind to the Taylors, and often invited them to their beautiful house on the outskirts of Chicago.

At the University of Chicago, Geography was housed with Geology in Rosenwald Hall. Grif found the building crowded and the private offices very small. He was dismayed that laboratory space was not considered essential for geography at Chicago and although excellent field camps were arranged, they were not compulsory, so few students attended.

Grif gave eight or nine lectures a week on Environment and Race, Polar Studies, and Navigation, but he was not familiar with the physical environment in the United States and this bothered him. He found that everyone in Chicago seemed to work harder and longer than in Sydney, and this suited him since he always had several projects underway at the same time. He began to write several new books. One was *Antarctic Adventure and Research*, an explanation of scientific purpose in the Antarctic. This was topical since at the time Admiral Byrd's exploits in that area were receiving much publicity in the United States, and the book was chosen as the scientific book-of-the-month.

Taylor had a number of articles published in a wide variety of journals in the years 1928-30. Among the more important journals and topics were "Climatic relations between Antarctica and Australia" in the American Geographical Society special publication *Problems of Polar Research*; "New Lands And Old Education,""This Human Family: Problems of Population and Migration"and "Why Explore the Antarctic?", all in *Pacific Affairs*, and "Byrd's Scientific Achievement in the Antarctic" in *Current History*. Perhaps one of the most important articles was the "Agricultural Regions of Australia", one of a series on world agriculture. Its publication in *Economic Geography* in 1930 was recognition of Grif's position as a world authority on Australia. The paper was comprehensive and well-organized and divided Australia into ten agricultural regions, gave a history of agricultural production, supplied state-by-state statistics; and contained a discussion of major crops.

In January 1929, the very first month of Taylor's sojourn at Chicago, he had a letter from Harold Innis at the University of Toronto. Since Innis played the leading role in the establishment of a department of geography at Toronto, it is perhaps interesting to look at his background as well as the historical development of geography at the University of Toronto. A course in economic geography had been taught as early as 1908-09 by James Mavor in the Department of Political Economy. Mavor encouraged Robert Falconer, the President of the University, to establish a separate department of geography in the years after the First World War, but nothing concrete was done. Harold Innis was a Canadian who had done his doctorate at the University of Chicago, and was hired by the University of Toronto in 1921 to teach political economy; and he took over Mavor's course in economic geography, and also his commitment to a department of geography.

In his annual report for 1924-25 President Falconer of the University of Toronto had written:

As soon as the finances of the University permit, a chair of Geography should be established. This subject is now receiving great attention in England, but except in so far as it is dealt with on the physical side it has not yet been given adequate recognition in Canadian universities, though it is essential for historical, economic and commercial studies (2).

Although an economist, Innis had become interested in the fur trade in Canada and the effect of geography on this trade, and in 1928 he read a paper on this topic at the International Geographical Congress in Cambridge. While at the meetings, he wrote President Falconer that he had talked to several candidates for the position of geographer but had found them too oriented toward physical geography. He seemed convinced that the department should have a Canadian rather than a British or American emphasis.

> I am more and more impressed with the fact that we could find the material in Canada for establishing a department. By drawing on the resources of the University and of the government departments a start could be made and the position generally strengthened by bringing in men from outside as they are needed. This arrangement would ensure a department rooted in Canada and would promote the co-operation necessary for a strong department (3).

Innis knew Isaiah Bowman and depended on him for advice on the study of geography. He wrote Bowman in 1929:

> I am always appalled at some of the work done in geography. In many cases it is bad descriptive economics. I do not deny that economists do bad geography but a compromise is badly needed (4).

Innis asked Bowman for suggestions for a young man for Toronto, and Bowman suggested Glen Trewartha at Wisconsin, an outstanding young geographer and Henry Leppard at Chicago, a Canadian graduate. However, Wisconsin was loath to let Trewartha leave and Leppard was not considered because Bowman thought he was not "up to the job of heading" a department, and besides, "his eyes are crossed ." Innis visited Leppard in Chicago and agreed with Bowman's evaluation. Innis met Taylor during this Chicago visit, but did not immediately consider him a candidate since Innis' preference was for a Canadian and a younger geographer. Grif at this time was 48 years old. However, when no obvious Canadian candidate appeared, Innis wrote again to Bowman and the latter replied

> I would go right after Griffith Taylor if I were you and attach him to Toronto . . . . . while he has an outer fringe of lunacy like most of us, yet at the same time he has done extraordinarily good work. He is a pioneer in spirit and drives ahead with tremendous energy (5).

Innis consequently wrote to Grif rather circumspectly in January 1929, not offering him the job but asking his advice:

> I am writing to you regarding problems with which we are faced in Toronto in connection with the establishment of a geography department. We have discussed the matter with Professor Burns. The President has suggested we ask you to come to Toronto . . . give us the benefit of your advice on our future course of action. We have

done very little in the subject in this country and are anxious to get a good man who will build it up (6).

Grif accepted the invitation to Toronto and spoke to the Royal Canadian Institute on March 2. He described the trip in a letter to his mother on March 3.

Two professors, Innis and McIlwraith, met me and drove me to the University. I had breakfast at Hart House [he stayed there] and spent the morning at the Museum. Then we had a conference for three hours after lunch, 2 anthropologists, 2 economists, 2 geologists. Parks (geology) was very urgent that the proposed new man shouldn't touch physiography. Currelly wanted him joined to anthropology, and Innis thought he ought to be joined to economics. I told them he must be independent. Innis said several times that G.T. was the man he was trying to get, to start geography in Canada. They haven't <u>one lecturer</u> [Grif's underline] in six universities. Well, I told them what I thought and left a six page report for Falconer (in bed with sinus — didn't meet him). In the evening I spoke to the Canadian Institute — big audience. Next day I had a long talk with Innis in the pine woods north of Toronto. It is a friendly town like Sydney (not a collection of fortresses like Chicago) (7).

It should be noted that in Grif's letter to his mother he said he would not be compromised in having geography an independent department, despite the attempts to have it linked with anthropology or economics. The letter also shows that Grif liked Toronto on that first visit, and preferred it to Chicago. On 25 March 1929 in a letter to President Falconer, Innis had obviously decided that Taylor was the best man:

I am aware of the difficulties of appointing a full professor in charge of a department but once we have realized that it seems impossible to get a younger man as we had earlier hoped the appointment of Professor Taylor remains as the only alternate. With his international reputation and strong connections in the United States, England (Cambridge) and Australia, Toronto and Canada would be placed at one stroke in a position to develop the subject under most favourable circumstances. He has had a thorough scientific training from the geographic point of view and has gone over into the human side. He is an excellent traveller and his knowledge of Australia and the Antarctic would be valuable to work on Canada and the Arctic. As would be expected from his success with geography in Australia he is a pleasing, forceful and energetic speaker with ability to stimulate interest among students and audiences. Consequently he would push the subject in the schools where it is most needed and in the government departments. By the time he retires he will have left a body of graduates in other Canadian

Universities and in government departments and a Canadian who could take his position as successor. He is an ardent imperialist and is not anxious to remain in the United States and left Australia only because he felt the need of meeting men in his field in the United States and England. His experience and success in pioneering the subject of geography in one country of the British Empire would be invaluable in the task of establishing the subject in Canada (8).

It is obvious from the above that in 1929 Innis correctly predicted Taylor's influence on Canadian geography both in his stimulation of students and his desire to incorporate geography in the school system. However, such predictions were not immediately realized. Nothing happened that year as far as establishing a department of geography at the University of Toronto was concerned, since the great depression began and money became a problem.

Grif returned to Chicago and Doris and the boys arrived on 26 March. The family, re-united, moved to 5524 Kimbark Avenue in Hyde Park (Fig. 15). Grif, and Doris too, disliked the mid-western climate. The winters were too cold and the summers too hot. They found they could not afford a house and neither liked apartment living, since they had always had a garden.

Grif was almost never sick, but in August 1929 he was taken to hospital where the physician diagnosed a tumor in the caecum. While in hospital, he wrote as usual in his diary — of his letters, the books he was reading, and also, the night before the operation on August 12th, this note: "Operation 11 a.m. tomorrow. Hope if things go wrong, they give Doris a pension." While Grif was in hospital Doris and the boys stayed with the Platts. But the operation was successful and the tumor was not malignant. Grif's strong constitution had him eating solid foods in a few days and out of the hospital by August 25. It is interesting that in his autobiography Taylor called the operation an appendectomy. However, the operation and his weakness made Grif very depressed, as Doris wrote to Grif's mother on August 19:

No idea how depressed and pessimistic Grif has been since his operation (9).

As usual Dorothy wrote to console him:

Actually you do find pleasure and thrill in your new life, don't you? I am waiting to hear that most of your clouds and worries have vanished (10).

Doris was not always happy in their new home and she missed Dorothy and her Australian friends (11). Both she and Grif worried a great deal about the high cost of living. In a letter to his mother that winter he sounded as if he were already planning to leave Chicago:

We can't keep expenses within my official salary — You'd have no society, get no maids, schooling would be harder and it's so jolly in

131

Figure 15. Doris and Grif, David and Bill at their home in Chicago. October 1930. National Library of Australia.

winter — making long journeys in -12° F. We may do something in 12 months (12).

But by October Grif was feeling better. He was invited by Professor Hobbs to the University of Michigan and by President Atwood for a week's visit to Clark University, and had a very good time. He gave a series of twelve lectures on Australia, Antarctica and racial distribution. He enjoyed visits with Atwood and Ekblaw. In his diary Grif said of President Atwood:

> He is the oldest geographer in the U.S. now. He started the school in Chicago, then succeeded Davis at Harvard. Agreed professors badly paid. . . . I was pretty frank that we don't like living in Chicago (13).

At Clark, Grif enjoyed meeting Ellen Semple:

> The geographer I particularly wanted to meet was Ellen Semple, into whose room I soon walked in order to introduce myself. She and I had a gratifying discussion on the evils of too much of the Classics in university education (14).

Grif wrote to Professor David that they did not like Chicago and said that his complaints to Atwood could not do any harm and would perhaps lead to their leaving Chicago. Grif and Doris were finding it difficult to live well in Chicago and Grif again wrote to his mother about the inadequacy of his salary:

> Wrote the President a pretty frank letter about the relative costs in Chicago and Sydney.

And he complained about the department and the lack of lab work:

> They do so little lab work here. I think our scheme in Sydney is a much better program and turns out a much better average student (15).

The Priestleys in England certainly heard of Grif's dissatisfaction with Chicago. Brother-in-law Ray Priestley wrote to him in June 1930:

> Professorship of geography at Birkbeck will fall vacant at the end of the present session. Are you interested? There are rumours that things have not been too satisfactory with you from the point of view of cost of living (16).

However, nothing came of the Birkbeck position, and Grif's first year at Chicago so impressed Barrows that he succeeded in obtaining an increase in Grif's salary from $6,200 to $7,000. This made Grif the highest paid member of the faculty with the exception of Barrows himself.

Grif's writings during the early 1930s were chiefly on two themes — his racial-migration zones theory and the limits of settlement in Australia. He began writing for journals other than geographic — *Human Biology* in 1930, the *American Journal of Sociology* in 1931, and *Ecology* in 1934. He correctly realized that his novel ideas on race and his geographic methods would be refreshing and stimulating to other scientists. His articles repeated much of what he had already published in the *Geographical Review*, but also showed that he had read widely in the current anthropology and sociology journals. He published nothing on the United States or on geography in that country. He was not enamoured of the then current emphasis in U.S. geography on regional micro studies. He was much happier addressing large global themes.

Grif was always interested in anything to do with the Antarctic and noted in his diary the day that Admiral Byrd reached the South Pole. The *New York Times* commissioned him to do an article on the scientific results of the Byrd discoveries, on the advice of Isaiah Bowman who told the *Times* that they should offer Grif payment for the article because of his modest salary. Dr. Frederick Cook, the controversial discoverer of the North Pole visited the University in 1930, and had lunch with Grif. Cook presented him with a copy of his book *My Attainment of the Pole*, and in the fly leaf he wrote: "To Griffith Taylor. All which life implies is but a halo between the past and the future. Frederick A. Cook." Grif made the most of the public interest in the Antarctic to publish two articles — one on the Byrd discoveries in *Current History* and "Why explore the Antarctic?" for *Pacific Affairs*.

Bowman knew that Grif was unhappy at Chicago, and suggested that he make a trip to Colombia and Central America that autumn for the American Geographical Society. Grif was pleased at the opportunity to visit a part of the world he had never seen, and left Chicago in mid-November of 1930 on his "free quarter." He visited Panama, Cartagena and Santa Marta and then proceeded to climb the Sierra Nevada behind Santa Marta with a Colombian guide. At 9,000 feet the guide refused to go on, so Grif proceeded on alone to 10,500 feet. On the way he celebrated his 50th birthday. When he returned to Chicago he assisted Ray Platt with the new contour map of the area, pleased, he said, that he had a small part in the preparation of the American Geographical Society's millionth map of South America. Grif could now claim to have set foot on all seven continents, a feat that no other professional geographer could then claim.

Taylor published an article in the *Geographical Review* in 1931 on this trip entitled "Settlement Zones of the Sierra Nevada de Santa Marta, Colombia." It was a study of the physical geography, economic history and settlement pattern of the Santa Marta area, again an interesting example of man-land relations. It is interesting that in the same year the *American Journal of Sociology* published Taylor's article "Nordic and Alpine Races and their Kin: A Study of Ethnological Trends." This was a study of the racial characteristics he thought important — hair texture and skull type and their distribution.

In 1931, Dr. Robert Hutchins, the "boy wonder," became president of Chicago and radically changed the undergraduate curriculum. Some knowledge of geography was now regarded as fundamental in undergraduate training. Geography became a liaison subject with status in both the physical and social sciences, a position it still retains in Chicago. This coincided with Grif's concept of geography's place in education and pleased him very much. Grif certainly agreed with the description of geography as it appeared in the University of Chicago calendar that year, stating that geography was neither a natural science nor a social science but that its field lay between the domains of those subjects, its point of view unique among the sciences dealing with the earth or with humanity.

In 1931 Rand and McNally published Grif's book *Australia*. It was part of a series for elementary schools under the editorship of Isaiah Bowman, but in fact was more suitable as a reference book for teachers. It included a record of his travels through northern, central, and western Australia, and served later as a model for a similar work on Canada.

During 1931 Grif's "off term" occurred in the fall, and he made use of the time to return to Europe and tour Scandinavia and Central Europe with his sister Dorothy. He combined business with pleasure, planning to attend the International Geographical Congress meeting in Paris in September and the British Association meeting in London in October. It was like the old days in Australia — just Grif and Dorothy travelling cheaply with rucksacks on their backs over the less travelled roads of Europe. Grif and Dorothy usually got on well together but he confided to his diary:

> Five solid weeks is a severe test. We had a spat or two, chiefly because
> I am too conventional . . . I'll be glad to be home (17).

A highlight of the trip for Grif was a visit to Graz in Austria to meet the famous Wladimir Koppen, with whom he had corresponded and for whom he had written the chapters on the "Climatology of Australia" for Koppen's *Handbuch der Klimatologie*. Koppen's daughter, who had married the scientist Wegener of Continental Drift fame, was living with her father after her husband's tragic death in Greenland, and Grif and Dorothy found them charming.

In Paris Grif met Marion Newbigin, editor of the *Scottish Geographical Magazine* which published, in January 1932, Grif's address to the British Association for the Advancement of Science, "The Geographer's Aid in Nation-Planning." In this article, Grif reviewed his career in geography in Australia and pointed out a number of areas in which he began by collecting data and consequently became interested in reasons and predictions. In this speech he reiterated his strong statements against the "White Only" policy then popular in Australia. "Race prejudice is but another name for ethnological ignorance" (18).

Part Two of the same speech was published in March 1932 — "The Inner Arid Limits of Economic Settlement in Australia." Taylor mustered quantities of scientific evidence, especially Koppen's, to support his views regarding settlement in arid areas. Some statements revealed that the treatment he received in Australia because of these views still rankled.

> Because, however, this southern area is slowly being occupied by
> wheat farmers, Brady implies that all other Australian areas
> described as deserts are also wrongly named. One would not discuss

this type of opinion were it not that the volume in question has been widely distributed by the government (19).

Grif enjoyed the conference in England and meeting scientists whose works he had read, including Halford Mackinder, who nominated him as a Vice-President of the British Association, and H.R. Mill, a veteran geographer and meteorologist, who had a lifelong interest in Antarctic exploration and later wrote a biography of Ernest Shackleton.

Grif used his time in England to try to advance his chances of being elected a Fellow of the Royal Society. He visited his Antarctic colleague Simpson at the Weather Office and the latter told Grif that no geographer had a hope of an FRS because only six sections had a vote and they voted for their own groups. In his diary he wrote: "Plenty of men live and die happy without an FRS — so I'd better do the same."

Back in Chicago, in November 1931, the possibility of going to the University of Toronto again surfaced. Good news came in a letter from Harold Innis asking him if he would consider coming to Toronto:

> If we could possibly persuade you to come it could only be as a full professor and head of department. Anxious to act quickly as the President retires at the end of this year, and the President Elect becomes a new problem (20).

Taylor replied on November 12:

> . . . Other things being equal I would rather work among Britishers — though all my American friends have been most kindly. But my salary this year is $7450, which is more than twice what your trustees have voted. Dr. Atwood wrote me some months ago that he urged upon your President the advisability of starting with a senior man. Indeed he was good enough to recommend my name very strongly, I understand.
>
> This is a huge institution with a remarkable group of men — and I have half each day for research, so that my output has been larger than in Australia. . . .
>
> On the other hand Canada offers the best opportunity for valuable work in the world. . . .
>
> How do costs compare in Toronto? What does a pleasant house like your own rent at? . . . I could not entertain any drop in status.
>
> I realize that money is scarce; but my experience has been that a department of geography doing real Empire-building becomes the most popular department in Science. Surely a big University like Toronto could step out boldly (21).

And again to Innis in November:

> Thanks for your letter with the information concerning the living expenses. I feel that you now know what sort of an offer would be

attractive to me. I have had several tentative offers from England which I did not take up; and there is another appointment soon to be made for which some of my friends there hope that I will apply.

I have, moreover, to consider the readjustment of my wife and sons. The latter are now doing excellently at the University High School.

I feel that I should enjoy building up a School of Geography in Canada as I did in Australia. But I have naturally no wish to start off with inadequate salary or quarters; and with no help until some time has elapsed. That was my trouble in Sydney, where I had only two instructors to help me with over 200 students and three years of laboratory work.

It seems to me that it should now be possible for your University to make a definite offer. I shall of course discuss this with our Chairman (Professor Barrows), with whom my relations have always been most cordial. I may add that I rank next to him in this School, which is I think the largest in the world. I receive a much higher salary than my remaining colleagues (22).

Harold Innis wrote again on November 18:

Many thanks for your letter. It is the best you can possibly do and I am grateful to you for it. . . . I am not optimistic as to the probable outcome. If we fail to persuade the authorities, the alternative is the appointment of one of our own men. We have canvassed the field rather thoroughly in the last few years and had almost decided on the appointment of a very able young man connected with the government at Ottawa but I feel that such an appointment would involve years of patient effort. Your appointment would solve all problems — give us a strong department to start out. The cause of geography would be enormously advanced in Canada . . . you may rest assured that I shall do my very best with the hope that we may offer you something definite and worthy of your consideration (23).

The University of Toronto archives of the Department of Political Economy do indeed show that the University had been searching for the proper candidate to start a department of geography at Toronto. Letters of application from Bowen of Aberystwyth in Wales, Wolfanger of Columbia and Stilgenbauer of Detroit are on file. The candidate from the Federal Government to whom Innis referred was J. Mackintosh Bell of the Geological Survey. Innis was changing his priorities and now felt that the candidate should have a strong background in geology. He had written to President Falconer on 6 July 1931:

I have felt more and more that the ideal appointment should have reference to the department of geology. The great handicap to my own work in the field of Canadian economics is the lack of

137

knowledge of geographic features. This knowledge can only be gained through research over a long period by a man thoroughly familiar with the geological background and at the same time acquainted with the significance of this background to economic, social and political developments. Research in Canadian human geography can only rest secure on a foundation built up especially in relation to geology. I admit frankly a bias in favour of this development (24).

Innis again asked Bowman for his opinion, and Isaiah Bowman wrote to Innis concerning Mackintosh Bell, stating that he considered him a suitable candidate. But the problem was one of money. President Falconer wrote to Innis, 20 November 1931:

Unquestionably Professor Griffith Taylor would bring great distinction to the University . . . but . . . it seems to me out of the question for us at this period of the University's finances to secure enough money both for his salary and for equipment, and for assistance as would be necessary for a man of his distinction.
My only hope for the present lies in the possibility of securing some younger man (25).

Meanwhile, in Chicago, Grif was not idle. He was very pleased to be invited to speak to the annual meeting of the National Council of Geography Teachers in December 1931. He spoke on "The Margins of Geography" explaining the nature of the "new" geography to the geography teachers. In spite of his hatred of Latin he even began by using a Latin quotation — "Scire vere est per causas scire" (True knowledge involves the study of causes). He stated that three subjects seem vital in the scheme of education:

Biology, which deals with the evolution of man as an animal; secondly history which deals largely with the growth of his ideals and institutions and thirdly, geography which deals with his present, often varying, environment (26).

In this talk Grif declared outright his belief that geographers should have a basic scientific training. He rightly anticipated the arguments of geographers in the 1960s:

I am sure that if geography is to command a place of honour in the learned world, the devotees must be trained in science; and not creep into geography "because anyone can teach it" as I have heard it crudely expressed (27).

Grif had not given up hope for an Oxford position. W. A. Craigie, a professor of Engineering at Chicago, who was an honorary fellow of Oriel College at Oxford, wrote on his behalf to the Electors to the Professorship of Geography at Oxford. His letter was dated 9 January 1932:

As one who for a number of years was in close contact with two successive heads of the School of Geography in Oxford, I am of the opinion that G.T. would be an ideal person to occupy the position of professor in that subject. . . . From intimate personal knowledge of him I am confident that he would fit unusually well into College and university life at Oxford and maintain the reputation of Oxford scholarship (28).

In Taylor's application he cited as referees Sir Halford Mackinder and Frank Debenham. Debenham was at that time in the geography department at Cambridge and Grif had visited him while in England in 1931. He wrote in his diary:

We talked about Oxford a great deal. He thinks they're keen on Roxby but says I'm much better in every respect except I'm not a graduate of Oxford. . . . He says he's going to do his best for me . . . says that the Oxford crowd quarrel a lot (29).

In spite of such strong support, the post went to a Major Mason, and Grif was very disappointed. One wonders how Oxford would have fared if Taylor had been appointed. Many years later his brother-in-law Sir Raymond Priestley wrote that Oxford and geography in England would have been much more stimulating if Grif had been selected for the position.

Harold Innis persisted in trying to persuade the University of Toronto to hire Taylor. President Falconer resigned in 1932 and in his final report, he regretted his inability to establish a department of geography at Toronto:

A factor in my regret on leaving the University has been my inability to effect the establishment of departments of geography and of fine arts, including larger provision for the study of music by undergraduates. From the Governors I have always had sympathetic support for such developments. Geography, it is true, has for years been partially provided for in geology and economics, but there is need of an independent department in which it will become in its wider phases a more comprehensive subject for study and investigation, and this requires well-appointed quarters and a geographer of special training (30).

In a letter in June 1932 Innis wrote Grif:

We are crossing horns at present. Sir Robert Falconer has retired and his place is taken by Canon Cody. Geography will be at a standstill as a result. The effects of the depression have of course not helped matters. However, we shall press on and I hope I may be able to use the request in that connection (31).

Again nothing happened. The new President at Toronto, Canon Cody, had other problems and the question of a new department of geography was put aside. Cody wrote to Innis on 12 September 1932:

Many thanks for your letter, containing your views on the proposed chair of geography. As you know on account of the financial stringency the appropriation for this chair was left out of the estimates for the current year. I hope that we shall be able to restore such an item next year (32).

And again on 14 March 1933, Cody made the decision definite:

In regard to the chair in geography I feel that we really cannot, owing to financial conditions, make even a beginning this year (33).

And that seemed to be that! Grif was obliged to wait another two years for the Toronto position. However, he did not waste time in regrets and his literary output during these years was prodigious. During 1932, he began working on a course which eventually would become the book *Environment and Nation* published in 1936. He used his considerable knowledge of Europe to examine the geographical factors in the cultural and political history of that continent, a perspective that most historians lacked. It was a new interest of Grif's and one he approached with his usual vigour and perception. Also in 1933, the *Geographical Review* published Taylor's paper "The Soils of Australia in Relation to Topography and Climate" in which his thesis, novel at that time, was that soils depend on climate more than on underlying structure.

Many of Grif's students in Chicago became famous in their chosen field and most of them considered Taylor to be an excellent and imaginative teacher. Tomkins wrote to many of them when he was doing his doctoral thesis on Taylor and several of their replies are quoted here. Chauncy Harris considered him a person of enormous imagination and great energy and drive; Donald Hudson thought him a stimulating teacher and original thinker; John K. Rose mentioned his breadth and originality, but noted that he was out of the mainstream of the trend in geography of the time since he had no interest in the detailed study of small areas that were currently popular. Many of his Chicago students felt that Grif's personal relations in the department were not ideal. Charles Colby especially did not get on well with Taylor, although describing him as "an able and even brilliant lecturer." Colby stated:

We were not sorry when he decided to leave Chicago . . . he was a fine geographer, an outstanding man, but he was not ready for the theory of equality in the United States (34).

Colby was probably correct. Grif, however, considered his position in Chicago as marking time until another opportunity arose. In the spring of 1933, he complained to Harlan Barrows that he had not had any summer vacation for two years so at the end of term he was given leave and set out to see the southwestern parts of the United States. With a young Japanese biologist, Watanabé, he travelled some 6,000 miles.

Grif kept in touch with friends in Australia and in 1934 learned of the death of his great friend, Sir Edgeworth David. Grif was saddened by the death of his oldest and dearest friend, and wrote the following:

It is as a teacher, lecturer, and, one may say, orator that his innumerable friends will perhaps best remember him. When deeply interested in his lecture his voice would ring out like a clarion, awakening enthusiasm in all types of audience. He was on every important scientific committee and was ever willing to give his too crowded time to aid any attempt to improve the status of science in Australia. His students loved him for his camaraderie, for his old hat and his still older umbrella, for his courtesy and aid given equally to nervous freshman or senior colleague. Those of us who were privileged to work closely with him owe him our worldly advancement as well as an abiding and a many-sided love of science. To many of the younger generation he seemed a modern Bayard, le chevalier sans peur et sans reproche (35).

Grif was very interested in the American involvement in the Antarctic in 1934, and during the fall of that year he received radio messages from his ex-student Paul Siple who was in the Antarctic with Admiral Byrd. In December Byrd himself radioed to Grif to ask his advice. Grif carefully recorded his reply in his diary:

Advise geological party attempt to make base about one week sledging east of Thorne Glacier. Remain week and climb to reach viewpoint. . . . Obviously closer airplane view desirable also (36).

Although Grif had heard nothing about the Toronto position for some time, he was surprised and pleased in January 1935 to hear from Harold Innis that the Board of Governors had finally given President Cody permission to hire a geographer as a professor of a separate department:

The prospects of a geography department are brightening again and the President, Rev. H.J. Cody, has asked me to ask you whether you could see him at the Union League Club, on Sunday, February 10 . . . much depends on the results (37).

Again on February 2,

I have just sent a note to the President regarding the appointment. I have pushed and held persistently the view that you should be appointed to a chair in geography in Toronto because of the tremendous advantages which both Toronto and Geography would gain from such an arrangement. We have so much to do in the subject and it occupies such an important place that I have been convinced that your appointment was the only solution. The President is worried about finances of course and I appreciate also your difficulties. An appointment or a chair at the highest salary paid would involve sacrifices on your part which you might not care to take. However, I do hope we can make an arrangement (38).

Evidently the financial support for this new chair came partly from the Governors, with the remainder coming from the Provincial Department of Education. The latter's support was contingent on the grounds that the successful applicant would also teach geography in the Ontario College of Education. Grif subsequently met Canon Cody at 2 p.m. at the Union League and Grif's diary indicates that they spoke about specifics. Grif said he would consider a $6500 salary, and Cody suggested that the appointment, if made, could continue until Taylor reached the age of 70, that his salary would begin in July, and he would start to work in September.

On March 5, Grif received a letter from Cody offering $6250, and he replied asking for $6500 and assistants for the laboratories. On March 14 Cody wired, "I think everything will be alright at the figure you suggest." Taylor was to receive $6500 of which $4000 was paid by the University and $2500 by the Ontario Department of Education. The latter subsidized Taylor's salary during his 16 years at Toronto, in return for which he lectured to a generation of high school teachers.

In his President's report for 1934-35 Cody stated his reasons for appointing Taylor:

> We had to choose as the first professor either a younger scholar with his reputation still unmade, or some one whose scientific work was known throughout the learned world and whose coming would bring prestige to the University. We felt that in establishing so important a chair — the first of its kind in a Canadian University — it would be wiser to choose for its incumbent a tried scholar of maturity and accomplishment. Our first professor will be Dr. Griffith Taylor, of the department of geography in the University of Chicago (one of the chief research institutions in America). He is an Englishman by birth and an Australian by early training. He held the first chair of geography in Australia, in the University of Sydney, and so organized this department that it became famous throughout the Empire. [Actually Taylor was head of the department as an Associate Professor] (39).

Harold Innis had won at last! It had been a six-year battle but geography was at last to be established as a separate department at Toronto. All was agreed upon, and on April 13 Grif sent his resignation to Harlan Barrows and wrote the following to Innis on 24 April 1935:

> I want to thank you for your long fight to start Geography on a professional basis at the University. I hope you will feel that it has been successful, since I handed in my resignation to Barrows — and have just accepted Dr. Cody's offer. . . . I have all sorts of plans for a live department, and I think Imperial Geography owes you a good deal! (40)

Taylor and Innis were to become great friends during the 1940s, as did their families. Mary Quayle Innis liked Doris Taylor, and Harold's son Donald, who eventually entered the geography program at Toronto, was David Taylor's best friend.

Very shortly, Grif, with Bill driving, started off on a trip to see something of his new country. They crossed the Ambassador Bridge into Windsor and spent their first night in Canada in Essex, Ontario, then drove on to Toronto, Montreal and the Maritimes, then back to Toronto to see Innis and the new quarters at the University of Toronto. He had a meeting with President Cody and reported in his diary:

> He was very affable but hasn't done much to finalize anything. I talked a lot about laboratories but he doesn't seem to know anything about space or apparatus (41).

Grif continued his observations about Toronto and his pleasure in being again in the Commonwealth.

> The campus looks fine and the city seems fresh and free from factories and foreigners. . . . The real estate agent drove us around Rosedale and Forest Hill where the second house was quite new, with a garden, across from Upper Canada College ($75 month). . . . Nice to see the Union Jack and the helmeted bobbies.

Grif and Bill returned to Chicago by way of the shores of Lake Huron. Grif liked the Ontario landscape, stating in his diary:

> I feel ever so much surer of Canadian topography and geology and history etc. that it has paid splendidly I think.

The Taylors rented the house at 110 Forest Hill Road and later bought it for $15,000. Grif felt that he did not have good luck with finances as he wrote to his brother Evan, February 1936:

> When we left Australia we lost £2,000 on the house. In Chicago, we lost £2,000 in bonds. When we leave Toronto, we'll probably not be able to sell this place (42).

On May 25, back in Chicago, Grif wrote to President Hutchins:

> The President of Toronto University has offered me the newly initiated Chair of Geography as I notified Mr. Barrows on April 13. I have accepted this duty of inaugurating the Department of Geography in Canada — as I had the privilege of doing in Australia.
>
> I shall always be proud of my seven years service with the University of Chicago which I consider the most interesting and one of the two greatest schools of research in America. . . . (43).

The final days in Chicago were hectic. Numerous farewell parties were given for the Taylors, perhaps the most pleasing an outdoor supper at the Platts. On this occasion, as again at Grif's farewell party many years later at Toronto, he was urged to sing "Waltzing Matilda." Then, as in Toronto, he had to explain the Australian meaning of the words to his audience. He was not sorry that he was leaving Chicago but felt a little hurt by the lack of friendliness he had felt there. This is evident from a letter Grif wrote to Wellington Jones from Toronto:

> It seems to me that Barrows and Colby gave me up as a friend and colleague after I proposed going to Toronto. . . . I felt very much in the cold except for the Platts (44).

It is interesting that Taylor was still analyzing his position in Chicago four years after leaving. In his autobiography he stated "I had never been able to feel myself securely established there" (45). In his personal diary he recalled in April 1939:

> I am rather surprized that Barrows and I had no friction until the last 6 months because we disagreed amicably on many important points. However he was much annoyed when I mentioned that 5½ months of lecturing was enough for any Chairman to expect. Like Henry 1, he never smiled again (46).

When Grif left Chicago in August 1935, he had been in the United States for seven years, and it seems surprising that he had published nothing that concerned the American landscape. His publications at Chicago drew on his Australian and Antarctic material and any new approaches focused on environment and history. He had travelled considerably in the United States and usually an article resulted from each of his major trips. Perhaps he did not consider himself the expert in the United States as he had been in Australia or Europe or Antarctica. However, he published a prodigious number of papers during these seven years, many of them in biology, history or popular journals. His writings on Australia, the Antarctic and in climatology were considered to be those of an expert in the field. His book *Environment and Race* had earned him much notoriety in disciplines other than geography. He had begun to explore a new area — geography and nation planning, a topic that interested him until his death. Certainly the thought of founding a new department of geography at Toronto, the first in Canada, excited him. He had the experience of founding a department in Australia, so he had the necessary self-confidence. He never doubted that he would accomplish the task.

References

1. Tomkins, George: "Griffith Taylor and Canadian Geography," p. 107.
2. University of Toronto. Falconer Presidential Papers, 1924-25, Box 118.
3. University of Toronto. Falconer Presidential Papers, 1924-25, Box 118.
4. Dunbar, Gary. Unpublished manuscript sent to author, 1984.
5. Dunbar, Gary. Unpublished manuscript, 1984.
6. National Library, Canberra, MS 1003/5/29.
7. National Library, Canberra, MS 1003/5/33.
8. University of Toronto. Falconer Presidential Papers, 1924-25, Box 118.

9. National Library, Canberra, MS 1003/5/21.
10. National Library, Canberra, MS 1003/5/25.
11. National Library, Canberra, MS 1003/5/26.
12. National Library, Canberra, MS 1003/5/23.
13. Griffith Taylor. Private Diary, 1929.
14. Taylor, Griffith: *Journeyman Taylor.* p. 211.
15. National Library, Canberra, MS 1003/5/23.
16. National Library, Canberra, MS 1003/9/1263.
17. Griffith Taylor. Private Diary, 1931.
18. Taylor, Griffith: "The Geographer's Aid in Nation — Planning," *Scottish Geographical Magazine*, Vol. XLVIII, January, 1932, p. 17.
19. Taylor, Griffith: *Scottish Geographical Magazine*, Vol. XLVIII, March, 1932, p. 68.
20. National Library, Canberra, MS 1003/9/1432.
21. National Library, Canberra, MS 1003/9/1433.
22. National Library, Canberra, MS 1003/9/1435.
23. National Library, Canberra, MS 1003/6/73.
24. University of Toronto. Falconer Papers, Box 118.
25. University of Toronto. Falconer Papers, Box 118.
26. Taylor, Griffith: "The Margins of Geography," *The American Schoolmaster*, December, 1931, p. 56.
27. Taylor, Griffith: "The Margins of Geography," p. 56.
28. National Library, Canberra, MS 1003/5/50.
29. Griffith Taylor. Private Diary, 1931.
30. University of Toronto. Falconer Papers, Box 118.
31. National Library, Canberra, MS 1003/6/74.
32. University of Toronto. Cody Papers. Letter from Cody to Innis, September 12, 1932.
33. Cody Papers. Letter from Cody to Innis, March 14, 1933.
34. Tomkins, George: "Griffith Taylor and Canadian Geography," pp. 114-133.
35. Taylor, Griffith: "Obituary, T.W.E. David," *The Australian Geographer*, Vol. II, no. 3, 1934, pp. 5-6.
36. Griffith Taylor. Private Diary, 1934.
37. National Library, Canberra, MS1003/6/75.
38. National Library, Canberra, MS1003/6/76.
39. University of Toronto. Cody Papers. 1934-35, p. 11.
40. National Library, Canberra, MS1003/6/79.
41. Griffith Taylor. Private Diary, 1935.
42. National Library, Canberra, MS1003/6/85.
43. Griffith Taylor. Private Diary, 1936.
44. Griffith Taylor. Private Diary, 1935.
45. Taylor, Griffith: *Journeyman Taylor*, p. 249.
46. Griffith Taylor. Private Diary, 1939.

CHAPTER 10

New Beginnings —
University of Toronto

Griffith Taylor was 56 years of age when he moved from Chicago to Toronto but his enthusiasm for geography and his capacity for hard work in his chosen profession were undiminished. At Toronto he was no longer an Australian geographer in North America, but a geographer of international repute (Fig. 16).

On 1 September 1935, the Taylors arrived at their new home in the posh Forest Hill Village section of Toronto. David was enrolled at Upper Canada College across the street from their home on Forest Hill Road, although Bill stayed in Chicago to finish his engineering course at the University of Chicago. A maid was hired. At last Grif was happy with his life style. He and Doris were entertained by President Cody, and Grif was invited to dine at the prestigious York Club. He met Sir Joseph Flavelle and Sir Robert Falconer. In October he was introduced to the Senate by President Cody:

> We are to be congratulated to have obtained a world famous scientist
> to start the (geography) department. He is the whole of it at
> present (1).

A committee with Cody as Chairman was formed to determine what form the department would take. Grif argued that it should be housed in the Science faculty, and that there should be no honours program at first. He insisted on a laboratory assistant. Cody agreed. One room in the old McMaster building on Bloor Street was allotted to Taylor, and later some basement rooms, previously used for storing blood supplies, were floored and used for laboratories.

Taylor's installation at the University of Toronto in November 1935 was attended by many dignitaries, among them the Lieutenant Governor of Ontario, Dr. Joerg of the American Geographical Society, and Dr. Preston James of the University of Michigan. President Cody described the occasion in his annual report:

> Thus was auspiciously launched the University's new venture in
> geography — the story of the background of man's history; the
> description, localization and explanation of the facts which relate
> man to his physical environment (2).

It is interesting to speculate who wrote the words spoken by President Cody. Whether Innis or Taylor, it is obvious that the new department would focus on man's relation to his physical environment. There was no disagreement between Innis and Taylor on that point. Another person who attended Taylor's

Figure 16. Griffith Taylor at the University of Toronto, 1935. (Photo from Bill Taylor)

inauguration that day in Convocation Hall was Charles Camsell, the distinguished explorer of the Canadian Northwest, who was invited in his capacity as President of the Canadian Geographical Society. His remarks, later published in the *Canadian Geographical Journal*, were entitled "What Geography means to Canada." He stated:

> To me this occasion marking the setting up of the first Chair in Geography in any of our Canadian Universities, is a memorable one. I again congratulate you upon the establishment of this new Department of Geography in your university, and upon your good fortune in securing Dr. Griffith Taylor as its Head. His wide achievements in the field of geography, particularly in Australia, are well known. It gives me much pleasure to tell you that the Board of Directors of the Canadian Geographical Society at a recent meeting elected Dr. Taylor a Fellow of the Society in appreciation of his appointment; and to extend my best wishes, as well as those of the Society, to him in his great responsibility of making his new Department the success which its importance warrants (3).

Taylor's first speech at the University of Toronto understandably concerned his ideas about geography. He called it "Illustrations of the New Geography," and it was later published in the *Canadian Journal of Economics and Political Science* with the title "Geography the Correlative Science." The talk and resulting paper expressed Grif's viewpoint of geography at the start of his Canadian career. Because of his concern over what faculty the new department would belong to, he spoke of the position of geography at Chicago and emphasized its liaison character:

> At the University of Chicago, one of the three leading research institutions in America, the four general divisions of undergraduate study are the social, physical and biological sciences and the humanities. It was found desirable to give geography a place in the first two divisions, thus emphasizing its liaison character (4).

He defined geography as the description, localization and explanation of the facts relating man to his material environment. He used again his diagram illustrating the realm of geography as the correlative science linking eight other sciences: anthropology, sociology, economics, botany, physics, geology, astronomy, history. He also outlined the history of geographical thought, and an elaboration of his zones and strata concept. He spoke of urban ecology or town planning, again anticipating a role that future geographers would play in urban geography. He used material from his new book *Environment and Nation* then in press to discuss the environmental influences on European history. Grif usually gave his audience a full fare of interesting concepts and this occasion was no exception.

As soon as Grif was settled in his new department, in June 1936, he set off to visit the western and northern areas of his new country: Winnipeg, Calgary, the Rockies, Victoria, then north to Edmonton, Waterways and Lac la Biche. He wanted to see the frontier areas of Canada as he had the frontiers of Australia. He made copious notes which he used later in his book on Canada.

The academic year 1936-37 was the first in which geography was listed as a separate department at the University of Toronto, although Grif was the only staff member. During his first year he gave only one course, a physical-economic geography taken by Commerce and Finance and General Arts first year students. To this was added the next year, a course in cultural geography, while at the same time Grif inaugurated a course in geography for high school teachers at the Ontario College of Education, and he began also to offer geography as an evening extension course.

Andrew Clark and Ann Nicholls (later Marshall) were hired as demonstrators. Clark had graduated from Brandon College in Mathematics and Physics and then had worked for the Manufacturers Life Insurance Company in Toronto. In September 1935 he entered graduate school at Toronto, working in economic history with Harold Innis. He needed funds, as did most graduate students, and when Innis told him work was available in the new Department of Geography, he was quick to apply. He was a general helper — teaching, errand-running, researching, doing whatever Taylor needed done. In 1938 Andrew

Clark was awarded the Masters degree in Geography — the first in Canada. He left Toronto, on the advice of Harold Innis, to go to Berkeley where he did his Ph.D. He went on to become one of North America's foremost historical geographers, and remained one of Grif's life-long friends.

Marshall, who later became a Senior Lecturer in Geography at the University of Adelaide in Australia, remembered Taylor as a dynamo in those days:

> He drew his own maps — on untidy sheets of paper which I then had to transfer to wax sheets and run off on a mimeograph machine discarded by some other department. He had his students cut out contours in cardboard to model the Toronto region and in response to lifted eyebrows said, "All right, it's kindergarten stuff but these kids will understand contours for the rest of their lives" — and how true it was (5).

Grif also found time to complete his book, *Environment and Nation*, which he had begun before leaving Chicago, and which was eventually published by the University of Toronto Press in 1936. Grif considered this book a sequel to his earlier work on *Environment and Race*. He was fascinated by the effect of the physical environment on man — first on the general distribution of races over the surface of the globe as in his early book on race, then on the effect on smaller units, or nations as he called them. He was already planning his third book in the trilogy — the relationship between environment and settlement, a book that ultimately was published as *Urban Geography*.

In a sense *Environment and Nation* was a reaction to the overwhelming concern of geographers of the period with economic geography and was a protest against narrowing the fields of science unduly. He felt that the application of his unique geographic technique — the use of maps, isopleths and block diagrams — to historical problems would be interesting to geographers and historians alike. *Environment and Nation* focused on Europe, an area Grif knew extremely well. He felt that no one could understand the politics of Europe without knowing the fundamentals of the cultural and topographic background. The subtitle of the book was "Factors in the Cultural and Political History of Europe," and Taylor hoped it might help to contribute to peace:

> The foregoing study is an attempt to investigate some of the cultural and historical problems of Europe. If it helps in however small a degree to promote the brotherhood of man, the writer's main objective will have been accomplished (6).

Taylor's purpose in the book, one that would overwhelm any geographer with lesser courage, was to explore the relationship between history and geography, to correlate such diverse factors as race, religion, language, temperature, and rainfall with the cultural development of the 74 natural regions of Europe. His hand-drawn maps and three dimensional diagrams presented material that was unconventional and stimulating, especially to the non-geographer. Grif used the book as his text for the second-year course in Toronto and it was exciting fare for the students of history, or anthropology, or economics who crowded into that classroom in the old McMaster building on Bloor St. Grif was greatly concerned with the possibility of war in Europe, and there are numerous references to Hitler's Nordic policy and its fallacy:

> I have shown in Fig. 145 the boundary between the declining nations in the north-west and the increasing nations in the south-east. It presages a time where the "Nordic Fetish" will obviously lose its appeal, owing to the dwindling of the Nordic race (7).

He also spoke out against the persecution of the Jews:

> It is, of course, the economic aspects of Jewish culture which excite the hatred of powerful groups of Anti-Semites but the so-called racial and religious arguments lend themselves better to propaganda. The expulsion of the Jews because they are non-Christian is eminently un-Christian. Their persecution because they are a "Non Aryan Race" is the height of scientific absurdity. Indeed if the Nazis were logical most of the South Germans might equally well be expelled from Germany since they are of the same Alpine race as the Jews, and were clearly the originators of the hated Yiddish dialect (8).

The book was successful and was reviewed by historians as well as geographers. Although Richard Hartshorne commented on Taylor's "dubious generalization" he included the book in his famous study, *The Nature of Geography*. Jan Broek thought the book was full of stimulating suggestions but, like Hartshorne, was critical of Taylor's unsupported generalizations. Huntington, of course, liked the book since it echoed many of his own pet theories and he correctly identified Taylor's special ability, namely, "his capacity for overlooking minor details and seeing the whole pattern." Van Valkenburg reviewed *Environment and Nation* for the *Geographical Review* and was full of praise for its originality and the remarkable amount of knowledge it contained. However the comments that probably pleased Grif most were those of Arnold Toynbee who wrote him November 1936 commenting on the "extraordinarily illuminating" theories in the book (9).

Grif also lost no time in publishing about his adopted country. "Fundamental Factors in Canadian Geography" appeared in the *Canadian Geographical Journal* in 1936, and also in 1936 in the *Canadian Journal of Economics and Political Science* an article entitled "Topographic Control in the Toronto Region".

In 1936 Grif accepted an invitation from Isaiah Bowman to contribute to a symposium he was editing under the auspices of the Institute of Intellectual Co-operation, a branch of the League of Nations. This symposium was published in 1937 under the title *Limits of Land Settlement*, and Grif's article concerned

Australia, "The Possibilities of Settlement in Australia." Taylor was now the acknowledged expert on Australian geography.

In 1937, Donald Putnam, a soil scientist from the Maritimes who had a keen interest in geography, came to Grif and asked for a job in the new department. Grif spoke to the President and Putnam was offered a position as lecturer in geography at $1200 per year. Grif recognized Putnam's good qualities and the two men, although so different in temperament and interests, got on remarkably well during the next 14 years. Putnam was a practical geographer, meticulous in detail and rather slow-moving. A story is told by some of his students that he actually fell asleep during one of his own lectures. He took over the field trips since Taylor was too busy to do them, and the stories of his driving off the road while pointing out some geographical feature on those occasions are legion. Grif certainly encouraged Putty in his monumental work with Lyman Chapman, *The Physiography of Southern Ontario*. Together each summer they walked the fields and roads of Southern Ontario and published the first definitive work on the retreat of the glaciers from this part of Canada.

There were 100 students in the first year geography course in the fall of 1937, one of whom was Lloyd Reeds. Grif made a lasting impression on the young student, and convinced him that maps were the essence of geography as Reeds recalled many years later:

> I recall having included more than 20 sketch maps on a single examination I had written for Griffith Taylor. He called me into his office after he had read my paper to congratulate me and to say that he had noted in his diary that I had set a record in having illustrated my answers with more maps on a single examination than any of his students had ever done previously. He mentioned that I had the earmarks of a true geographer and that I should be successful if I ever decided to join the profession (10).

Mildred Brookstone, a physics graduate, was hired to assist in the labs, and obtained her M.A. in geography in 1940. Miss Brookstone (now Mrs. Zacks) was a demonstrator in the department until 1945 and her first and second year labs stressed quantitative techniques long before it was fashionable in most geography schools.

Grif wrote a great deal during those years. In 1937 he published the "The Structural Basis of Canadian Geography" in the *Canadian Geographical Journal*, a "Comparison of the American and Australian Deserts" in *Economic Geography*, and "The Distribution of Pasture in Australia" in the *Geographical Review*. Also, in 1937 one of Grif's most popular books was published by the University of Toronto Press. He called it *Environment, Race and Migration* and used it as a text for his very popular first year geography course. In reality it was a new edition of *Environment and Race*. He had greatly increased the section on environmental control of modern migration, and had added several new chapters on settlement in Canada. He explained his philosophy of environmental or "Stop and Go" determinism:

152

Exaggerating somewhat, I feel that Man's part in the programme of a country's material evolution is not unlike that of a traffic policeman. He can accelerate, slow or halt traffic, but he does not alter its direction. This "Stop and Go" determinism has no supporters among the historians and not many even among geographers. But it expresses something of the conclusions that the writer has arrived at from a lengthier study of difficult environments than has fallen to the lot of most geographers (11).

In this book, as in earlier ones, Grif tried to demonstrate the correlative nature of geography, linking the environmental to the human sciences. At a time when many racial myths abounded in Hitler's Europe, Grif hoped to dispel myths, and promote, even to a small degree, the brotherhood of man. It was heady stuff for a first year university course, and his students, whether geography, commerce and finance, or economics majors were excited and stimulated by his lectures. This book *Environment, Race and Migration*, like *Environment and Nation*, gained him a wider audience than the geographic community. The eminent Harvard anthropologist Ernest Hooton called the book a splendid piece of work and wrote to Grif that he was thoroughly sold on his Zones and Strata Theory, and that he had made an extremely important contribution to anthropology.

I have been in a state of exaltation while I have been reading your book and have communicated a great deal of my enthusiasm to my colleagues (12).

Even if all anthropologists did not agree with Hooton, Taylor was encouraged in his anthropogeography writings and was on his way to becoming a world famous anthropogeographer.

Grif was pleased to be elected President of Section E (Geography) of the British Association in 1938, and asked to give the presidential address in Cambridge in August of that year. As he usually did, Grif took the opportunity to see parts of the world still unknown to him, and left New York in May to travel to Africa and the Sahara, Greece, and Paris before arriving in Cambridge for the meetings. Travel for Grif was never dull. He was arrested in Tunisia and again in Northern Italy where he was taken for a spy. Grif was wandering along the Adige River sketching when a soldier arrested him. His notes, photographs and sketches were taken from him, and confusion existed since the guards could speak no English, or German, and Grif no Italian. He was finally released after promising to take no more photographs and make no more sketches.

Finally arriving in Cambridge, he was the guest of his old Antarctic friend Frank Debenham, then Professor of Geography at Cambridge. Grif spoke to the British Association on "Correlations and Culture," a plea for the use of isopleth diagrams and maps in cultural geography. Later, he managed to have this paper published in three different journals — *Nature*, the *Scottish Geographical Magazine*, and the *Pan-American Geologist*. At the meeting Grif was pleased to make the acquaintance of H.G. Wells, who entertained him at his home in

Regent's Park and with whom he enjoyed many good arguments. Wells pleased Grif by quoting the latter's racial views in his book *Outline of History*.

Back in Toronto in September, Taylor found the numbers of geography students increasing and spoke to President Cody about augmenting his staff by hiring a young Welsh geographer George Tatham. During the 1938-39 academic year, Stephen Jones from the University of Hawaii had been hired, but he had stayed only one year and a replacement was urgently needed. Tatham had been a student of Rosby's in England and then had gone to Clark University in 1932 for his Ph.D. Back in England he had taught at Birmingham, and was at the University of Hull when he received a letter from Taylor asking him to apply for the Toronto position. On 14 February 1939, Grif wrote to Tatham:

> I was glad to receive your prompt letter. I am authorized by the President to invite you to join us as Senior Lecturer at $2200-salary to start in July. We should hope to see you early in September (13).

George Tatham accepted the offer and came to Toronto (Fig. 17). Grif showed great perception in his choice of staff. While Putnam was chosen for his practical ideas of geography, Tatham was his opposite. A geographer who lectured about Kant and Aristotle, who was interested in the history of geographic thought and made it exciting to his students, who played the piano brilliantly and wrote funny poems on occasion, Tatham was the right choice. More than slightly left wing in his politics, Tatham was sometimes in trouble for his political views, but always remained a friend of Grif's. George Tatham contributed a great deal to the department in Toronto in those early days, although he published very little. He later moved to the Department of Geography at York University, just north of Toronto.

In 1939 Grif attended the meeting of the Association of American Geographers at Harvard, where he was elected Vice-President, and renewed his acquaintance with Paul Siple, an ex-student of his from Chicago days. He was also pleased to make the acquaintance of Ernest Hooton who had reviewed his *Environment, Race and Migration*. At the meeting in Harvard, Grif spoke of his recent research in the Sahara, which was subsequently published in the *Geographical Review* in 1939 as "Sea to Sahara — Settlement Zones in eastern Algeria."

Talk of war increased, and Grif noted in his diary in July, "Hitler swallows Baldwin's pipe and Chamberlain's brolly," and in September, England declared war on Germany. At a meeting with Grif in November, President Cody said that geography was surprisingly popular and that more geographers than ever were needed in war-time.

Taylor felt that geography had little influence in the University without an Honours program, and lobbied for the inauguration of a four-year Honours course. He knew how to play university politics, and in April 1940 the honours geography program was passed unanimously by the Faculty of Arts, since Grif said that he would not need more money or staff and that he expected only six

Figure 17. The Geography staff, University of Toronto, 1940. Putnam, Brookstone, Tatham, Taylor, behind old McMaster Building. (Photo from Bill Taylor)

Honours students per year. Preparations for the Honours program began, and Grif asked Putnam to collect ideas for the timetable.

Putnam, with the help of Tatham and Taylor outlined a very rigorous program. The Honours students began their geography program in the second year. The first year was done in either the physical sciences or a general course called "Social and Philosophical Studies," or "Sock and Fill" as it was called by all the undergraduates. The course load was heavy and included regional courses dealing with every continent including the polar regions. Grif anticipated the quantitative revolution in geography by insisting that the second year students take Mathematical Geography, a rigorous course well taught by Miss Brookstone. Urban Geography and Advanced Climatology were taught by Taylor and History of Geographical Thought by George Tatham. The second year Honours students took four geography courses and four options, including sciences such as geology, botany or physics, as well as history or economic history with Harold Innis. In the third and fourth years, 12 hours of geography courses were required plus 10 hours of outside courses and reading courses in French and German. An Honours thesis was required. The number of teaching hours that Taylor managed was prodigious. He asked no more of his staff than he did of himself.

Two Honours students enrolled that first year — Jim Hamilton and Mary Parker. And students began to come for graduate work, Nadine Hooper for a

Master's degree and Chun-fen Lee from Shanghai for a doctorate. Lee had won a Boxer scholarship to study geography in Great Britain, but because of the war, was permitted to go to Canada instead. Lee got on very well with Grif. His doctoral dissertation was entitled "Land Utilization in the Middle Grand River Valley of Western Ontario," and he was awarded the doctorate in 1943. It was the first Ph.D. degree in Geography granted in Canada. Dr. Lee now lectures at the East China Normal University in Shanghai.

In November 1940, Grif noted in his diary that Roosevelt was re-elected President of the United States, and Coventry in England was largely destroyed by German bombers. The letters from the Priestley relatives in England were full of the bad news and the possibility of an invasion of Britain. Grif was upset by the war since he was a pacifist, and did his best in his published articles to stress the need for cultural harmony. He used material that he had previously gathered in Europe for several articles on the geography of Europe. In an article in the *Geographical Review* entitled "Trento to the Reschen Pass — A Cultural Traverse of the Adige Corridor," he stated:

> To the geographer, however, the outstanding features of interest are surely the interrelations of topography and human occupation along the glacier cut routes leading to one of the lowest branches in the Alpine barrier to Europe (14).

In the *Canadian Geographical Journal* Taylor published an article entitled "Cultural Geography Along the Rome-Berlin Axis" in which he made the sound statement that education was part of the solution to war.

> ... universal employment must have preference over profits; backward countries must be mandated rather than exploited and the vanquished nations must immediately be helped towards rehabilitation. Only in some such fashion, Utopian though it may seem at present, shall we ever reach the main objective of civilization, a World at Peace (15).

Again in the *Canadian Geographical Journal*, January 1940, his article "Cultural Aspects of Romania, Yugoslavia and Hungary" contained an excellent discussion of the physical, historic and cultural bases of these nations and suggestions for their future.

In 1940, Grif's new book on Australia was published by Dutton. Using material from his earlier books, from the first in 1911 with Herbertson, to the 1931 text published by Rand McNally, and with added material from his many scientific articles on Australia, Grif's new *Australia* was indeed the most complete and authoritative text on that continent yet published.

During the summer of 1941, Grif taught summer school, and since the war precluded travel abroad, he set off to see more of Canada: Winnipeg, British Columbia, Prince Rupert, Calgary. He returned in September to a busy schedule. Andrew Thomson, Director of the Weather Service in Canada, at that time the Meteorological Branch of the Department of Transport, asked him to give 20 lectures in climatology to the meteorologists-in-training, further adding to Grif's teaching load.

In 1941, Don Kerr, a graduate of the University of British Columbia, moved to Toronto for graduate work with Grif, and to begin an association with the Department of Geography at Toronto that continues today. He was to leave the department in 1943, after completing his master's degree, for a job with the Meteorological Branch of the Department of Transport. After a short period on the west coast and two semesters at the University of California at Berkeley, he returned to Toronto in 1946. Lloyd Reeds was appointed as a teaching assistant in 1941 in his final undergraduate year, and joined the Royal Canadian Navy when he graduated in 1942. Reeds recalls the help he received from Grif in the advancement of his career:

> Grif volunteered a letter to Naval Headquarters to point out that a recruit by the name of Reeds was joining the service and that if they were wise they would advance him immediately to the Intelligence Branch where they could benefit from his knowledge of all countries of the world. When I became an instructor, I had access to my confidential file and discovered Grif's letter. When the war ended in 1945 he convinced the President to contact the Navy and to arrange my immediate release. Within 72 hours, I was discharged and was in the classroom at University of Toronto (16).

Reeds finished his Ph.D. in 1948 and was hired by the new department at McMaster in Hamilton. Wreford Watson had been invited to McMaster in 1939 to start the department, while he worked on his Ph.D. degree with Grif at Toronto. The dissertation which earned him a Ph.D. in 1945 — the third from the University of Toronto — was entitled "The Geography of the Niagara Peninsula." Richard Ruggles also spent some time at McMaster, from 1947 until 1952, when he left to begin work on his Ph.D. at Syracuse. Thus Grif's ideas of geography influenced the department at McMaster in those early days.

Always interested in the topic of geography in education, Grif was pleased to be invited by the U.S. National Foundation for Education to write a paper on "Education for Citizen Responsibilities" and he returned to his old theme — the Classics versus Geography. He used the opportunity to air his views of what constitutes a university geography course and a plea for the study of cultural geography.

One of the greatest honours Taylor received came in 1941 when he was elected President of the Association of American Geographers — the first geographer in Canada to be so named. Mark Jefferson was on the committee which chose Taylor as president, and he wrote to Grif:

> The office will bring us more distinction than it will you. [And further] There has been no man fitter for the Presidency since we lost our founder, W. M. Davis (17).

Figure 18. Grif and Ph.D. student, Chun-fen Lee, in the Taylor's garden 1941. (Photo from Dr. Chun-fen Lee)

For his presidential address Grif decided to talk about one of his new interests — urban geography. He was now working on the third book in his trilogy on environment and human settlement, to complement his books on environment and race and environment and nation. He wrote about his talk to Preston James, stressing his "deterministic" stance and his arguments with the "possibilists:"

Dear James:

I have finished the rough draft of my address, about 50 pages plus a number of what Zierer calls "taylor style" sketches. What happens to it now? In my Cambridge address it was printed before the meeting, and I was able to use a proof copy for my evening of responsibility. As you know I am trying to integrate Urban Geography in the same heterodox way that I have done with racial geography and historical geography. I have got some novel ideas I think, regarding infantile to senile towns in the paleotechnic type of settlement. My formula seems to me to be useful since you can take the formula and draw a fairly good and descriptive map of the town. You may be sure that I have boosted determinism and made the ultra possibilist writhe. Unfortunately candour compels me to state that possibilism must be considered in the building of towns. Anyhow I am trying to evaluate the importance of the two ideologies.

He went on to give James some advice about the nature of AAG meetings, interesting advice which is still valid today:

> I wish we could do something about the character of the lectures during the meeting. I see no reason why we should not prohibit reading of manuscript. The talker always has slides, and surely he can readily find out how much he can say in 10 or 20 minutes. Very good practice for them, and of course many already realize how much better a talk is than a long-winded reading. I saw a long article in Science on this very point about a year ago, and I am thoroughly in accord. I promise to talk without notes for 50 minutes of my address, though I may want to read the peroration (if any) (18).

In December 1941 Grif travelled to New York to give his presidential address to the AAG. His talk on the effect of environment on villages and cities, entitled "Environment, Village and City," was published in the *Annals* in 1942 and expanded later to become a book he called, *Urban Geography*. Here again, Grif was a pioneer for in his examination of the relationships between settlements and the environment, he explored new ground that marked the beginning of the interest of geographers in planning and urban geography.

Grif had never been busier lecturing and writing, and he wrote on many different topics and for many different journals: "Geography at the University of Toronto" for the *Canadian Geographical Journal* in 1984, "Structure and Settlement in Canada" for the *Canadian Banker* in 1940-41, and "Races of the World" for *Human Biology*, in 1941.

During the summer vacation in 1942, Grif again set out to learn more about Canada, this time travelling to Quebec, the Saguenay and Gaspé and the Maritime provinces. At the same time Grif was redoubling his efforts to gain status for geography at the University of Toronto. He tried to have the subject accepted as an option for entrance to the Faculty of Arts, while confiding to his diary,

> Canada is slow to emerge from her state of geographic illiteracy in spite of all my efforts (19).

In June 1943 the first two graduates in Honours Geography (Parker and Hamilton) received their degrees from Chancellor Sir William Mulock. Chun-fen Lee successfully defended his doctoral dissertation on the Grand River Valley and was invited for tea in the Taylor garden on Forest Hill Road (Fig. 18). In 1943, the number of students taking the Honours program was still very small: Don Kirk, Arnold Boggs and Marie Lustig were entering final year, Dick Ruggles third year, and Bill Wonders and Ruth Braffette second year. Arnold Boggs subsequently became a high school teacher in Kitchener and Don Kirk, who completed a doctorate at the University of Illinois, was tragically killed in the crash of an RCAF Lancaster aircraft at Alert in Canada's Northwest Territories in 1950. Ruggles who, at the instigation of Wreford Watson, later founded the

Department of Geography at Queen's University, remembers standing a little in awe of "the Professor." He describes his impressions of Grif's lectures:

> One of the most vivid memories of courses at Toronto was Grif's first year course in Geography. It may be that his "slides with annotations" approach suited my visual orientation, but I received from him the ability to "see" geographical aspects — it was a continuous kaleidoscope. It taught me to see both geographical and historical data as graphics, and although this can go too far, and can generalize too much, I never will regret having this course as the beginning one.

Ruggles also has memories of Grif at home, when the students were invited to parties in the house in Forest Hill.

> I thought that Grif "at home" with his family, when they had us there on several occasions, was an enlightening experience. The Professor, off the pedestal on which I held him, was so warm and pleasant, and the two of them such a devoted couple, it was a "growing-up" experience for me. They made young people very welcome (20).

Honours continued to come Grif's way during the war years. He was invited to speak in New York at the Herald-Tribune Forum in October 1943, sharing the platform with such notables as Eleanor Roosevelt, Wendell Wilkie, Henry Wallace and Greer Garson. Grif was a little nonplussed to find his talk on nation planning was followed by a speech on the possibilities of robots picking peaches. Lewis Mumford was there and spoke to Grif about his theories of urban geography: "I am probably closer to your point of departure than most sociologists." He met Stephen Leacock who was then teaching at McGill, and who proved himself a champion of geography, confiding to Grif that he had written 4000 words entitled "a plea for geographical science" for the *Encyclopaedia Britannica.*

It was a great honour for Taylor to be invited to give the Messenger lectures at Cornell University in 1944. The President of the University had written Grif in 1941 stating that the topic of the lectures was to be the evolution of civilization. The honorarium was astronomical in Grif's eyes — $1500 — and the lectures were to be published as a book. This was a real challenge for Grif who worked hard at the six Messenger lectures which he gave in April in Ithaca. The topics were ecology and evolution, environment and race, environment and nation, environment and city, environment and war and environment and peace. In addition to these, Grif managed to fit in some lectures on military geography to soldier groups on campus. But he had trouble with the Cornell Press when it came to the publishing of his work, writing to them on 15 June 1944:

> I do not understand yet why Cornell should differ in its methods from all other Presses with which I have had dealings. I have published in the last few years three larger books than "Our Evolving

Civilization" on cognate subjects. The maps and diagram were of the same type. A few were redrawn, but any geographer will tell you that my block diagrams are accepted by the leading American "Geographical Society" or by the professional "Geographers Association" without change. How many do you wish to be redrawn? As regard my text I have published three editions of "Environment Race and Migration" and the editors have been content to accept my manuscript as I typed it with changes in hardly a dozen lines. The same treatment was accorded my book "Australia" by Methuen (21).

The day Grif wrote the above letter, he left for Canada's northwest as a member of a party doing a reconnaissance survey of the Northwest Territories and Yukon settlements with a grant from the Social Science Council. He was in his element, again in the frontier settlements of Canada, making copious notes and diagrams, filling his diaries and writing long letters to his family. He took a boat down the Mackenzie, visiting all the settlements along the way and on July 22 finally reached Tuktoyaktuk, where he ate muktuk and took part in a whale

Figure 19. Grif in Canada's Arctic. Tuktoyaktuk N.W.T., 1944. (Photo from Bill Taylor)

hunt (Fig. 19). He made a side trip to the Yukon, visiting Whitehorse and Dawson City, and finally arrived home August 18. He wrote two articles about the Northwest: "A Mackenzie Domesday" and "A Yukon Domesday" which appeared in a book entitled *The New Northwest.*

Grif was not slowing down in 1944. Rather, he was working on his books *Canada* and *Our Evolving Civilization* and was still battling Dr. Althouse, the director of the Ontario College of Education, about the role of geography:

> In all my public lectures and in most of my articles I remind the Canadian public how far their schools are behind the rest of the educated world in this respect. There is a chance for Premier Drew make a name for himself in Canadian education if he could spare time to tackle the geographic problem (22).

He went to battle also for his staff and his students. He requested from President Cody raises for Tatham and Putnam, and $100 for field work for Putnam, since he and Lyman Chapman of the Ontario Research Foundation were devoting their summers to the work that would appear in 1951 as *The Physiography of Southern Ontario*. Grif told Cody it was "slave labour." Taylor also believed in getting his geography message to the ordinary reader and wrote a piece for *Chatelaine Magazine* in February 1945 entitled "Canada — 100 Years from Now." The article began:

> I think it likely that in 100 years the population of Canada may be some 40 million. I think it likely that the area of densest population in the Dominion will have shifted to Alberta.

He sent a copy of the article to fellow professor and economist Vincent Bladen, with whom he often argued about the future population of Canada.

> Dear Vincent — Give this to your granddaughter as an heirloom — and in 2045 we'll meet and see who is right — you or me!

And then a reminder that his prophesies for Australia had come true:

> I think I can say that the figures I predicted 25 years ago for Australia are now accepted. At any rate it seems safe to challenge anyone to come back in a hundred years and disprove my forecast for Canada (23).

In 1945 the war ended, and the veterans flocked to the universities, interested in learning more about the world which they had seen. More than 750 students registered in the freshman course in geography at Toronto, posing almost insuperable problems of staff, classroom space and timetables. During the post-war period, and indeed right up to his retirement, Taylor undoubtedly worked harder than he had ever done before.

The book that had developed from the Messenger lectures, *Our Evolving Civilization*, appeared in 1946, published by the University of Toronto Press.

Taylor had lived through two World Wars and hoped that this book which he subtitled "An introduction to geopacifics" would contribute in some way to the path toward world peace. In the book, the original six Messenger lectures were reduced to four parts. The first three contained material that Taylor had published before, on the importance of the physical environment and its influence on human history. Taylor again used his "dynograph" or graph of power, to compare the natural resources of various countries. He recognized oil and population as resources, something he had not done in his earlier books, and again he prophesied correctly in stating that the United States, Russia and in the future, China, would be world powers.

The last section of the book concerned Taylor's new ideas on geopolitics and geopacifics. Grif coined the word "geopacifics", and although it has not caught on in geographic circles, the notion that geographers can help promote world peace is not without merit. In a sense he offered his idea of geopacifics as an antidote to the perverted geography of Hitler's and Haushofer's geopolitics. One chapter in the book is a critique of Karl Haushofer's geopolitics, and Taylor observed in a footnote that the closing years of this famous geographer's life were filled with tragedy. His son Albrecht was involved in the attempt on Hitler's life in 1944, and was imprisoned and murdered, and Karl and his wife both committed suicide in March 1946.

Perhaps the most interesting part of the book was the last chapter on future world population in which Grif predicted a world population of four billion, a prediction that would have many supporters some 40 years later. He predicted that the Soviet Union would be predominant in Europe, and China would take precedence over Japan in the Asian world. He accurately predicted the struggle between the developed and developing countries. In this book, Taylor also re-stated his views of "stop-and-go determinism."

> Man is like the traffic controller in a large city, who alters the rate,
> but not the direction of progress. So also, man is able to accelerate,
> slow or stop the progress of a country's development (24).

This type of "determinism" is one with which few people would argue, and typified the neat turn-of-phrase that Grif was noted for. He considered too that geographers were well qualified to study civilization, stating in the concluding chapter that the chief aim of civilization is not to prepare for a better world beyond this earth but to prepare a better world on this earth. This he said can be attained only by studying world problems, especially those involving other nations and regions.

The book was reviewed for the *Canadian Historical Review* by Wreford Watson. Grif's ex-student, who was then Professor of Geography at McMaster University, considered that Taylor influenced the whole trend of modern geography with this book and that his insistence on the influence of the physical environment was essential for historians.

In the post-war years, 1946-1951, the staff members of the Toronto department worked long hours. The number of students enrolled in geography classes increased from 804 in 1946 to 1191 in 1947. George Tatham recalled in the tape he made on the early days of the department that on many days he lectured from 9 a.m. to 6 p.m. One day he was a little surprised to return to his office at 6 p.m. to find a note from Grif.

> Why don't you spend more time in your office? I can never find you (25).

But Tatham also pointed out that the department at Toronto was a very happy one. It was a stimulating place to be and the staff and students had fun together. The Taylors were very hospitable and had many parties at their house. There were also departmental parties at Christmas, and on special occasions, all of which were marked by poems or songs composed and sung by members of the faculty or students. Grif, of course, was always invited to sing that perennial Australian favourite "Waltzing Matilda."

In 1946 the Taylors' son Bill left Canada to return to Australia. This was probably one of the reasons that led Grif and Doris to decide they would return to Australia when Grif retired, but there was no time to think of retirement in post-war University of Toronto.

At this time Grif was working on the book which he tentatively called *Environment and Settlement*, his interest in the history of settlements perhaps stemming from his meeting with Lewis Mumford in 1943 in New York. As usual, Taylor became excited by his new interest in the relationship of environment and city. Three articles in 1945 dealt with this new theme: "Town and Township in Southern Ontario" and "The Seven Ages of Towns" in *Economic Geography* and "Town Patterns on the Gulf of St. Lawrence" in the *Canadian Geographical Journal*. He finally finished his manuscript in 1946 and sent it to Prentice-Hall, but they turned it down, as did McGraw-Hill. In a letter dated 26 August 1946, the representative of the latter publisher wrote:

> Although we should like very much to act as your publisher, we have been forced to the conclusion that we shall not be in the position to do so in this case.
>
> We may, of course, be wrong in our estimate, but we feel that the market for the type of volume you have projected would be rather limited, especially so as we would be given only the American rights (26).

Refusals never daunted Taylor. He changed the title to *Urban Geography* and it was finally published by Methuen in London in 1948. Grif realized that urban studies were popular in all geography departments but that sociologists and town planners had cornered the market on text books. He rightly stated that no geographer had published a book on urban geography. Again he drew from his voluminous journals, his diaries and his published articles on settlements and cities. He was familiar with settlements on seven continents and used that knowledge well in his book. The historical parts taken from Mumford were not so interesting, but in all, it was a good first attempt to link topography and history to human settlement. It resulted in a course in urban geography in Toronto, probably the first of its kind in Canada.

Taylor was very pleased when Donald Innis, the son of his great friend Harold Innis, and a friend of his son David, enrolled in the honours geography program. Innis, now Professor of Geography at the State University of New York at Geneseo, remembers Grif with fondness but also recalls one of Grif's disconcerting habits. Don recalls being summoned to Taylor's office for a critique of his thesis:

> As soon as I started to talk, he started to whistle. I couldn't believe it, but I tried to keep on talking. I had the feeling that Taylor was a little concerned that you might have nothing to say — so he whistled while you were talking in case what you said made no sense, and that way he avoided wasting time (27).

Grif needed additional staff for the increasing number of students taking geography, and Don Kerr, who, as noted earlier, had gone to California, was offered $2000 a year to move to Toronto as a junior lecturer. He did so in 1946 and began work on his Ph.D., at the same time helping with the labs and doing some lecturing. He was advised on his dissertation on the climate of British Columbia by Grif, but also by Ken Hare at McGill. On July 1st of that same year Brian Bird from Cambridge was appointed to augment the geography staff. In this appointment Grif was again very astute. The department needed the infusion of a younger man, one unafraid of hard work and with physical geography interests, and of course, Grif was always partial to Cambridge graduates. Brian Bird was an excellent addition to the department, and Brian and his wife Beryl became good friends of the Taylors. Brian, now Professor of Geography at McGill, recalls his arrival in Toronto:

> Grif wrote telling me to arrive in Toronto on Monday September 1. This I did, arriving at 9:30 a.m. at the Old McMaster building straight from the New York train. Nobody had told me it was Labour Day so I was a little surprised to find the front door locked. After a time Mac (the janitor) came and opened the door — "You're lucky" he said "the only professor who will appear today is already here" — and there was Grif sitting in his office!
>
> Grif was extremely friendly and invited me to stay with Doris and himself. This I did for about a week until I found a place to live. During that week Grif had a constant stream of visitors — Sir Charles and Lady Wright were staying with them (we all went to the 'Ex' and had great fun) three of the University of Toronto senior historians, Chester-Martin, Brown and Wilkinson came round and we saw the Innis' (Harold and his wife) twice: very impressive for a young man — particularly when he was brought into several highly intellectual discussions (28).

The number of Grif's publications during the 1940s was really quite remarkable. In addition to his long hours of lecturing, he managed to complete five books in those ten years as well as dozens of articles. His text on Canada was published in 1947 by Methuen and was to be the standard geography text on Canada for many years, although Donald Putnam believed that Grif erred in trying to make it fit the mold he had used for his "Australia" texts. Taylor called the book *A study of cool continental environments and their effect on British and French settlement*. Again, Grif drew on his wide knowledge of the country, since he had travelled to every corner of Canada except the Arctic islands. His accounts of the Mackenzie area of the Northwest Territories and the Yukon are classics and it is unfortunate that he was unable to do the same for the high Arctic. The book was very rational in its organization. First, the geology and climate were explained, then the soils and vegetation. His division of Canada into seven natural regions was excellent and was copied by many later geographers. Lastly, he described man's use of the environment and concluded with a forecast of Canada's population for the year 2050. The population of Canada when Grif wrote was some 12 million, but he predicted 40 million in 100 years time. Perhaps he will be proved correct as he was in predicting Australia's population!

The Taylors had not seen Australia since 1928 so Grif was very pleased to receive in May 1947 an invitation from Professor Mills of Australia to visit that country and assist the Interim Council in planning the new National University. Grif suggested that he leave Toronto in April of 1948 and spend three months in Australia. He had not travelled abroad for some years, and he was restless to go again. He was keen to see Australia, but in his reply to Mills he could not resist making some remarks about the Australian desert:

> I was most struck with the pronouncement of the pastoral experts in the recent book "Australia", 1947 (edited by G.C. Wood) that "two-fifths of Australia is a great desert, and not likely to carry any stock."
> In 1911-12 my first geography book was put on the black list in Western Australia for suggesting there was any desert in the Commonwealth! (29).

In February 1948, there was a farewell party in the geography department for Grif before he left on his Australian tour. He took the train to Vancouver, then a plane from San Francisco to Honolulu. There he visited an old friend from Australian days, Professor Porteus, who was then teaching at the University of Hawaii. He travelled to the Big Island and also saw every part of Oahu, before flying on to Fiji, where he revisited the places he had seen in 1907. On April 1, he arrived at Sydney to be met by son Bill and his new daughter-in-law, Dot. After 20 years he again visited the University of Sydney and met Macdonald Holmes and John Andrews, and Vice Chancellor Roberts. He spoke to the Royal Society and was considered a great success. He gave radio talks and interviews with reporters. He was the prodigal son returned and it was a heady experience for him. From Sydney he visited Armidale, Melbourne and Hobart in Tasmania. His days were filled with luncheons, dinners and meetings. He spent a pleasant few days in Adelaide with his old friend Douglas Mawson. Mawson had indeed done well. He was now a "Sir." His new premises at Adelaide University had been named in his honor — the Mawson Geological Laboratory. Of all Grif's friends, he had remained the most active.

Grif then travelled to Western Australia where he gave four lectures in Perth. The *West Australia Times* reported a statement from one of his speeches:

> The empty lands of Canada offer greater settlement possibilities than do those of Australia (30).

He could not help noticing the change from the 1920s when his books were banned in Western Australia! Then it was north to Darwin before following the east coast south from Townsville to Brisbane — and in June back to Sydney for a formal dinner and on to Canberra. How different was the Canberra of 1948 from the one Grif knew in 1910, and how differently did the Australians greet Grif from those early days! He found he had showers of compliments for his earlier pronouncements on the future population of Australia, ideas that had been so unpopular twenty years previously. In Canberra, Grif met the Canadian High Commissioner and his diary of June 17 has the signature of the Prime Minister. He finally departed Australia on July 10 and was back in Toronto on July 15, after 30,000 air miles and five months of travel. For a man of 68, even a man with Grif's constitution, it had been an exhilarating but exhausting experience.

Even before going to Australia, Grif had begun work on one of his most important books *Geography in the 20th Century*. The initiative came from the Philosophical Library of New York which asked him to be the editor and gave him complete control in the matter of contents and authors. He enlisted the help of his friends, who were the outstanding geographers of the mid-century, so the list of authors is a "who's who" of geography at the time; Harrison Church, Samuel van Valkenburg, S.W. Woodridge, F.K. Hare, Stephen Visher, Isaiah Bowman, A.L. Washburn, Karl Pelzer, E.W. Gilbert, Dudley Stamp, Charles Fawcett, Ellsworth Huntington, J.K. Wright, J.K. Rose, H.C. Darby, Wreford Watson as well as his colleagues George Tatham and Donald Putnam. So, when he returned from Australia, he was immediately busy with *Geography in the 20th Century* and received manuscripts from Visher, Rose, Stamp, Gilbert, Church and Watson.

In September, Jacob Spelt from the Netherlands joined the department and in the year 1948-49, 980 people took geography courses. Grif welcomed graduate student Bill Wonders back from his travels in the Arctic to Cornwallis Island, where the base at Resolute was being built. Bill recalls that one day he brought his fiancee Lillian in to see the great man. Now Professor of Geography at the University of Alberta, a department that he founded, Bill recalls that meeting:

> In the midst of our conversation the telephone rang but it was nowhere in sight. I think Grif stood up and listened to it ring with his

167

head half cocked to one side rather like a robin. He glanced around the room which was almost totally inundated with papers. He then proceeded across the room and dug through them to emerge triumphantly with the telephone in time for him to give an answer. This made an indelible impression on Lillian's mind (31).

Also in 1949 the Taylors were very pleased, and Grif a little envious, to hear that Doris' brother, Ray Priestley, had received a knighthood. Grif had promised Doris that one day she would be a "lady." Time was slipping by and in 1951 he would be forced to retire. Ray visited Toronto in 1949 and invited Grif to come to Britain in 1950. Priestley had arranged a busy lecture tour for Grif under the auspices of the British Council. He lectured in the University of Birmingham where Ray was installed as Vice-Chancellor, and also in Edinburgh and Cambridge. He toured in his spare time — to Cornwall, to the Lake District, to London. And, as always when he travelled, he wrote to Doris every day and she faithfully wrote to him letters full of news of Toronto friends and departmental problems. She told him of a visit with George Tatham:

> He has a problem on his shoulders because Bird has been invited to take a job at McGill. George has seen [Dean] Beatty and felt it was such an unsatisfactory interview that he went right to the President himself and Smith gave him over half an hour to hear all sides. Bird feels Kerr has waited five years for promotion and sees no sign of it so how long would he too have to wait? Now the president is to see Bird himself (32).

However, the attempts to keep Bird in Toronto failed and he and Beryl left for Montreal and the department at McGill in 1951.

The British trip was strenuous and Grif was glad to arrive home in June 1950. He was not feeling well, and this was very unusual. On July 22 he was admitted to hospital for an operation for a bowel obstruction and discovered that he had cancer. For the first time since he was 21, Grif did not write in his diary. From July 22 until August 12 the pages are blank. He had blood transfusions and a relapse on August 24. He did not go to the University until October 3, and even then did not feel very well. There was a party in the map room to welcome him back, and Putnam and Tatham tried to cheer him by saying that there were plenty of troubles for him to clear up.

It was depressing for Grif to learn that Harold Innis and another friend, Professor Cassidy, also had contracted a similar cancer. They were all told that their days were numbered and that they had perhaps one to two years to live. This turned out to be true for Grif's two friends but he surprised his doctors by living for another 12 years! He was proven right when he wrote to Scott in 1909 that he came from hardy stock.

Understandably, Grif was depressed about his own future and he did not like the idea of retiring in May 1951. He confided to George Tatham that there was nothing more for him to do in life, and nothing left to write. George tried to cheer him up by saying that his important contribution would be to continue to make people *think*. The fact that he had also heard from the Royal Geographical Society that he was turned down for Fellowship did not help his frame of mind. His old friend Debenham, now director of the Scott Polar Research Institute at Cambridge, wrote that he could not understand the RGS. In October Grif started preparing for their departure from Canada. He wrote Cunard about tickets for Australia, and put up the house on Forest Hill Road for sale. The list price was $28,000, although he finally sold it for $23,000, a sum which satisfied him.

Sidney Smith, the President of the University, was concerned about the future of the geography department and the position of chairman was offered to British geographer Professor W.B. Fisher. However, Grif stated in his diary that a letter from Fisher indicated that he was "not keen on the job." President Smith then asked Ken Hare at McGill to accept the position, but Hare declined to come unless both Putnam and Tatham agreed. Putnam did not agree and finally the problem was solved by making Putnam and Tatham joint heads of the department.

During Grif's last semester, he was busy as usual — the best antidote for depression. His old friend Dudley Stamp visited the University and stayed with the Taylors. Grif was also busy completing his editing of *Geography in the 20th Century*, having received manuscripts from most of the contributors. He had asked his old friend Huntington to write the introductory chapter, but Huntington died before he could comply. Mrs. Huntington offered Taylor the last article her husband had written, "Geography and Aviation," which Taylor of course accepted for his book.

The book was published by the Philosophical Library in New York and by Methuen in England in 1951, the year the Taylors left Canada. It was the last major work Taylor completed in Canada and his last purely academic book. The objective, of course, was to discuss the status and philosophy of the discipline in mid-century. I think the book accomplished that purpose extremely well, perhaps better than a similar volume which appeared in 1954, *American Geography — Inventory and Prospect*. Two of the best chapters in Grif's book were those of George Tatham, "Geography in the Nineteenth Century" and "Environmentalism and Possibilism." Since Tatham was not a prolific writer, these two chapters are unique in presenting his well-thought-out philosophy of geography in the twentieth century. In the chapter on "Environmentalism and Possibilism," Tatham quite clearly explained the difference between the views of the earlier determinists such as Ratzel and Semple who spoke of environmental "control" and those of Griffith Taylor who, despite his earlier position, had come to believe in "Stop and Go determinism." He stated that Taylor believed that man has choice of action and his philosophy could equally be called "pragmatic possibilism." These arguments over labels seem much less important today.

169

Grif's contributions included chapters on the Antarctic, urban geography and geopacifics. It seems fitting that in this last academic book, Grif wrote on his first and last loves — the Antarctic and geopacifics. The book was very well received and is still a standard reference in the history of geographic thought.

On April 27 the department gave a farewell party for Grif. He described it thus in a letter to me, 7 May 1951:

> There was a big roll-up of old students, with Mrs. Zaks [Miss Brookstone] from Kitchener, and the two Birds from McGill. Dean Beatty unveiled a large portrait of G.T., which hangs on the north wall of the library — looking down grimly on students who dare to smoke in that room! The Dean told a story about an Australian orator (Nelson, M.H.R. for Darwin!) who dared to oppose Taylor's ideas, and pretty soon was lying on his back dying of thirst in central Australia. I hope this will lead my students to pay heed to my ideas about race, determinism, and geopacifics; though in this country it would be hard to find an appropriate desert, if they fall from grace.
>
> Tea and cakes were handed around by Miss Moore and helpers, and the latest development was to have — not only lots of wives, like Mrs. Taylor, and Tatham and Putnam, and uncounted student wives — but also four tiny tots of the third generation, who will we hope be students in a dozen years. (Mrs. Deacon, Spelt and Tatham brought their offspring).
>
> I give my last lecture tomorrow — appropriately on Geopacifics, which I have been developing in the last five years. I feel sure that only geographers can get the salient features of politics and strategy and economics and internationalism (in the form of simple maps) across to a nation in the limited time that is available to prevent world-wars. After all, Hitler and Haushofer with their geopolitics tried to do the similar job in propaganda — but for war, whereas we should be teaching for peace. However it has taken 30 years to put across various ideas of mine regarding deserts and races — and so I suppose geo-pacifics — if it is ever of general importance, will take the same time.
>
> On Wednesday night they are giving me an official dinner, when Dean Beatty warns me that some ragging will be indulged in. I must try to think of some comebacks.

On May 9, the University gave a big party for Grif. In addition to the geographers — Putnam, Tatham, Kerr, Wonders and Spelt — there were Dean Beatty and other associates and friends, among them Harold Innis of course, and Althouse of the Ontario College of Education. Grif's final convocation took place on June 8 in Convocation Hall and 13 Honours degrees in Geography were awarded. Especially pleasing to Grif was the awarding of Ph.D. degrees to Don Kerr and Bill Wonders (Fig. 20). In June, Putnam informed Grif that he had

Figure 20. Bill Wonders with Grif, after receiving Ph.D. degree June, 1951. (Photo from Bill Taylor)

been made the Honorary President of the new Canadian Association of Geographers. Sidney Smith, the President of the University of Toronto, also honoured Grif by making him a Professor Emeritus. On July 1 his diary noted, "Out of work," and on July 24, the Toronto newspaper the Globe ran an article, "Top geographer, University of Toronto professor, off to Australia . . . one of the world's leading geographers."

With Doris and son David, Grif sailed from Quebec on August 1. He had accomplished a great deal in his 16 years in Canada. He had travelled far and wide in his adopted country. He saw in Canada the same sort of challenges he had known in Australia, a chance to demonstrate that human settlement should be planned to fit the resources of the environment. Whereas in Australia his interpretation of nature's plan ran afoul of popular opinion because it gave too small a population, not more than 30 million, he disturbed Canadians by forecasting that Canada might easily accommodate 50 million people.

He had worked hard to establish the department in Toronto as a solid department, the first department in a Canadian University. In 16 years the department had grown from a single professor — Taylor — to one with six professors — Putnam, Tatham, Kerr, Bird, and Spelt. The Honours program was well established and hundreds of students took the general geography courses. The department was straining its allotted space in the old MacMaster

Building on Bloor Street and would soon be moved to spacious new quarters in Sidney Smith Hall.

Grif's students liked and respected him, as is obvious from their statements quoted in this chapter. Under his gruff exterior, he was a warm and friendly human being. He was genuinely interested in their welfare. That is obvious from reading his diaries, in which he noted the marks they obtained in individual term papers, and statements about their good and bad points. He obtained graduate scholarships for them and summer jobs. He wrote glowing testimonials to obtain employment for them and most important, he passed on to them his enthusiasm for geography and his unflagging curiosity about the world. Consequently they graduated with a zeal to work in the new geography: Kerr at Toronto, Ruggles, Reeds and Gentilore at McMaster, Ruggles later at Queens in Kingston, Wonders at the University of Alberta, and Innis at the State University of New York at Geneseo.

Grif had tried very hard to promote geography in high schools but felt that he had failed. He confided to his diary:

> In my most sincere effort, I feel that I have failed, for after 16 years of pleading, I can see no signs of any change of status for geography in the schools of Ontario (33).

Yet, a few years after Grif's retirement, the situation had changed and high school geography examinations were written by 2,500 Ontario students. The chief examiner and chairman of the examining group were both former students of Grif's. He could be justly proud of his accomplishments.

Grif's writings during these years earned him an international reputation. He was never afraid to tackle interesting global problems. He prophesied the future course of settlement in Canada and future population. He wrote stimulating books on the relation between history and the environment and the geographical factors affecting world peace.

However, Canadians with a few exceptions seem to have forgotten Grif. In Australia there is a building at the University of Sydney named for him; his picture hangs in a place of honour; and the Geographical Society of New South Wales has inaugurated a Griffith Taylor Memorial Lecture. Such honour is not obvious in Canada. George Tomkins in 1965 wrote his Ph.D. dissertation on Grif's contributions to geography, and several articles about him written by David Jones have appeared in the *Toronto Star*. It is time that his contribution to geography in Canada is more generally acknowledged.

It is probable that Grif never thought of any of these things as he sailed from Quebec. He was not in the habit of looking back on his life. He looked to the future. He was keen to see his relatives and friends in England, and live again in the pleasant climate of Sydney, Australia.

References

1. Griffith Taylor. Private Diary, 1935.
2. University of Toronto. Cody Papers. Annual report. 1936.
3. Camsell, Charles: "What Geography Means to Canada." *Canadian Geographical Journal* Vol. XI, no. 5, 1935, pp. 214-216.
4. Taylor, Griffith. "Geography the Correlative Science". *Canadian Journal of Economics and Political Science*, Vol.I, November, 1935, p. 536.
5. Marshall, Ann: "Griffith Taylor's Correlative Science," 1972. p. 192.
6. Taylor, Griffith: *Environment and Nation.* University of Toronto Press, 1936, p. 545.
7. Taylor, Griffith: *Environment and Nation*, p. 537.
8. Taylor, Griffith: *Environment and Nation*, p. 418.
9. Tomkins, George: "Griffith Taylor and Canadian Geography," pp. 214-221.
10. Letter from Reeds to author, 1983.
11. Taylor, Griffith: *Environment, Race and Migration*, University of Toronto Press, 1937, p. 459.
12. University of Toronto. Fisher Rare Book Room Manuscript Collection 20, Box 4.
13. Griffith Taylor. Private Diary, 1939.
14. Taylor, Griffith: "Trente to the Reschen Pass - A Cultural Traverse of the Adige Corridor," *Geographical Review*, Vol. 30, 1940, p. 237.
15. Taylor, Griffith: "Cultural Geography along the Rome - Berlin Axis," *Canadian Geographical Journal*, Vol. 20, 1940, p. 301.
16. Letter from Reeds to author, 1983.
17. Tomkins, George: "Griffith Taylor and Canadian Geography," p. 234.
18. Letter from Taylor to Preston James, July 7, 1941. University of Toronto, Fisher Rare Book Room, Manuscript Collection 20. Box 4.
19. Griffith Taylor. Private Diary, 1942.
20. Letter from Ruggles to author, 1984.
21. University of Toronto, Fisher Rare Book Room, Manuscript Collection 20, Box 3.
22. Griffith Taylor. Private Diary, 1944.
23. University of Toronto, Fisher Rare Book Room, Manuscript Collection 20, Box 3.
24. Taylor, Griffith: *Our Evolving Civilization.* University of Toronto Press, 1946, p. 361.
25. Interview with George Tatham. Tape, University of Toronto, Thomas Fisher Library.
26. University of Toronto, Fisher Rare Book Room, Manuscript Collection 20, Box 11.
27. Letter from Innis to author, 1984.
28. Letter from Bird to author, 1984.
29. National Library, Canberra, MS 1003/6/20.
30. *West Australia Times*, May 15, 1948.
31. Letter from Wonders to author, 1984.
32. University of Toronto. Thomas Fisher Rare Book Room. Manuscript Collection 20, Box 28.
33. Griffith Taylor. Private Diary, 1951.

CHAPTER 11

Retirement

Grif, with Doris and son David, arrived in Liverpool and had an enjoyable holiday touring England and Scotland, and visiting the Priestley relatives. Grif visited his Antarctic friend Cherry-Garrard and talked of old times before the family left England for Australia on the steamship *Oronsay* on August 23.

The Taylors were met in Sydney by Bill and Dot. Grif wrote in his diary that it was pleasant to come home to "the best climate in the world, to relations and old friends." Bill had been looking for a house for his parents and showed them the one he had chosen across the bay from Sydney at Seaforth, 28 Alan Avenue. Grif and Doris liked the house with its lovely garden, and lived there for the years that were left to them. Grif described their location in a letter to me, January 1952:

> We live in a brick bungalow about 5 miles due north of the centre of the city. But we are on Seaforth Bluff, 200 feet above Middle Harbour, and are quite isolated from the madding crowd. Unfortunately we are also quite isolated from rapid transport! and have to walk a mile to get a bus or tram to town. A mile or so around us are solid suburbs, but our outlook is to wooded hills; not touched since Cook's visit in 1770. I suppose all will be a mass of red-roofed bungalows in 20 years. I manage to grow good vegetables, and my wife is keen on flowers. Our fruit trees died from flood last year, and drought this year; plus the horrible fruit-fly, which has wiped out orchards around Sydney.

Grif enjoyed working in the garden with its peach, apricot, lemon and fig trees. What a change from Toronto!

Grif continued to live his life in retirement as he had when he had been employed. He wrote every day, setting himself an allotted number of pages, kept up his voluminous correspondence, and did manual labour of some kind. He and Doris played bridge every week and went to the movies. He went to the University of Sydney and met old friends.

Grif found that one of his old friends, Marcel Aurousseau, was living nearby in Seaforth. The latter had also retired to Sydney after a geographic career which included working with Bowman at the American Geographical Society in New York, and lived there until April 1983. Grif and Doris often walked over to the Aurousseaus' for bridge or tea and Marcel accompanied Grif to meetings of the Geographical Society of New South Wales.

In October Grif was invited to speak to the Science Society of the University of Sydney and gave the following advice to the young scientists, "Make notes all the time, travel all you can," and he spoke of the great debt he owed to his friend

Sir Edgeworth David. But he made new acquaintances also. The novelist Nevil Shute and Grif began a correspondence that lasted until Grif's death. Among the Australian geographers Oskar Spate became a good friend. During the twelve years that Grif lived in Australia, he was visited by many American and Canadian geographers, since any geographer who visited Australia naturally wished to see the great man.

In retirement Grif continued his considerable output of books and articles (Fig. 21). Two very popular books appeared in 1953 and 1954, *Southern Lands* and *Lands of Europe and Asia* with Dorothy Seivewright and Trevor Lloyd. The royalties from his many books provided a welcome addition to Grif's income, and he carefully noted the amounts in his diaries.

Grif was very pleased to have his earlier views of the Australian climate vindicated. Australian geographer Langford-Smith wrote in an article entitled "Economic Resources of Australia" in 1951:

> G.T. some 30 years ago, drew attention to the limitations which climate imposes on the development of Australia. His views were unpopular at the time, and raised quite a storm of criticism — in fact in 1924 he was publicly censured in the Commonwealth Parliament. There is irony in the fact that if due notice had been taken of his investigations there would have been enormous savings in Government expenditure thrown away in fruitless efforts to develop areas that are now known as "marginal" or even "desert" (1).

Grif also kept in touch with events in Toronto. He heard from Professor Wilkinson in June that Donald Putnam was confirmed as the head of the department of geography. He also heard in November that Harold Innis had died, and he was saddened by the death of his old friend. Harold and Mary had been good friends in Toronto. Mary Quayle Innis, who was a successful writer herself, became Dean of Women at University College at the University of Toronto and kept in touch with the Taylors until they died. Their son, Donald Quayle Innis, also kept up his correspondence with Grif until the latter's death.

In April 1952, Grif started writing his autobiography which he eventually entitled *Journeyman Taylor*. It was his last book to be published although there was to be another *Journeyman* which never appeared in print. By April 1953, he had finished his book, 1114 pages, quite an accomplishment in one year. Grif sent the manuscript to Methuen, but to his surprise and disappointment they turned it down. In May, Grif met a most enterprising young man Alasdair MacGregor, who persuaded Grif to let him undertake the editing and publishing of the book. Grif liked him — a vegetarian and teetotaler. But the co-operative venture was not entirely satisfactory and in the years before the book was finally published by Hale in 1958, Grif had cause to regret his decision.

On 26 March 1954, Grif received a letter from Robert Hale saying that he would publish the autobiography, before he had even seen it. After seeing it, Hale wrote that the chief readers suggested that the manuscript should be cut from 250,000 words to 100,000 words, since the best part of Grif's story, the Antarctic chapter, had appeared in print before. MacGregor wrote Grif in November,

> You will remember that I was mainly interested in bringing you and the publisher together. What he expected from you was the autobiography of a man famous in the world of science — a really first class autobiography, which of course, I have to say to you my dear Grif, is just what the present work is *not*. It will have to be largely rewritten.

By this, MacGregor meant that he would do the rewriting and continued to Grif:

> Naturally you would have to approve my handiwork but I should have to have a modicum of payment (2).

Grif sent money to MacGregor and months passed, and then years, and Grif never saw the manuscript. The senior Hale died and his son took over the business and it was years until the book was finally published.

In June 1953, when he was 73, Grif was ill again — and he did not have much patience with sickness. However, he realized he had reached the "threescore and ten" milestone and had some thought of death. In his diary he stated:

> Do our minds have any continued existence after death? Curious that Christians don't say how eternity is to be spent.

and again:

> We all hope to permanently affect the direction of civilization — become immortals (3).

Grif was pleased to have a letter in August 1953, from Pierre Camu who was president that year of the two-year-old Canadian Association of Geographers, saying that he had been made a permanent Honorary President of the Association. He wrote Pierre Camu the following:

> I am very gratified that you have elected me a permanent Honorary President of the Canadian Association of Geographers. My interests in Canada have by no means ceased, and it may interest the members of the Association that my Presidential Address to the geographers at the Aus. Assoc. Adv. Science — to be given at Canberra in a few months — consists of a comparison of the resources of the two great Dominions of Canada and Australia.
>
> Geography has gone ahead a good deal in the universities of Australia in the last few years, and many folk are kind enough to say that my lengthy tour of Australian Universities in 1948 contributed to this desired result.
>
> I much miss my pleasure in lecturing to earnest students after 50 years of such work. However I gave a course of 12 lectures to

engineering graduates at the new University of Technology in Sydney, during May and June; and I trust I may continue this course next year.

With renewed thanks (4).

In 1954, the meeting of the Australian Association for the Advancement of Science was held in Canberra and Spate was the chairman. Grif attended the meeting and was elected its first president. Shortly afterwards, the Queen and the Duke of Edinburgh were in Sydney where the Queen gave a charter to the Australian Academy of Science. She stated that it had been 300 years since Charles II had given a charter to the Royal Society. Sixty-four fellows were elected to the Academy, among them Sir Douglas Mawson and Griffith Taylor. Grif gave a copy of his book *Australia* to the Duke of Edinburgh, and was pleased to receive the following letter,

> Government House, 6-2-54,
> I have been instructed by the Duke of Edinburgh to thank you most sincerely for your book Australia which His Royal Highness is delighted to accept.
> Yours sincerely, Michael Parker (5).

It would have been the perfect time for Grif to receive a knighthood, but it did not happen, and when approval was finally given it was too late for Grif to be a "Sir," or Doris a "Lady" as he had promised her!

In 1954, Dorothy persuaded Grif to have his portrait painted. The artist, Doris Toovey, produced a very fine portrait which Dorothy donated in 1962 to the Geography Department of Sydney University. It now hangs in the Great Hall of the University. Grif wrote to her in August, 1962:

> Dear Dorothy: It is very generous of you to donate the portrait by Doris Toovey to the Geography department at Sydney. Our mutual unfriend devoted his first months in Sydney to rooting out memories of my unworthy self, including the best demonstrator in geography — my sister, with discourtesy in the latter case which I have never known equalled. He did little to enhance geography and has not left many admirers in our discipline (6).

It seems a shame that in his later years Grif dwelt so much on what he believed to be a slight from his successor in the department of geography, Macdonald Holmes. Perhaps Holmes had erred in getting rid of Dorothy but it was so long ago.

Grif never lost touch with his Antarctic friends and the Cherry-Garrards visited Australia in 1955 — the last time that Grif saw Cherry. They discussed the Scott expedition, of course, and after 40 years were candid with each other. Cherry-Garrard spoke of Scott's "sense of failure." Four years later, in December 1959, Grif heard of Cherry's death and that he had left an estate of some £400,000. In a letter to Grif, Frank Debenham wrote of Cherry:

Figure 21. Grif in retirement in Sydney. Probably 1955. (Photo from Bill Taylor)

He was a very much altered man from what we knew at Cape Evans and I rather lost patience with him of recent years.

Deb also kept in touch with the Antarctic crowd and gave news of the others to Grif:

Sunny Jim is still moderately active although very hard of hearing. Saw Silas [Wright] in Vancouver and gave him a shock since I had an angina attack while talking to him (7).

Grif, as always, was interested in the press and in February 1956 wrote to the editor of the *Seaforth Morning Herald*. His letter was acknowledged in the paper thus:

The stencilled sheet was signed by one of Australia's most famous men, Professor Griffith Taylor the Geographer. But when I read it, I found it mainly about sewerage, road safety and the painting of bus shelters. You see, he's also the honorary secretary of the Seaforth Progress Association (8).

That same month, at 75 years of age, Grif began a new book. He had always wanted to write about Sydney, the city that he considered the most beautiful in the world. The book was completed in December 1956 and published in 1958 as *Sydneyside Scenery*. It was very different from Grif's earlier books. His purpose in writing this book was to combine the fields of geology, geography and history for the benefit of the intelligent layman. He was successful in showing the interrelatedness of man's physical environment and the economic and social pattern of his existence. He drew on his notes from his early researches in the Sydney area before he went to the Antarctic, as well as his field research in the 1920s.

Grif dedicated this, his last book, to the memory of Sir Edgeworth David. It proved to be a successful book and a new edition was published in 1970. In this later edition, Professor J.A. Mabbutt of the University of New South Wales wrote a 28-page introduction about Grif, his life, and how he came to write the book. He said of Grif,

Griffith Taylor was a man of outstanding character . . . . and in reading this book we learn something of his enthusiasm for his subject, his restless individualism, his compulsive wish to teach, and of his great interest in the interrelationships between man and his physical environment . . . . It is not difficult in this later day to criticize the book on technical grounds . . . . but these faults still leave much of merit. The residual value of Sydneyside Scenery is that it expresses with such clarity the personal force and charm of its author (9).

It was a measure of the respect that Taylor inspired that he was invited at the age of 77 in 1957 to give a series of 50 lectures at the University of Queensland in Brisbane. He described his time in Brisbane in a letter to me:

I have just finished a course of 50 lectures at the new University in Brisbane. It is a huge quadrangle of cut-stone buildings 3 stories high, with lovely cloisters on the inner side. A doctor gave about 100 acres in a bend of Brisbane River, 5 miles West of the city, and 3 colleges are already erected near the University. I lived in Cromwell College (Congregational). There are 64 students in it, and one-third are Asians. It was fine to see the Malays and Chinese mixing in all activities, and sitting at meals on equality in every way. This result of the Colombo plan will do more to promote world peace than missionaries or books on Geo-pacifics!!!

Brisbane was a very dusty city, since they have missed their summer monsoon. (We have also missed our usual autumn rains here in Sydney — probably from the same break in the inflow of wet tropical air from the north). Brisbane has lovely poinciana trees like huge green umbrellas with lovely big red flowers in the season. Their big fig trees are handsome trees too — very close to the Indian Banyan. Gerberas and crucifixion plants were the commonest garden flowers — I don't know if you know them. Mango trees line some of the roads, and bananas and pawpaws are found in every garden. I was surprised to see fields of strawberries near Nambour, and a big jam factory near Buderim. Here we were stranded 20 miles from anywhere, when our axle snapped on a steep hill. However we were picked up later, and managed to reach Brisbane in an 85-mile taxi ride — which cost a little as you may imagine.

He was also involved with the new generation of geographers of New South Wales. That December he led a field trip to Mt. Kosciusko for the department at Sydney. The mountain, the highest in Australia, was very special to Grif and he wrote in his will that he wished to be cremated and have his ashes scattered over Mt. Kosciusko.

In 1958, Grif was pleased that the Antarctic was again in the news and on January 3 noted in capital letters in his diary, "HILLARY AT POLE." He was asked to be on television to comment on Hillary's expedition, but he refused, probably because he realized that he was becoming hard-of-hearing. He noted also that on January 19, Fuchs reached the Pole and on March 2 that Fuchs was at the Scott base. Grif wrote to Washburn on 18 November 1958:

pleased to find that they have named the new weather base in Mac Robertson Land 161° E Taylor — a glacier and a penguin rookery close by have the same name (10).

In March, on the anniversary of Edgeworth David's birth, he wrote in his diary in a philosophical mood, obviously thinking that the time left to him was short:

Life isn't joy and it isn't sorrow. It's something one gets through and if you ask me how — I can only say that we have to, and that's the end of it (11).

However, he still had problems to solve with his writing. He was displeased to hear from the junior Hale that his book *Journeyman Taylor*, when finally printed would contain a map. He wrote Hale, April 1957:

> I am perplexed by the phrase "illustrations and map." I hope this is a slip since my reputation as a scientist depends largely on my use of maps, I have pointed this out ad nauseam to your father and to Mr. MacGregor (12).

The final version of *Journeyman* did indeed appear with one map and Grif was not at all pleased. In July he was very upset to receive the proofs of the book — with 53 misprints and irrelevant photos — and in August he wrote to publisher Hale about changes free from "MacGregor's high handedness." Grif complained that he had never seen page proofs of *Journeyman Taylor* and wrote to Hale in September:

> I am afraid "very amusing" is not the way I view Mr. MacGregor's treatment of my illustrations. I feel it reasonable to ask that 8 of my photographs replace 8 of MacGregor's which have little bearing in my story (13).

The book as it finally appeared is not worthy of Grif. The illustrations in *Journeyman* are indeed irrelevant and it is certainly not obvious why MacGregor included them. They do distract from Taylor's interesting story. The book was based on diaries kept meticulously year after year, and is strictly factual. The great exponent of determinism is seen himself to be the product of possibilism, his life shaped by series of accidental happenings such as the casual invitation which led to his participation as geologist in Scott's Antarctic Expedition (1910-12) and the regulations of the Exhibition Commissioners which led to his two years at Cambridge. Dudley Stamp, the premier British geographer of the time said of the book:

> No serious geographer should miss the opportunity of reading Griffith Taylor's Autobiography — the life seen by himself of one of the most stimulating if controversial figures of our time. For the mind of Grif is evolution in action, producing plenty of sprouts destined to wither and die, plenty of sound ideas a generation before their time, still others such as his climographs — so apt as to be absorbed immediately into current thought and literature (14).

In October 1958, Grif's great friend Douglas Mawson died, and the number of "Antarctickers" remaining became few. But Grif managed a reunion, which was to be their last, with Debenham and Priestley at the Australian Association for the Advancement of Science meetings in Canberra in 1959.

182

Grif realized that he was getting older and becoming deaf, and tried a hearing aid, but although it slipped off his ear and was a bother to turn on and off, it did not slow him down. In April 1959, he was awarded an honorary degree by the University of Sydney and he noted the procedure in his diary, recalling the similar occasion in London when he received the Antarctic medal from King George. Also in 1959 the Institute of Australian Geographers was formed and Grif was elected the first president. In a letter to me January 1960 he wrote:

> In a week or two I go to Melbourne for the inaugural meeting of the Institute of Australian Geographers. We have 50 professional fellows, and no one is eligible without original research. So things have changed lately. No less than six full profs in geography have been appointed in the last two years, so that the subject is now receiving the attention it deserves. My address is "Geographers and World Peace" — along the lines of the Cultural Geography which you know about. I hope that geographers will realize that they are in a better position in education than most folk — to link science with human problems involved in war and peace. I haven't made many converts in geography, but now geographers can expand a bit, and are recognized, I hope they will take up this branch fairly generally. Geopolitics spread like mad with some evil encouragement. Why shouldn't Geo-pacifics do likewise? We all want peace.

Oskar Spate and Macdonald Holmes were vice-presidents of the new Institute. Grif wrote to Doris about the meeting:

> I couldn't hear anybody except in the front row. I'm the last rose of summer . . . but I finished in a blaze of glory. Greenwood (my room mate) said I made the congress. Spate at the end called for special claps. Said he never before had the founder of Geography in a country live to preside at the first modern Congress on the subject (15).

Grif sent a copy of his speech to Prime Minister Menzies and received this reply dated 20 December 1960.

> Thank you for sending me a copy of the Presidential address given by you to the Australian Institute of Geographers. I note that you have recently reached your 80th birthday. Please accept my congratulations and my thanks for your distinguished work (16).

His talk was published in the first volume of *Australian Geographical Studies* in 1963, as "Geographers and World Peace."

In June of 1959, in his 80th year, Grif began writing his last book, the one that was never published, that he titled *Journeyman at Cambridge*. He finished the manuscript by December — 90,000 words, and sent it off to his publisher Hale in London. In 1960, he was disappointed that Hale declined to publish it. Grif probably realized that he would not have time to find another publisher so sent the manuscript to the Scott Polar Research Institute in Cambridge where it is kept with the rest of the Taylor material.

Grif was concerned about his voluminous correspondence and journals and wondered where to send them. He finally decided that the bulk of the material should go to the National Library in Canberra, and they agreed. When he was in his 80th year, he was invited to open the new geography department at the University of New England at Armidale. In appreciation, he gave them some of his Antarctic material.

The year 1960 marked the 50th Anniversary of the Scott Expedition and there was a party at the Scott Polar Research Institute on November 26. Grif was invited, of course, but since he could not go, he recorded a speech and sent it to Cambridge. Director Robin sent the anniversary pictures to Grif, noting that three members of the expedition were there, Debenham, Simpson, and Priestley.

In August 1960, when he was almost 80 years old, Grif tried to prove to Dr. Barbara Moore, a professional pedestrian, that he could walk to Canberra. He trained for weeks by taking 20-mile walks each day. The day he set off from Sydney he managed to walk 21 miles, to Liverpool, to find that the first hotel he went to turned him away because of his unkempt appearance. The next day he reached Narellan, another 17 miles. However, that was as far as he got. He became very weary and although hating to admit defeat, took a train home. He described his walk in a letter to Silas Wright:

> I tried to copy our 1910 walk to London. I planned to do 20 miles a day but 2 days was all I could manage. I returned home and had a sprained Achilles tendon for 2 months. I did plenty of practice beforehand, all to no purpose. So I guess I'll have to stick to writing cards and novels from 80 on (17).

Grif spent a good deal of time that year sorting his letters and papers and arranging to send them to various libraries. In a letter to me in January 1960, he wrote:

> I am now in my 80th year, but still going strong I am glad to say, for I find that writing keeps me busy. I have published 2 books, part of another, and finished the mss. of the third in the last couple of years. Mostly biographical, which seem to please the critics in the geog. journals. I don't know who will want to publish a book on my life at Cambridge — but it keeps me busy, and that's the main reason. Last year I led an excursion some 50 miles away, which involved a good deal of tramping; and may do a similar one for the Geog. Soc. next April.

In April 1961 he was honoured by the bronze medal of the Royal Society of Australia. In May he spoke of World Peace at a conference in Brisbane and in

June he gave three radio talks on the Scott expedition. In one of these talks he stated: "If he had taken dogs, Scott would have lived." To the end, Grif was interested in the Antarctic and one of his last publications was a review of Sir Edmund Hillary's *No Latitude for Error* in 1961. It was published in *The Australian Geographer* and in it Grif stated:

> With his [Hillary's] huge Snocats he had the same time available as had Scott to reach the vicinity of Mount Erebus. There was no undue risk of his motor caravan being delayed into the terrible weather of the end of March . . . To the reviewer, the receipt by Hillary of his wife's letter on the high Plateau, only 2 days after it left New Zealand, is the most striking commentary on the changes in Polar Exploration since 1911 (18).

In his latter years, letters were more than ever important to Grif. All his life he had written at least ten letters a day, keeping them all in his files and answering each one noting the date of his answer. He frequently heard from Debenham, Priestley and Wright. Wright had visited the Antarctic that year and sent Grif a picture of the Taylor glacier. Grif replied:

> I thought with my 20 mile a day walk at 79 I would beat all you folks, but I did too much I guess for I've not been able to do much but scrap books since. Thank goodness I can still read and play bridge (19).

Grif confessed in a letter to Oskar Spate October 25 that he was slowing down:

> I've done 6 publications at 82, so you live and do more at that age. Now I've nothing to do until I touch the century, if such is to be my fate. I don't get out of the house nowadays, so I fear I shall not get to Armidale again (20).

In January 1963 he finished an article — a piece for the Royal Geographical Society on the possible disintegration of Antarctica. He wrote to a friend in May 1963:

> I have just sent back proofs of a short article, probably my last, to the London RGS. "The probable disintegration of Antarctica." I have gradually begun to realize that Wegener (whose house I visited in Graz) was right in the drift ideas (21).

Grif was correct. It was his last published article, again a novel and stimulating one, and published several years before the theory of plate tectonics illustrated that Wegener was right in his ideas of continental drift.

In March, Professor Holmes wrote to Grif that the new Geography building at the University of Sydney was to be called the Griffith Taylor Building. Holmes evidently still worried about the old feud with Grif:

> This is excellent and may do something to redress what you deemed a wrong when your sister left the department. Your sister's dismissal

from the department had been planned before I came to Australia. There is not the least doubt about that (22).

Obviously, the question of Dorothy's dismissal had been bothering Professor Holmes for all those years, and he wanted to exonerate himself in Grif's eyes. Grif was surprised and sent the letter to Dorothy asking her how he should reply. She answered with her typical common sense:

May 19, 1963

I have to thank you for your championship of my ancient cause. I remember the facts quite vividly. The bitterness no longer remains. I am sorry for the mean soul that Holmes has to carry around with him. We are all getting too old for hard feelings. Professor Dury has nice thoughts about you. I think it is lovely to have a GT building (23).

With this good advice, Grif's answer to Professor Holmes was this:

March 24, 1963

I appreciate your pleasant opinions regarding the naming of the new Griffith Taylor Building. Since it is now some 30 years back to the controversy as to my sister's resignation from her position in the geography department, and as we are both 80 years old now, it seems useless to discuss the matter. You and I are unlikely to have much to do with each other in the future (24).

In June he wrote to Lady Mawson:

I get giddy and rather tired quickly these days — although I can read all day and sleep all the rest of the time. I used to write at least a book a year but I had to give all that up about a year ago. I have spent much of the last year in collating all my letters (25).

In August, he suffered a bad fall and broke three ribs. Although Doris looked after him for a while at home, she finally had to take him to the hospital in Manly in October. His mind was clear and active up to the last weekend. Doris wrote in a letter to me 5 March 1964 that:

I had shown him a photo during his last week of his name on the outside of the new Geography building at the University of Sydney. It gave him great pleasure and satisfaction.

On 18 October 1963, Grif wrote to Mrs. Middleton at the Royal Geographical Society in London,

I shall reach 83 in a couple of months. My doctor does not hope for much activity in the future. Journeyman Taylor has done all his travels (26).

186

Grif's last letter was to Debenham, his oldest and probably dearest friend. Dated October 23, it reads:

> I fear my geographic research is over. I have read lots of novels the last being Queed which Professor David sent me as a present in December 11 on the Terra Nova. I fancy David thought it might do me good. There are resemblances in his career and my own.
>
> They have just named the new Geography department after me. Dury appreciates my work, and my old opponent with 33 years of running geography since 1928 has been rather ignored as far as I can judge, while my rather gloomy ideas of arid Australia have met with universal approval (27).

For 2 and 3 November 1963, the writing in Grif's diary is illegible and the page for November 4 has, in Doris' writing, the entry

> Grif died today about 5:30 a.m.

References

1. Langford-Smith, G: "Economic Resources of Australia," *Regional Development Journal*, 1951, pp. 11-25.
2. National Library, Canberra, MS 1003/8/59.
3. Griffith Taylor. Private Diary, 1953.
4. Griffith Taylor. Private Diary, 1953.
5. Griffith Taylor. Private Diary, 1954.
6. National Library, Canberra, MS 1003/8/341.
7. National Library, Canberra, MS 1003/8/578.
8. *Seaforth Morning Herald*. Feb. 9, 1956.
9. Taylor, Griffith. *Sydneyside Scenery*. Angus and Robertson, Sydney, 1958, p. xxx-xxxi.
10. National Library, Canberra, MS 1003/8/341.
11. National Library, Canberra, MS 1003/8/249.
12. National Library, Canberra, MS 1003/8/250.
13. National Library, Canberra, MS 1003/8/258.
14. Stamp, Dudley: *Review of Journeyman Taylor. Geographical Journal*, March, 1959.
15. Griffith Taylor. Private Diary, 1959.
16. National Library, Canberra, MS 1003/8/350.
17. Griffith Taylor. Private Diary, 1961.
18. Taylor, Griffith: Review of "No Latitude for Error," *Australian Geographer*, Vol. 8, no. 3, 1961, p. 140.
19. Griffith Taylor. Private Diary, 1962.
20. Griffith Taylor. Private Diary, 1962.
21. National Library, Canberra, MS 1003/8/452.
22. National Library, Canberra, MS 1003/8/452.
23. National Library, Canberra, MS 1003/9/220.
24. National Library, Canberra, MS 1003/9/221.
25. Griffith Taylor. Private Diary, 1963.
26. Griffith Taylor. Private Diary, October 1963.
27. National Library, Canberra, MS 1003/9/229.

CHAPTER 12

Taylor's Contribution to Geography

Doris wrote the month after Grif died:

> The house is so very quiet without him ... I have had some wonderful tributes and kind messages from so many old students.

His old friend Marcel Aurousseau, who knew Grif well, said:

> He deliberately provoked discussion because it forced people, especially students, to think hard and even to develop convictions. He admired conviction ... and it is, in fact, very easy to find fault with his work in matters of detail. But the man was like Bernard Shaw, a perennial fountain of ideas and he was a teacher who aroused lasting interest in geography in several generations of students (1).

I talked to Aurousseau about Grif in Sydney in 1980 and he said that he believed Grif received honours far less than his due. He thought it was interesting that the research student who began as an invertebrate paleontologist became in the end an advocate of what he called "geopacifics" (2). The new generation of Australian geographers had gotten to know Grif when he retired to Australia. John Andrews spoke for them when he wrote:

> To most Australian geographers, the passing of Griffith Taylor marks the end of a chapter in Australian geography .... one of the giants who established geography in the Universities, an international figure of extraordinarily wide-ranging achievements in research; and for his knowledge, his humanity and his friendliness he was respected and loved .... We shall remember Grif for many things: his maps, ... the fertility in ideas, ... his kindness to the young and the interested .... the bigness of mind (3).

Another Australian geographer, Ann Marshall, who first knew Grif from his early years in Toronto, wrote the obituary for the *Geographical Review*:

> The quality of greatness is indefinable, but it is unmistakable. With the death of Griffith Taylor on November 5, 1963, geography, and particularly Australian geography, lost a great man. To most of us in Australia he has always been there, an almost legendary figure, continually in the midst of some battle of ideas. To those who worked with him his death means not only the loss of a great geographer; it means also the loss of a great friend (4).

189

An Australian who was neither an academic nor a geographer also wrote about Grif after he died. D'Arcy Niland, a journalist with the Australian magazine *Walkabout*, had written two articles in 1962 about the Scott Expedition. The byline read, "As told to D'Arcy Niland by Professor Griffith Taylor." Niland had spent many days with Grif, and had gotten to know and admire him during his last years, and in April 1964, after Grif's death, wrote another article for *Walkabout* entitled, "Griffith Taylor, a man for all seasons." Even at the age of 82, Grif communicated to Niland his love of geography as the keystone of the edifice of mankind, and Niland remembered him thus:

> I saw the physical crumbling of a great frame and the slow run-down
> of a dynamo. But I never saw capitulation to the defects of age and
> illness. He travelled, he wrote, he lectured, he taught and he walked.
> He always had to have something to do. He put the globe at his feet
> and searched it for what it had to tell him (5).

In England the *Geographical Journal* carried a short obituary, followed by a note by Raymond Priestley who said:

> The world of geography has lost one of its outstanding and most
> colorful personalities . . . He was one of those rather infuriating
> persons who is always certain he is right and unfortunately for his
> neighbour's peace of mind, usually is (6).

In Canada, Donald Putnam was asked to write Grif's obituary for the *Canadian Geographer*. "Putty" as he was known to a generation of Canadian geographers, grasped, I think, the essence of Taylor as a geographer:

> To Canadian geographers, his death marks the end of an era. Taylor
> was a pioneer, and a pioneer was needed to set Canadian geography
> on its feet (7).

Only two years earlier, I had written to Putty to ask him his assessment of Grif's contribution to geographic thought, and I quote from his letter to me:

> He put a spoke into nearly every wheel in the machine. He was
> intensely stimulating, whether you agreed with what he was saying or
> not.

John K. Rose, Grif's student at Chicago and in 1964 a geographer at the Library of Congress, wrote of his old friend in the *Annals of the Association of American Geographers*:

> Griffith Taylor was possibly the most controversial person the field
> of geography has produced . . . His enthusiasms, his curiosity, and
> his wide range of friends were notable, he was crisp but not
> unemotional . . . He was an unusual man not overpowering in
> physique but with "presence"; his high degree of energy and vigor,
> both physical and mental, continued little diminished at later life (8).

It is noteworthy that Grif's Australian fellow-geographers have continued to praise him. John Andrews in 1966 edited a book entitled *Frontiers and Men — a Volume in Memory of Griffith Taylor*. In it, Raymond Priestley wrote:

> No-one could know Grif without being aware of him as a man of unusual quality and parts. He was very sure of himself and his opinions and had reason so to be. He was one of these rather annoying people who are quite certain their own particular view of a problem is the right one and are the more aggravating because they are often correct in so thinking, certainly if the problem happens to be in their own field of specialization. Very few people of his generation made a greater impact on his particular subject of which he was the first professor both in Australia and Canada (9).

In 1972, on the occasion of the 50th anniversary of Grif's founding of the Department of Geography at the University of Sydney, Oskar Spate gave the Griffith Taylor memorial lecture "Journeyman Taylor: Some Aspects of his Work." Spate thought Grif's *Environment and Nation* his best book. He knew Grif personally only after Taylor's return to Australia, past his 70th birthday, but he had read enough Griffiana to have seen the true Grif. The following quote is from Spate's article:

> By god, the old boy had tremendous intellectual guts. A lot of this [referring to *Geography in the 20th Century*] may be nonsense, some is certainly sense; . . . The elements were very mixed in Griffith Taylor; but they made an interesting human person, mentally alive and acute, honest, courageous, resilient. We shall not soon see another like Grif (10).

Another Australian geographer, Joe Powell, wrote the article "Thomas Griffith Taylor" for *Geographers: Bio-Bibliographical Studies* in 1978. He believed that Taylor was never so bravely or completely deterministic as some authors claimed, even if he liked to think of himself as an "enfant terrible."

> It was Taylor's capacity for hard work and his personality as much as any real intellectual achievements which made such a huge impact on the growth of geography during his lifetime. The unique qualities of the man himself must stand out in very bold profile in any interpretation of the geographical profession over the past 50 years (11).

In Canada not much has been written about Grif, with the exception of George Tomkins' Ph.D. thesis "Griffith Taylor and Canadian Geography" in 1965. Although Tomkins never knew Grif personally, he stressed the contribution of the man to Canadian geography:

> It could be said of Griffith Taylor that "he builded better than he knew" and that his shadow would be cast across the Canadian geographic landscape for many years to come (12).

Some twelve years after Grif's death, Donald Jones, a free-lance writer in Toronto, wrote an article in the *Toronto Star* describing Grif's ideas of Canada's future and concluded:

> It is only now, that Griffith Taylor is being considered a prophetic genius who may have been the first to accurately foretell the future of Canada (13).

In summing up Taylor's contributions to science in general and to geography in particular, we should begin with his work as chief geologist in the Antarctic with the Scott expedition. His geological work included the detailed topographic mapping of that part of Antarctica called Victoria Land. This detailed mapping, done with primitive equipment and with the help of fellow-geologist Frank Debenham, laid the foundation for a description of the Antarctic continent which was not surpassed until the age of aerial photography.

Grif was interested, as both a geologist and geographer, in the then-unknown structure of the Antarctic continent. He developed the theory that Antarctica resembled Australia in its structure, consisting of four elements, low shield, line of plateaux, downfold and young mountains. He regarded the mountains of West Antarctica as a continuation of the South American Andes, the faults and blocks of the Ross Sea area like those of southeast Australia, and Victoria Land and East Antarctica as bearing a close resemblance to the granite shield of West Australia. These theories have been corroborated by more recent findings. In 1959 the American glaciologist Neuberg explored the hinterland of the Filchner Ice Shelf and adopted Taylor's thesis for this downfold area and the upthrust blocks across the continent. It has also been verified that East Antarctica is mainly a low shield area like West Australia, as Taylor had predicted.

Taylor was also found to be correct in his interpretation of the Ferrar glacier and the Taylor arm of that glacier. American and New Zealand geologists reported in 1960 that the upper Ferrar glacier, as it had been called, should actually be the upper Taylor glacier as Taylor had stated in 1911.

Although he had been trained in geology, Taylor called his scientific field "physiography", that area of science between geology and geography which studied the action of wind, frost, water and ice upon the landscape. Before going to Antarctica, he had believed in Davis' theory that the primary agent of erosion in that continent was ice, but his first-hand investigations changed those beliefs. He realized that the issue was a complex one and that frost, wind and water action were also important in moulding that continent — a novel idea at the time and one corroborated by later investigation.

The Antarctic experience succeeded in establishing Taylor's reputation in physiography. His next job experience at the Weather Bureau in Australia established his reputation as a climatologist. He was never interested in weather forecasting, but he was intrigued by the relationship between climate and crops and climate and settlement. He was the first to write of Australian climate and drew the first climatic maps of Australia. In doing so, he pointed out the dry nature of much of Australia and made many enemies among Australian politicians and boosters. However, his climatic papers laid the foundation for the study of Australian climate on which others would build and his ideas of the "empty heart of Australia" were finally vindicated. It must be realized, however, that the criticism really bothered Taylor and was the reason that he decided to leave Australia in 1928.

During the years 1921 to 1928 while Grif was the first Professor of Geography at the University of Sydney, he made his mark in another area of scholarship, anthropogeography. Grif's work in climatology and his friendship with Ellsworth Huntington and admiration for Huntington's work encouraged him to write his book *Environment and Race* in 1927. This book was probably his most controversial and earned him a reputation beyond the realm of geography. His Zones and Strata Theory, borrowed from geology and applied to race and culture was an innovative and interesting concept, earning him an admiring reply from world figures such as H.G. Wells and H.L. Mencken. Taylor's belief in climate control, and the importance of the physical environment to man's development would be re-stated and redefined throughout his lifetime and earn for him the title of environmental determinist.

Grif spent only seven years at the University of Chicago and his writings during the period 1928-1935 did not contribute a great deal to his geographical reputation. He refined his definition of geography at Chicago, since at that time it was defined as a liaison subject with status both in physical and social sciences, a concept that has been lost in many modern departments. In Chicago, he began work on his book *Environment and Nation* which was published in Toronto and was considered by many geographers to be his best work.

It was during his 16 years at the University of Toronto that Taylor made his greatest contributions to geography. He began his Canadian career auspiciously, with the founding of the first geography department in Canada, one that has achieved a world reputation and whose graduates established geography departments in universities across Canada. In Canada Taylor was considered an explorer not of distant and unknown places only, but of new and unfamiliar ideas as well. While he placed great emphasis upon the physical facts of geography he thought of geography basically as the study of civilization.

His next book *Environment Race and Migration* was perhaps the most popular since it contained his philosophy of environmental or "stop and go" determinism, earning him a world reputation as an anthropogeographer. Probably the reason this book was so successful was because of Taylor's imaginative concepts and his ability to integrate all the fragments of knowledge which he had gathered during his travels on all the continents and carefully recorded in his detailed journals.

During his Toronto years, Grif turned his attention to urban geography, a new branch of his discipline. His lively curiosity about settlements in Canada resulted in a study of environment and settlement which was one of the first books to be titled *Urban Geography*. It was the third in a series which included *Environment and Race* and *Environment and Nation*. His last major work while in Canada was editing *Geography in the Twentieth Century*, a book which is the classic description of the status and philosophy of geography in the mid-20th century and which is stimulating both for Grif's choice of authors and for his imaginative editing.

Grif's two books published in Australia after his retirement illustrate a different Taylor. His autobiography, as I have mentioned, does not do him justice since it was badly cut and changed by his editorial assistant Alasdair MacGregor. But *Sydneyside Scenery*, his gift to the people of the city he loved best, will remain a monument to that city's premier geographer.

In all, Taylor wrote some 20 books and hundreds of papers, and kept up a voluminous correspondence, in addition to his daily journals. It is obvious that geography never lost its fascination for him. He had a curiosity about the world which made every subject he researched of absorbing interest. He also had that quality of intuition which allowed him to integrate the knowledge he amassed during his long career to formulate ideas that were interdisciplinary and controversial.

Why is Grif remembered? What made him a great geographer in Canada and in Australia? It is perhaps because in Canada as in Australia, he was the pioneer, willing to do battle for what he believed to be the role of geography in the university, in education in general, and in national and world affairs. Quite simply, he believed that a knowledge of the physical environment is essential to understanding the history of mankind. He believed that geography is neither a natural science nor a social science but that its field lies between the domains of those subjects and its point of view is unique. He agreed with University of Toronto President Cody's view that geography is the "description, localization and explanations of the facts which relate man to his physical environment" and had an unremitting devotion throughout his lifetime to the advancement of his chosen subject.

Taylor started his career as a geologist and perhaps for that reason, when he became a geographer he never lost sight of the role of the earth, the "ge" in geography. As Niland said, "He put the globe at his feet and searched it for what it had to tell him." His curiosity about the world was insatiable.

Grif will be remembered, too, because he was a colourful character, and in comparison, he makes most geographers look pale! His colleagues agreed that he was intensely stimulating and gave him their personal loyalty, responding by being creative, hardworking and enthusiastic. Yet the man was kind and generous to his staff and students and his personality was more gentle than his vigorous writing. He was a happy man.

And he worked hard. Not many geographers of his era, or any era, can claim 20 books and 200 articles to their credit. He loved his chosen field. As noted earlier, in the Antarctic, he chose as the motto for his sledging flag *Expergiscamine* which he translated as "get a move on." He lived up to this motto during the 83 years of his life. His influence on geography will be enduring, not only because what he did was interesting and important, as well as geographical, but because of his personal honesty and magnetism.

This book has been about an explorer, a geographer, a writer, but in the final analysis, it is the story of a human mind — a mind that never stopped questioning, that stretched beyond the furthest horizons.

References

1. Aurousseau, M. "Obituary: T. Griffith Taylor, 1880-1963," *The Australian Geographer*, Vol. XIV, 1964, pp. 131-133.
2. Aurousseau, M. "Obituary: Professor Griffith Taylor, F.A.A." *Nature*, February 1964, pp. 555-556.
3. Andrews, John. "Obituary: Griffith Taylor 1880-1963," *Australian Geographical Studies*, Vol. II, no. 1, 1964.
4. Marshall, Ann: "Obituary: Griffith Taylor 1880-1963," *Geographical Review*, Vol. 54, 1964, pp. 427-429.
5. Niland, D'Arcy: "Griffith Taylor. A man for all seasons," *Walkabout*, Vol. 30, no. 4, April 1964, pp. 17-30.
6. Priestley, Raymond: "Obituary: Thomas Griffith Taylor," *Geographical Journal*, Vol. 130, 1964, pp. 189-190.
7. Putman, Donald: "Obituary Griffith Taylor," *Canadian Geographer*, Vol. VII, pp. 197-200.
8. Rose, J.K: "Obituary Griffith Taylor," *Annals, Association of American Geographers*, Vol. 54, 1964, p. 624.
9. Priestley, Raymond in *Frontiers and Men*. John Andrews, ed. F.W. Cheshire and Co, 1966, p. 4.
10. Spate, Oskar: "Journeyman Taylor: Some Aspects of his Work." *The Australian Geographer*, Vol. XII, no. 2, 1972, p. 122.
11. Powell, J: "Thomas Griffith Taylor" in *Geographers: Biobibliographical Studies*, 1978, pp. 141-146.
12. Tomkins, George: "Griffith Taylor and Canadian Geography," p. 485.
13. Jones, Donald: *The Toronto Star*, November 7, 1979.

APPENDIX I

Documentary Materials

1) The Taylor Collection in the National Library of Australia, Canberra

The collection (MS 1003) is extensive, comprising 48 boxes of material organized into 13 series: (1) Early years 1880-1910, (2) Antarctica 1910-1912, (3) Canberra and surrounding district 1910, 1912-1913, (4) Commonwealth Weather Service and Sydney University, 1913-1928, (5) Chicago University, 1929-1935, (6) Toronto University, 1935-1951, (7) Australian Institute of Geographers, Australian Academy of Science and A.N.Z.A.A.S., (8) Retirement, 1951-1963, (9) Scrapbooks, 1880-1963, (10) Wanderyears, 1907-1915, (11) Manuscripts and Proof Copies, (12) Publications, (13) Miscellaneous. The magnitude of the collection is seen from the library's descriptions, as below:

Series 1   Early Years, 1880-1910

Correspondence, field notebooks, press clippings, photographs, maps, sketches etc. relating to Taylor's early years, first as a schoolboy and later as a student at Sydney University and at Cambridge. The series includes extensive correspondence between Taylor and the various members of his family which contain a detailed account of his travels in the Pacific, North America and Europe as well as in Australia. Further material from this period may be found in series 9 and 10.

Series 2   Antarctica, 1910-1912

Correspondence, diaries, notebooks, press clippings, photographs, maps, sketches etc. relating to Taylor's work as Senior Geologist with the British (Terra Nova) Antarctic Expedition. He also held the position of Physiographer with the Federal Meteorological Service during this period. The series includes a diary of day to day events, sledging diaries and other material giving details of the two sledging journeys of the Western Party of which Taylor was the leader, and extensive correspondence between Taylor and his family and friends giving detailed descriptions of conditions in Antarctica and comments on the various members of the expedition. There are also manuscripts of articles by Taylor for the *South Polar Times* and the manuscript of *With Scott: The Silver Lining*, and four original drawings by David Low for the book *With Scott: The Silver Lining*. The series also contains material relating to glacial studies in Europe and New Zealand in preparation for the expedition. Further material relating to Taylor's work in the Antarctic may be found in series 9 and 10.

Series 3   Canberra and Surrounding District, 1910, 1912-1913

From 1912 to 1913, Taylor, as Physiographer with the Federal Meteorological Service, participated in a survey of the Federal Capital Site. The series includes a Report of geology along the proposed railway to Jervis Bay, and material relating to the opening of Canberra on 13 March 1913. There is also a field notebook of a physiographic survey of the capital site made by Taylor in 1910, photographs of early Canberra, and correspondence between Taylor and his family and friends. Further material may be found in series 9 and 10.

Series 4   Commonwealth Weather Service and Sydney University, 1913-1928

Correspondence, maps, field notebooks, newspaper articles and clippings, sketches, photographs, reviews etc. relating to Taylor's career in the Commonwealth Weather Service till 1920 and at Sydney University from 1920 to 1928. During this period he travelled widely in Europe, South Africa, New Zealand, Japan and the Pacific as well as in Australia. There is extensive correspondence between Taylor and the various members of his family giving detailed accounts of his travels and including much scientific observation. The material reflects Taylor's special interest in the problems of settlement in tropical and in arid areas in Australia. It also illustrates Professor David's influence on the development of Taylor's career. Further material from this period may be found in series 9 and 10.

Series 5   Chicago University, 1929-1935

This series is mainly correspondence, much of which is between Taylor and his family containing detailed accounts of his work as Senior Professor of Geography at Chicago University, and of his travels in North America, the Pacific, Australia and Great Britain. There is also correspondence of a more general nature including material relating to the publication of various books and articles. As well as the correspondence, there are lecture notes, field notebooks, press cuttings, maps, photographs, etc. Further material covering this period may be found in series 9.

Series 6   Toronto University, 1935-1951

Correspondence, press clippings, photographs, maps, field notebooks, etc. relating to Taylor's work as head of the new Department of Geography at Toronto University. During this period he maintained his usual extensive correspondence with his family and friends giving detailed accounts of his work and his travels in North America, Europe and Australia. The correspondence also relates to numerous articles and books written by Taylor during this period. Further material may be found in series 9.

Series 7   Australian Institute of Geographers, Australian Academy of Science and A.N.Z.A.A.S.

After his retirement in 1951, Taylor returned to Australia. In 1961 he became the first President of the newly-constituted Institute of Australian Geographers. Most of the correspondence relates to his work for this organization, and to his work for the Australian Academy of Science. There is also material relating to his interest in A.N.Z.A.A.S.

Series 8   Retirement, 1951-1963

Correspondence, press cuttings, articles, maps, photographs, etc. relating to Taylor's life in Sydney after his retirement. The series consists largely of correspondence relating to various publications, particularly to his autobiography *Journeyman Taylor*. Further material may be found in series 9.

Series 9   Scrapbooks, 1880-1963

Scrapbooks containing correspondence, press cuttings, photographs, pamphlets, notes, manuscripts of articles and reviews, field notebooks, diagrams, sketches, etc. covering the period from 1880 to 1963. Much of the correspondence is personal and includes many letters between Taylor and his family while on various journeys and field trips to many parts of the world. The correspondence also reflects the development of Taylor's career, his interest in various geographical and scientific societies, and the publication of his many books and articles.

Series 10   Wanderyears, 1907-1915

A series of letter books containing carbon copies of letters written by Taylor and bound together to form 6 volumes which he has called Wanderyears. It was Taylor's practice to keep a record of his travels in the form of copies of letters sent mainly to his family giving detailed descriptions (often containing geographical and geological data) of places he had visited. The series covers the years 1907 to 1915 when Taylor travelled extensively in Europe, South Africa, North America, Antarctica and the Pacific. Although most letters are to his family, they frequently contain a record of observations of a scientific nature. Also included are copies of some more general correspondence and a few press cuttings, pamphlets, etc.

Series 11   Manuscripts and Proof Copies

Manuscripts and proofs of many of the books and articles written by Taylor, some of which are unpublished. Many of them are incomplete.

Series 12   Publications

Some of the many books, articles, reviews, etc. written, edited, or contributed to by Taylor, most of which are autographed or annotated. There are also some books and articles by other authors. Most of the reprints of Taylor's own articles have been collected together and bound.

Series 13   Miscellaneous

Various unidentified photographs, maps, sketches, press clippings, etc.

2) University of Sydney, Australia

The Thomas Fisher Rare Book Library has two boxes of Taylor material which date from pre-1928 and were given by Taylor to the Library before he went to Chicago (as listed below).

(1) Notebook containing T.G.T.'s notes on Professor David's lectures on physiography in 1899 *mss.* (2) Notebook containing T.G.T.'s third year notes from Professor David on Australian geology in 1902 — "a fair summary of the science at that date." *mss* (3) *Mss* of first geographical paper, published in Linnean Society of N.S.W., 1906, on Correlation of contour, climate and coal. (4) First public lecture on ethnology, entitled, "The antiquity of man", given to the Sydney University Science Society (1906?). *Typescript.* (5) Working notes at the Sedgwick Museum, Cambridge, as 1851 Exhibition Science Research Scholar. These were published later in the large quarto memoir of the Archeocyathinae by the Royal Society, South Australia, 1910. *mss* (6) First *mss* of the two papers on Climate control, published in American Geographical Review, N.Y., 1919 and 1921. (7) An attempt at a short story, written at Cambridge in 1909, entitled, "Wydotter and I go mammoth hunting" (The King's School Magazine, May 1922). *Printed* (8) First sledging diary, early in 1911. (Basis of chapter in *Scott's Last Expedition*, and of *With Scott: The Silver Lining* 1916). *mss* (9) Antarctic sledging diary, 1911-12: the Granite Harbour journey. Typescript (10) Notebook used in hut of T.G.T.'s study of glacial topography, 1911. *mss.*

(11) Original surveys by Geological party, based chiefly on Debenham, traced by T.G.T. in the Antarctic hut, 1911. *Drawings* (12) *Photograph,* 29th Jan. 1911, "Packing the sledges," with signatures, C.S. Wright, Frank Debenham, P.O. Evans, Griffith Taylor. (13) Page proof of "Antarctic book by an Australian Commonwealth Official," i.e. page proof of *With Scott: The Silver Lining*, by Griffith Taylor, (with plates and drawings) 17 Aug. 1915. *Printed* (14) Original sketches by T.G.T. as basis for David Low's drawings in "With Scott," including a letter to Low about the

drawings. *Drawings* (15) Queensland, Parliamentary paper, 1881. "Geological survey of Northern Queensland." *Printed*

3) University of Toronto

The Robarts Library at the University of Toronto, Fisher Rare Book Room (Manuscript Collection 20) has 28 boxes of Taylor material.

Box (1) contains Australian material, notes, papers, books, and revised galleys of books; (2) Articles and other material relating to Australia and the S.W. Pacific including correspondence re the Australian banning of Taylor's book "Australia — physiographic and economic" in 1921; (3) notes and MSS of "Our Evolving Civilization" and the Messenger lectures on civilization at Cornell University; (4) page proofs of "Environment and Race" and reviews of this book; his addresses to the British Association for the Advancement of Science, Cambridge, 1938 and his presidential address to the AAG New York, 1944; (5-8) notes, draft copy, maps, galleys and page proofs of the book, "Environment and Nation"; (9-11) notes, page proofs, maps of "Urban Geography"; (12-13) Canada — MSS — draft and notes, page proofs, and galleys; (14) miscellaneous, block diagrams of polar regions, articles on Canada; (15) MSS of "Geography in the 20th Century" (16) Typescripts of articles by various authors and also some letters; (17) additional page proofs of "Geography in the 20th Century"; (18) photographs and other illustrative material; (19) lecture notes in climatology; (20) sketch book and note books on Canada, and The Geographical Laboratory; (21) unbound copy of Antarctic Adventure and Research 1930, lecture to Sydney University Engineering Club in 1948 and other European articles; (22-27) reprints of some 40 articles of Taylor's — from 1920s to 1940s; (28) miscellaneous letters and papers, including the dinner menu of the Cambridge Philosophical Society at St. John's College, Cambridge 1909.

Other sources of Taylor material at the University of Toronto are:

Cody Papers, Papers of Canon Henry J. Cody, President, University of Toronto (1932-1945). University of Toronto Archives, Acquisition No. A42 (A-68-006).

Falconer Papers. Papers of Sir Robert A. Falconer, President, University of Toronto (1907-1932). University of Toronto Archives, Acquisition No. A10 (A-66-003).

Mavor Papers. Papers of James Mavor. Professor of Political Economy, University of Toronto (1892-1923). University of Toronto Rare Books Collection.

APPENDIX II

Griffith Taylor's Published Works

1903 "Geology of Mittagong," with D. Mawson, *Journal Royal Society of New South Wales*, XXXVII, 309-350.

1905 "The Occurrence of Pseudomorph Glendonite in New South Wales," with T.W.E. David, *Geological Survey of New South Wales*, VIII, 161-72.

1906 "The First Recorded Occurrence of Blastoidea in New South Wales," *Proceedings Linnean Society of New South Wales*, XXXI, 54-59.

1906 "A Striking Example of River Capture in the Coastal Districts of New South Wales," with W.G. Woolnough, *Proceedings Linnean Society of New South Wales*, XXXI, 546-54.

1906 "A Correlation of Contour, Climate and Coal: a Contribution to the Physiography of New South Wales," *Proceedings Linnean Society of New South Wales*, XXXI, 517-29.

1907 "The Lake George Senkungsfeld, A Study of the Evolution of Lakes George and Bathurst, New South Wales," *Proceedings Linnean Society of New South Wales*, XXXII, 325-45.

1907 "Coral Reefs of the Great Barrier, Queensland: A Study of Their Structure, Life Distribution and Relation to Mainland Physiography," 379-413. *Report of the Eleventh Meeting of the Australian Association for the Advancement of Science.* Adelaide, South Australia: The Association.

1907 "Preliminary Notes on the Archaeocyathinae from the Cambrian 'Coral Reefs' of South Australia," 423-37. *Report of the Eleventh Meeting of the Australian Association for the Advancement of Science.* Adelaide, South Australia: The Association.

1906 *The Physiography of the Proposed Federal Territory at Canberra, Australia.* Bureau of Meteorology, Bulletin, No. 6. Melbourne, The Bureau, 18pp.

1910 "The Archaeocyathinae from the Cambrian 'Coral Reefs' of South Australia, with an Account of the Morphology and Affinities of the Whole Class," *Memoirs Royal Society of South Australia*, II, 55-188.

1910 "Meteorological Divisions of the Australian Commonwealth." *Australian Monthly Weather Report*, I, 151-4.

1911 *The Physiography of Eastern Australia*, Bureau of Meteorology, Bulletin No. 8. Melbourne: The Bureau, 18 pp.

1911 "The Geology and Petrography of the Prospect Intrusion," with H. Stanley Jevons, H.I. Jenson and C.A. Sussmilch, *Journal Royal Society of New South Wales*, LXV, 445-553.

1911 "Salient Features of the Climate of Western Australia," *Australian Monthly Weather Report*, II, 176-84.

1911 *New South Wales: Historical Physiographical and Economic*, with A.W. Jose and W.G. Woolnough. Edited by T.W. Edgeworth David. Melbourne: Whitcomb and Tombs Limited, 372 pp.

1911 *Australia in its Physiographic and Economic Aspects*. Edited by A.J. Herbertson. Oxford: The Clarendon Press, 256 pp.

1912 "Review of Recent Research on Weather Cycles," *Australian Monthly Weather Report*, III, 261-262; 469-71.

1913 *Climate and Weather of Australia*, with H.A. Hunt and E.A. Quale. Bureau of Meteorology. Melbourne: The Bureau.

1913 *Report on a Geological Reconnaissance of the Federal Territory (with special reference to available building materials)*, with D.J. Mahony. Department of Home Affairs. Melbourne. The Department.

1913 "The Western Journeys," *Scott's Last Expedition*, Volume II. L. Huxley, editor. London: Smith, Elder, 182-290.

1913 "A Resume of the Physiography and Glacial Geology of Victoria Land, Antarctica," *Scott's Last Expedition*, Volume II. L. Huxley, editor, London: Smith, Elder, 416-29.

1914 "Short Notes on Palaeontology," with E.H. Goddard, *Scientific Report of the British Antarctic Expedition 1907-9*, Vol. I. London Heinemann.

1914 "The Physical and General Geography of Australia," *Federal Handbook . . . 84th Meeting of the British Association for the Advancement of Science in Australia*, August, G.H. Knibbs, editor. Melbourne, 86-121.

1914 "Physical Features and their Effect on Settlement," *Oxford Survey of the British Empire*, Vol. V, A.J. Herbertson and O.J.R. Howarth, editors. Oxford: The Clarendon Press, 34-91.

1914 "Climate and Weather," with H.A. Hunt, in *Oxford Survey of the British Empire*, Vol. V, A.J. Herbertson and O.J.R. Howarth, editors. Oxford: The Clarendon Press, 91-139.

1914 "Mining and Economic Geology," in *Oxford Survey of the British Empire*, Vol. V, A.J. Herbertson and O.J.R. Howarth, editors. Oxford: The Clarendon Press, 216-67.

1914 "Antarctica, the British Sector," in *Oxford Survey of the British Empire*, Vol. V, A.J. Herbertson and O.J.R. Howarth, editors. Oxford: The Clarendon Press, 518-38.

1914 "Evolution of a Capital, A Physiographic Study of the Foundation of Canberra, Australia," *Geographical Journal*, XLVIII, (April), 378-95; XLVIII (May), 536-54.

1914 "Physiography and Glacial Geology of East Antarctica," *Geographical Journal*, XLIV (October), 365-82; (November), 452-67; (December), 553-71.

1914 *A Geography of Australasia*. Edited by A.J. Herbertson. Oxford: The Clarendon Press, 176 pp.

1915 *Climatic Control of Australian Production: An Attempt to Gauge the Potential Weather of the Commonwealth*, Bureau of Meteorology, Bulletin No. 11. Melbourne: The Bureau. 32 pp.

1916 *Initial Investigations in the Upper Air of Australia.* Bureau of Meteorology, Bulletin No. 13. Melbourne, The Bureau. 16 pp.

1916 *The Control of Settlement By Temperature and Humidity With Special Reference to Australia and the Empire: An Introduction to Comparative Climatology.* Bureau of Meteorology, Bulletin No. 14. Melbourne: The Bureau. 32 pp.

1916 "What we Australians Are Up Against," *Inlander* III, 50-71.

1916 *With Scott: The Silver Lining.* London: Smith Elder, 464 pp.

1916 *The World and Australasia; Adapted for use in Australasian Schools With a Special Section on Australasia* (with O.J.R. Howarth). Edited by A.J. Herbertson, Oxford: The Clarendon Press, 423 pp.

1917 "Geographical Factors Controlling the Settlement of Tropical Australia," *Proceedings, Queensland Branch, Royal Geographical Society of Australasia.* Brisbane: The Society, 32-3; 1-67.

1917 "Antarctic Geology," *The Mining Magazine* XVII (December) 262-69.

1918 *The Australian Environment, Especially as Controlled by Rainfall — A Regional Study of the Topography, Drainage, Vegetation and Settlement and of the Character and Origin of the Rains.* Memoir No. 1, The Advisory Council of Science and Industry. Melbourne: The Council. 188 pp.

1918 *Atlas of Contour and Rainfall Maps of Australia.* Melbourne: The Advisory Council of Science and Industry.

1918 "Climate Factors Influencing Settlement in Australia," *Commonwealth Year Book*, No. 11. Melbourne: Government of Australia, 84-101.

1918 "The Settlement of Tropical Australia," United States Department of Agriculture, Weather Bureau, *Monthly Weather Review*, XLV (December), 589-90.

1919 "The Physiographic Control of Australian Exploration," *Geographical Journal*, LIII (February), 172-92.

1919 "Air Routes to Australia," *Geographical Review*, VII (April), 256-61.

1919 "The Settlement of Tropical Australia," *Geographical Review*, VII (August), 84-115.

1919 "Climate Cycles and Evolution," *Geographical Review*, VIII (December), 289-328.

1919 "Air Routes to Australia," United States Department of Agriculture, *Monthly Weather Review*, XLVII (February), 78-80.

1919 "Scientist in the Antarctic," *Victorian Naturalist*, XXXVI, 5-10.

1920 "The Physiographic Control of Settlement," *Australia, Economic and Political Studies*, M. Atkinson, editor. Melbourne: The Macmillan Company, 304-37.

1920 "Agricultural Climatology of Australia," *Quarterly Journal Royal Meteorological Society*, XLVI (October), 331-55.

1920 "A Geologist's Notes on Water Divining," *Proceedings, Royal Society of Victoria*, XXXIII, 79-86.

1920 "Nature Versus the Australian," *Science and Industry* (Melbourne), II, 459-72.

1920 Australian Meteorology: *A Text-book Including Sections on Aviation and Climatology.* Oxford: Clarendon Press, 312 pp.

1921 "The Evolution and Distribution of Race, Culture and Language," *Geographical Review,* XI (January), 54-119.

1922 "Some Geological Notes on a Model of the National Park at Mt. Field, Tasmania," *Proceedings Royal Society of Tasmania 1921.* Hobart: The Society, 188-98.

1922 "The Distribution of Future White Settlement, A World Survey Based on Physiographic Data," *Geographical Review,* XII, 375-402.

1922 "Land Settlement in Australia," *New Outlook,* I, 9-11.

1922 *British Antarctic (Terra Nova) Expedition 1910-13: The Physiography of McMurdo Sound and Granite Harbour Region.* London: Harrison, 246 pp.

1923 "Introduction," *Willis Island, a Storm Warning Station in the Coral Sea.* John King Davis, editor. Melbourne: Parker, 1-9.

1923 "The Warped Littoral Around Sydney," *Journal. Royal Society of New South Wales,* LVII, 58-79.

1923 "The Blue Mountain Plateau." Pan-Pacific Science Congress Australia 1923, *Guide Book to the Excursion to the Blue Mountains and Lithgow.* Sydney: The Congress, 17-29.

1923 "Migration Zones around the Pacific," *Proceedings, Pan-Pacific Science Congress Sydney, 1923,* Vol. 1. Sydney: The Congress, 251-55.

1923 "Zoning of Australia and Causes Thereof," *Proceedings, Pan-Pacific Science Congress Sydney, 1923.* Vol.1 Sydney: The Congress, 256-58.

1923 "Theory of Migration Zones," *Proceedings, Pan-Pacific Science Congress, Sydney, 1923.* Vol. 1. Sydney: The Congress, 256-58.

1923 "Uninhabited Australia; and the Reasons Therefor," *Proceedings, Pan-Pacific Science Congress Sydney, 1923,* Vol. 1. Sydney: The Congress, 659-64.

1924 "Kamilaroi and White, A Study of Racial Mixture in New South Wales," with F. Jardine, *Journal Royal Society of New South Wales,* LVIII, 268-94.

1924 "Climatic Control of Wheat Production in Australia," Australasian Association for the Advancement of Science, *Report of the 16th Meeting,* 132-8. Wellington: The Association.

1924 "Geography and Australian National Problems," Australasian Association for the Advancement of Science, *Report of the 16th Meeting Wellington, 1924,* 433-87. Wellington: The Association.

1924 "Geographical Control of Australia's Resources," *Mid-Pacific,* XXVIII, 555-61.

1925 "The Kosciusko Plateau, a Topographic Reconnaissance," with W.R. Browne and F. Jardine, *Journal Royal Society of New South Wales,* LIX, 200-05.

1925 *The Geographical Laboratory*, (with Dorothy Taylor) Sydney: Sydney University Union, 78 pp.

1926 "The Frontiers of Settlement in Australia," *Geographical Review*, XVI, 1-25.

1926 "Scientific Travel in Australia," *Practical Hints to Scientific Travellers*, H.A. Brouwer, editor. Den Haag: Nijhoff, 73-110.

1926 "Scientific Travel in Antarctica," *Practical Hints to Scientific Travellers*, H.A. Brouwer, editor. Den Haag: Nijhoff, 111-42.

1926 "Notes on the Glaciation of Ruapehu," *Transactions of the New Zealand Institute*, 57, 235-38.

1926 "Natural Regions in New South Wales," Australasian Association for the Advancement of Science, *Report of the 19th Meeting*, 474-77. Perth: The Association.

1926 "Race and Nation In Europe," *Australian Journal of Psychology and Philosophy*, IV, 1-7.

1927 "The Topography of Australia," *Commonwealth Year Book*, No. 20. Melbourne: Government of Australia, 75-90.

1927 "The Resources of Australia," Institute of Pacific Relations, *Problems of the Pacific: Proceedings of Second Conference, Honolulu 1927*. Honolulu: The Institute, 489-95.

1927 "Australia as a Field for Settlement," *Foreign Affairs*, V, 679-81.

1927 *Environment and Race: A Study of Evolution, Migration, Settlement and Status of the Races of Man*. London: Oxford University Press, 354 pp.

1928 *European Migrations: Past, Present and Future*, Livingstone Lecture, Camden College. Sydney: The College. 43 pp.

1928 "The Natural Resources of Australia," *Studies in Australian Affairs*. P.C. Campbell, R.C. Mills and G.V. Portus, editors. Melbourne: Melbourne University Press, 1-26.

1928 "Agricultural Regions of Australia," *Proceedings Pan-Pacific Science Congress, Tokyo, 1926*, Vol. II. Tokyo: The Congress, 1657-62.

1928 "Glaciation in the South West Pacific," *Proceedings Pan-Pacific Science Congress Tokyo 1926*, Vol. II. Tokyo: The Congress, 1819-25.

1928 "Variations among the Australian Aborigine, with Special Reference to Tawny Hair," *Proceedings Pan-Pacific Science Congress Tokyo, 1926*, Vol. II. Tokyo: The Congress, 2386-95.

1928 "White and Black Races in Australia," *Pacific Affairs*, I (July), 1-3.

1928 "Climatic Relations between Antarctica and Australia," *Problems of Polar Research*, American Geographical Society Special Publication No. 7, W.L.G. Joerg, editor. New York: The Society, 285-99.

1928 "The Status of the Australian States, a Study of Fundamental Geographical Controls," *Australian Geographer*, I, 7-28.

1928 "Geography in Secondary Schools," *Education*, October 15, 395-397.

1929 "New Lands and Old Education," *Pacific Affairs*, II, 54-7.

1929 "This Human Family: Problems of Population and Migration as Discussed at the Harris Institute, University of Chicago, 1929," *Pacific Affairs*, II (September), 575-9.

1930 "Agricultural Regions of Australia," *Economic Geography*, VI, (April), 109-34; VI (July), 213-42.

1930 "Racial Migration Zones," *Human Biology*, II (February), 34-62.

1930 "The Control of Settlement in Australia by Geographical Factors," Institute of International Relations, *Proceedings of Sixth Session*, Vol. VI. Berkeley: The Institute, 207-18.

1930 "Antarctica, Some Political and Scientific Aspects," Institute of International Relations, *Proceedings of Sixth Session*, Vol. VI. Berkeley: The Institute, 230-35.

1930 "A Quantitative Forecast of Future White Settlement," Institute of International Relations, *Proceedings of Sixth Session*, Vol. VI. Berkeley: The Institute.

1930 "Admiral Byrd's Discoveries in Antarctica," *Science Newsletter*, XVII (June 21), 391.

1930 "Why Explore the Antarctic? Its Meaning for Pacific Lands," *Pacific Affairs*, III (July), 625-36.

1930 "Byrd's Scientific Achievement in the Antarctic," *Current History*, XXXII (August), 968-70.

1930 *Antarctic Adventure and Research*. New York: Appleton, 244 pp.

1931 "The Limits of the Australian Desert," *Gerlands Beitrage zur Geophysik*, XXXIII, 16-30.

1931 "Meteorology of the British Antarctic Expedition, 1907-1909," *Geographical Review*, XXI (April), 328-9.

1931 "Settlement Zones of the Sierra Nevada de Santa Marta, Colombia," *Geographical Review*, XXI (July), 536-58.

1931 "The Nordic and Alpine Races and their Kin, A Study of Ethnological Trends," *American Journal of Sociology*, XXXVII (July), 67-81.

1931 "The Margins of Geography," *The American Schoolmaster*, December, 55-61.

1931 *Australia, A Geography Reader, Including Chapters on New Zealand and Neighbouring Islands*. Chicago: Rand McNally and Company, 440 pp.

1932 "The Pioneer Belts of Australia," *Pioneer Settlement*, American Geographical Society Special Publication, No. 14. New York: The Society, 360-91.

1932 "Climatology of Australia" in W. Koppen and R. Geiger, *Handbuch der Klimatologie*, Band IV. V Koppen and R. Geiger, editors. Berlin: Borntraeger.

1932 "The Geographer's Aid in National Planning," *Scottish Geographical Magazine*, XLVIII (January 15), 1-20.

1932 "The Inner Arid Limits of Economic Settlement in Australia," *Scottish Geographical Magazine*, XLVIII (March 15), 65-78.

1933 "The Australian Environment," *Cambridge History of the British Empire*, Vol. VII, Cambridge: Cambridge University Press, 3-23.

1933 "The Soils of Australia in Relation to Topography and Climate," *Geographical Review*, XXIII (January), 108-13.

1934 "Environment and Nation," *American Journal of Sociology*, XL (July), 21-33.

1934 "Obituary, T.W.E. David." *The Australian Geographer*, II, No. 3, 5-6.

1934 "The Ecology Basis of Anthropology," *Ecology*, XV (July) 223-42.

1934 "The Block Diagram, and its Ecological Uses," *Recueil de travaux dedie par la Societe geographique de Lwow a Eugenjusz Romer*, 1-6.

1935 "Geography — the Correlative Science," *Canadian Journal of Economics and Political Science*, I (November), 535-50.

1935 "Aryan, German, Nordic, Jew," *The University of Chicago Magazine*, November.

1936 "Topographic Control in the Toronto Region," *Canadian Journal of Economics and Political Science*, II (November), 493-511.

1936 "The Geographical Approach to European History," in Canadian Historical Association, *Report of the Annual Meeting, Ottawa May 1936*, 78-89. Ottawa: The Association.

1936 "Fundamental Factors in Canadian Geography," *Canadian Geographical Journal*, XII (March), 161-71.

1936 "The Zones and Strata Theory — A Biological Classification of Races," *Human Biology*, VIII (September), 348-67.

1936 *Environment and Nation: Geographical Factors in the Cultural and Political History of Europe*. Toronto: University of Toronto Press, 571 pp.

1937 "The Possibilities of Settlement in Australia," *Limits of Land Settlement*. Isaiah Bowman, editor. New York: Council of Foreign Relations, 195-227.

1937 "The Distribution of Pasture in Australia," *Geographical Review*, XXVII (April), 291-4.

1937 "The Structural Basis of Canadian Geography," *Canadian Geographical Journal*, XIV (May), 297-303.

1937 "Comparison of the American and Australian Deserts," *Economic Geography* XIII (July), 260-68.

1937 "Review of An Historical Geography of England by H.C. Darby," *American Historical Review*, XXXVII (July), 702-04.

1937 *Environment, Race and Migration: Fundamentals of Human Distribution, with Special Sections on Racial Classification and Settlement in Canada and Australia*, Toronto: University of Toronto Press, 483 pp.

1938 "Correlations and Culture — A study in Technique," *Report of Annual Meeting, British Association for the Advancement of Science*, 103-38. Cambridge: the Association.

1938 "Correlations and Culture: A Study in Technique," *Nature*, CXLII (October 22), 737-41.

1938 "Correlations and Culture: A Study in Technique," *Scottish Geographical Magazine*, LIV (November), 321-44.

1938 "Correlations and Culture: A Study in Technique," *Pan-American Geologist* LXX (November), 241-62; LXXI (March), 81-106.

1938 "Climate and Crop Isopleths for Southern Ontario," *Economic Geography*, XIV (January), 89-97.

1938 *The Geographical Laboratory, A Practical Handbook for a Three Years' Course in North American Universities.* Toronto: University of Toronto Press, 1938, 107 pp.

1939 "Sea to Sahara: Settlement Zones in Eastern Algeria," *Geographical Review*, XXIX (April), 177-95.

1940 *Australia.* E.P. Dutton, Co. 455 pp.

1940 "Trento to the Reschen Pass: A Cultural Traverse of the Adige Corridor," *Geographical Review*, XXX (April), 215-37.

1940 "Cultural Aspects of Romania, Yugoslavia and Hungary," *Canadian Geographical Journal*, XX (January), 23-39.

1940 "Cultural Geography Along the Rome-Berlin Axis," *Canadian Geographical Journal*, XX (June), 287-301.

1940 "Structure and Settlement in Canada," *The Canadian Banker*, XLVIII (October), 42-64.

1941 "Mediterranean Pilgrimage, A Study of Ancient Sites," *Canadian Geographical Journal*, XXII (May), 222-35.

1941 "Geography at the University of Toronto," *Canadian Geographical Journal*, XXIII (September), 152-54.

1941 "Races of the World, A Discussion of Recent Classifications" *Human Biology*, XIII (September), 390-97.

1941 "The Climates of Canada," *The Canadian Banker*, XLIX (October), 34-59.

1941 *Australia, A Study of Warm Environments and Their Effect on British Settlement.* London: Methuen and Company, 455 pp.

1942 *The New Western Front, A Geographical Approach.* Canadian Institute of International Affairs, Contemporary Affairs Series No. 14. Toronto: The Ryerson Press. 27 pp.

1942 *Canada's Role in Geopolitics, A Study in Situation and Status.* Canadian Institute of International Affairs, Contemporary Affairs Series No. 16. Toronto: The Ryerson Press. 28 pp.

1942 "The Role of Geography," in F.L. Burdette (ed.) *Education for Citizen Responsibilities.* Princeton: Princeton University Press, 44-61.

1942 "Environment, Village and City: A Genetic Approach to Urban Geography, with Some Reference to Possibilism," *Annals of the Association of American Geographers*, XXXII (March), 1-67.

1942 "British Columbia, A Study in Topographic Control," *Geographical Review*, XXXII (July), 372-402.

1943 "Dynograph of World Industry," *Vital Speeches*, X (December 15), 144-47.

1944 *European Cultural Geography, A Guide to Reading.* Ottawa: Canadian Legion Education Services.

1944 "Geography and Nation Planning," in *Pioneering for a Civilized World, Report of the New York Herald Tribune Twelfth Forum on Current Problems, November 16 and 17, 1943.* New York: New York Herald Tribune Inc., 129-39.

1944 "Geography and Nation Planning," *Canadian Geographical Journal,* XXVIII (June), 281-85.

1945 "Towns and Townships in Southern Ontario," *Economic Geography,* XXI (April), 88-96.

1945 "The Seven Ages of Towns," *Economic Geography,* XXI (July), 152-60.

1945 "A Mackenzie Domesday, 1944," *Canadian Journal of Economics and Political Science,* XI (May), 189-233.

1945 "A Yukon Domesday, 1944," *Canadian Journal of Economics and Political Science,* XI (August), 432-49.

1945 "Town Patterns on the Gulf of Saint Lawrence," *Canadian Geographical Journal,* XXX (June), 254-75.

1945 "Corridors into Germany," *The Scientific Monthly,* LX, (May), 353-57.

1946 *Newfoundland: A Study of Settlement with Maps and Illustrations,* Toronto: Canadian Institute of International Affairs. 32 pp.

1946 "Future Population in Canada — A Study in Technique," *Economic Geography* XXII (January), 67-74.

1946 "Parallels in Soviet and Canadian Settlement," *International Journal,* I (April), 144-58.

1946 *Our Evolving Civilization: An Introduction to Geopacifics.* Toronto: University of Toronto Press, 370 pp.

1947 "The Geography of Canada" in "Features of Present Day Canada," *Annals of the American Academy of Political and Social Science,* CCLIII (September), 1-9.

1947 "Review of Engineering and Society" by C.R. Young, H.A. Innis and J.H. Dales. *Annals of the American Academy of Political and Social Science,* CCLIII (September), 202-3.

1947 "A Mackenzie Domesday, 1944," in C.A. Dawson (ed.) *The New North-West.* Toronto: University of Toronto Press.

1947 "A Yukon Domesday, 1944," in C.A. Dawson (ed.) *The New North-West.* Toronto: University of Toronto Press.

1947 "Zones de Colonizacion en la Sierra de Santa Marta (Columbia)," trans. Eduardo P. Bermudez, *Boletin Sociedad Geografica de Colombia,* VII, 400-418.

1947 *Canada, A Study of Cool Continental Environments and Their Effects on British and French Settlement.* London: Methuen and Company, 524 pp.

1947 *Canada and Her Neighbours,* with Dorothy J. Seivewright and Trevor Lloyd. Toronto: Ginn and Company, 524 pp.

1947 *Friends in Far-away Lands* with Dorothy J. Seivewright and Trevor Lloyd. Toronto: Ginn and Company, 156 pp.

1948 "Present and Future Settlement along the Mackenzie River," Proceedings, *Royal Canadian Institute*, XXIII, 36-7.

1948 *Australia and Canada, A Geographic Contrast*, Sydney University Engineering Club, Annual War Memorial Lecture.

1949 "The Geographical Scene," in R.J. Kerner (ed.) *Yugoslavia*. Berkeley: University of California Press, 3-23.

1949 *Urban Geography, A Study of Site, Evolution, Pattern and Classification in Villages, Towns and Cities*. London: Methuen and Company, 439 pp.

1950 "The First Fourteen Years," *Shield*, 1, 3-7.

1950 "Northward Across Australia," *Proceedings Royal Canadian Institute*, XV, 32-3.

1950 "Hobart to Darwin: An Australian traverse," *Geographical Review*, XL (October), 548-74.

1950 "Migrations of the Tasmanians," *Mankind* (Sydney), IV, 44-47.

1951 *Geography in the Twentieth Century*. Edited by Griffith Taylor. New York: Philosophical Library Inc; London: Methuen and Company, 674 pp.

1951 "Fiji, A Study of Tropical Settlements" *Economic Geography*, XXVII (April), 148-62.

1952 "The Founding of the Society, 1927," (The Geographical Society of New South Wales, Silver Jubilee), *Australian Geographer*, VI (June), 3-4.

1953 *Southern Lands*, with Dorothy J. Seivewright and Trevor Lloyd. Toronto: Ginn and Company, 282 pp.

1954 *Lands of Europe and Asia*, with Dorothy J. Seivewright and Trevor Lloyd. Toronto: Ginn and Company, 346 pp.

1954 "Australia and Canada, A Comparison of Resources," *Report of the Thirtieth Meeting. Australian-New Zealand Association for the Advancement of Science*, 277-315. Canberra: The Association.

1955 "Australian Antarctica," *Proceedings Royal Australian Historical Society*, XLI, 158-74.

1956 "Australia: Continental Comparisons," *Pacific Discovery*, XXX (September-October), 1-2.

1956 "The Antarctic Today," *The Etruscan* (Staff magazine of the Bank of New South Wales), (September), 8-12.

1958 *Journeyman Taylor: The Education of a Scientist*. Edited by Alasdair Alpin MacGregor. London: Robert Hale Ltd., 352 pp.

1958 *Sydneyside Scenery, and How It Came About*. Sydney: Angus and Robertson, 239 pp.

1958 "Nueva Gales del Sur; un homoclima del Uruguay," *Estuario*, I, 29-31.

1959 "Human Ecology in Australia," in A. Keast, R.L. Crocker and C.S. Christian (eds.). *Biogeography and Ecology in Australia*. Den Haag: Junk, 52-68.

1959 "Obituary: Sir Douglas Mawson," *Australian Geographer*, VII (March), 164-5.

1960 "Sydney, Topography and Settlement," *Australian Museum Magazine*, XIII, 266-69.

1960 "Antarctic Structure," *Australian Journal of Science*, XXII, (January), 299-300.

1961 "Australia and Canada, A Study of Habitability as Determined by Environment," *Professional Geographer*, XIII (January), 1-5.

1961 *Douglas Mawson*, Obituary, Great Australians Series, Oxford University Press, Melbourne. 30 pp.

1961 "No latitude for Error (review). Sir Edmund Hillary," *The Australian Geographer*. IX, 139-140.

1962 "How Geographers May Promote World Peace," *Geographical Outlook* (Ranchi, India), III, 1-4.

1963 "Geographers and World Peace, A Plea for Geopacifics," *Australian Geographical Studies*, I (April), 3-17.

1963 "Probable Disintegration of Antarctica," *Geographical Journal*, CXXIX (June), 190-91.

Taylor's Medals
(with inscriptions)
National Archives: Canberra

Presented by the Royal Geographical Society for Antarctic Discovery, 1913, (silver). On the reverse side is Scott's likeness and the words Captain R.F. Scott, Commander of British Antarctic Expedition, 1910-1913.

Royal Geographical Society of Australia, Queensland, (gold) Instituted 1885, J.P. Thomas, Founder (no date).

The Royal Society of New South Wales, Sydney. On the reverse side are the words, "For Research in Geography and Service to Science."

Antarctic 1910-13. (silver), presented by King George V.

D.Sc. Examination 1915, Geology T.G. Taylor. On the reverse side is the Crest of the University of Sydney, N.S.W.

Syme Prize for Research — Melbourne Australia, T.G. Taylor, 1918.

David Livingstone medal (gold) 1923 — American Geographical Society. Griffith Taylor. For scientific achievement in the field of Geography in the Southern Hemisphere.

Royal Society of Tasmania, 1948, R.M. Johnston Memorial Medal Awarded to T. Griffith Taylor.

Bibliography

Andrews, John. "Griffith Taylor 1880-1963." *Australian Geographical Studies*, Vol. 2, no. 1 (1964), pp. 1-2.

Andrews, John (editor). *Frontiers and Men: A Volume in Memory of Griffith Taylor*. Melbourne: F.W. Cheshire Co., 1966.

Aurousseau, M. "Obituary. T. Griffith Taylor. 1880-1963." *The Australian Geographer*, Vol. XIV, no. 3 (1964), pp. 131-133.

Aurousseau, M. "Griffith Taylor 1880-1963." *Australian Geographical Studies*, Vol. 2, no. 1 (April, 1964), pp. 1-9.

Aurousseau, M. "Obituary. Professor Griffith Taylor, F.A.A." *Nature*, (February, 1964), pp. 555-556.

Brent, Peter. *Captain Scott and the Antarctic Tragedy*. New York: Saturday Review Press, 1974.

Camsell, Charles. "What Geography Means to Canada." *Canadian Geographical Journal*, Vol. 11, no. 5 (November, 1935), pp. 214-216.

Cherry-Garrard, Apsley. *The Worst Journey in the World*. London: Chatto and Windus, 1922.

Dunbar, G.S. "Harold Innis and Canadian Geography." *Canadian Geographer*, Vol. 29, No. 2 (1985), pp. 159-164.

Evans, E.R.G.R. *South With Scott*. London: Collins Clear Type Press, 1921.

Gallagher, Mathew. "'Birdie' Bowers. The Scot in Scott's Shadow." *The Scotsman* (February, 1983), pp. 179-187.

Gwynn, S. *Captain Scott*. New York: Harper and Brothers, 1930.

Hanley, Wayne. "Mapping Australia: The Difficult Years." *The Globe*, Journal of the Australian Map Curator's Circle, Vol. 9 (1978), pp. 27-35.

Hanley, Wayne S. *The Griffith Taylor Collection: Diaries and Letters of a Geographer in Antarctica*. Armidale, N.S.W.: University of New England, Research Series in Applied Geography, 1978.

Huntford, Roland. *Scott and Amundsen*. London, Sydney, Auckland, Toronto: Hodder and Staughton, 1979.

Huxley, Elspeth. *Scott of the Antarctic*. London: Weidenfield and Nicolson, 1977.

Langford-Smith, G. "Economic Resources of Australia." *Regional Development Journal* (1951), pp. 11-25.

Leighly, John B. "Environment and Race." Review in *American Anthropologist*, N.S. Vol. 30 (October 1928), pp. 685-688.

Limb, Sue and Cordingley, P. *Captain Oates: Soldier and Explorer*. London: Batsford Ltd., 1982.

Marshall, Ann. "Griffith Taylor 1880-1963." *The Geographical Review*, Vol. 54, no. 3 (1964), pp. 427-429.

Marshall, Ann. "Griffith Taylor's Correlative Science." *Australian Geographical Studies*, Vol. 12 (1972), pp. 184-192.

Marvin, Ursula B. "Granite House: 1911-1981." *Antarctic Journal of the United States*. National Science Foundation, Vol. 18 (March, 1983), pp. 15-19.

Mill, H.R. *The Life of Sir Ernest Shackleton*. London: William Heinemann, 1923.

Naughton, Patrick W. "The Development of the Department of Geography at the University of Toronto." Unpublished manuscript. Toronto: University of Toronto, Department of Geography, 1977.

Niland, D'Arcy. "Griffith Taylor: A Man for All Seasons." *Walkabout*, Vol. 30, no. 4 (April, 1964), pp. 17-30.

Ponting, Herbert. *The Great White South*. London: Robert M. McBride and Company, 1923.

Pound, Reginald. *Scott of the Antarctic*. London: Cassell and Co. Ltd., 1966.

Powell, J.M. "Thomas Griffith Taylor, 1880-1963." *Geographers: Bio-Bibliographical Studies*, Vol. 3 (1978), pp. 141-153.

Priestley, R.E. "Obituary. Thomas Griffith Taylor." *Geographical Journal*, Vol. 130 (1964), pp. 189-191.

Priestley, Raymond. "Griffith Taylor." In *Frontiers and Men: A Volume in Memory of Griffith Taylor*. John Andrews, editor. Melbourne: F.W. Cheshire Co., 1966.

Priestley, Raymond E. *Antarctic Adventure: Scott's Northern Party*. Toronto: McClelland and Stewart [1914], 1974.

"Professor Thomas Griffith Taylor." *The Polar Record*, Vol. 12, no. 77 (May, 1964), pp. 230-231.

Putman, D.F. "Obituary. Griffith Taylor 1880-1963." *Canadian Geographer*, Vol. 7, no. 4 (1963), pp. 197-200.

Rose, J.K. "Obituary. Griffith Taylor 1880-1963." *Annals of the Association of American Geographers*, Vol. 54 (1964), pp. 622-629.

Scott's Last Expedition. 2 Volumes. London: Smith Elder and Co., 1913.

"Scott's Last Expedition." Review in *The Times* of London, Literary Supplement, November 6 (1913), p. 502.

Spate, O.H.K. "Journeyman Taylor: Some Aspects of His Work." *Australian Geographer*, Vol. 12, no. 2 (1972), pp. 115-122.

Stamp, L. Dudley. Review of *Journeyman Taylor. Geographical Journal*, Vol. 125, no. 1 (March, 1959), pp. 121-122.

Tomkins, George. "Griffith Taylor and Canadian Geography." Unpublished Ph.D. Dissertation. Seattle: University of Washington, Department of Geography, 1965.

Wilson, Edward. *Diary of the 'Terra Nova' Expedition to the Antarctic 1910-1912*. Edited by H.G.R. King. London: Blandford Press, 1972.

Wright, Sir Charles. "Foreword." Edward Wilson, *Diary of the 'Terra Nova' Expedition to the Antarctic 1910-1912*. Edited by H.G.R. King. London: Blandford Press, 1972.

LaVergne, TN USA
19 October 2009
161368LV00005B/50/P